NATURE IN ITS PLACE

BASED ON THE RTE TV SERIES

NATURE IN ITS PLACE

The Habitats of Ireland

STEPHEN MILLS

The Bodley Head
London

To my parents who have shared with me, among many gifts,
their own love of nature.

All photographs by
Stephen Mills © Stephen Mills 1988.

Line illustrations and diagrams by
Chris Jones © The Bodley Head 1988.

Cataloguing in Publication
Data for this title is
available from the
British Library.
ISBN 0370 31168X
ISBN 0370 312171 (pbk)

Printed in Great Britain for
The Bodley Head
32 Bedford Square
London WC1B 3EL
by Butler and Tanner Ltd
Frome and London
Set in Linotron 202 Bembo by
Rowland Phototypesetting Ltd
Bury St Edmunds, Suffolk

Acknowledgements

I wish first to thank my co-producer, Dr Patricia Phillips, who shared with me all the long and sometimes onerous tasks of making a television series and who has so generously allowed her own ideas to disappear into the book without further acknowledgement.

The freedom to travel round Ireland, to camp for weeks on the dunes of Murlough, on the Burren, up in the Mourne Mountains and away on bird islands off the coast has been a privilege. It would not have been possible without the support of Radio Telefís Éireann and in particular of the head of co-productions, John Baragwanath, whose unstinting help and warm friendship have been greatly appreciated.

The botanist Declan Doogue has guided me on many a trip with patience and good humour for which I am most grateful.

I would also like to thank the following for all sorts of professional assistance and personal kindness: Dr Alan Craig, Tracey Curtis, Richard Ellis, Peter Gahan, Corinne Hall, Dr Peter Wyse-Jackson, Dr Daniel Kelly, Dr Noel Kirby, James McEvoy, Oscar Merne, Dora Murphy, Richard Nairn, Dr Jim O'Connor, The Office of Public Works, Liam O'Sullivan, Paddy O'Sullivan, David Shaw-Smith, Michael Starret, The Phillips family, May Phillips, Bill Quirk, Dr Julian Reynolds, Jo Whatmough, The wildlife rangers of Killarney National Park, John Wilson, The Woodman family, and Professor Peter Woodman.

Finally, I want to acknowledge a debt of inspiration to the many authors whose work I have consulted and listed at the end of the book, and especially to Dr David Bellamy, Dr James Fairley, Anthony Huxley and Professor Frank Mitchell.

Contents

List of Plates

41 Whooper swans with wigeon and mallard, regular winter visitors.
42 Grey heron fishing on the river bank.
43 Male and female common newt, Ireland's only species of newt.

List of maps and diagrams

Introduction

Ireland is a fragrant land, full of flowers, freshly washed, ever-changing, graceful in shadow and light—a land of green valleys and shining waters, of heather, peat and moss and of lonely oceanic headlands.

And best of all for the naturalist, it is still an unspoilt land, one, for instance, where meadows full of seven or more species of orchid can survive within a few kilometres of the capital city.

This book attempts to explain the nature of Ireland, not only in terms of its species and their histories, but also by looking at how those species live together and form communities.

The basis of every animal community is its plantlife. Different plants have different ways of nourishing themselves depending on the topography. Some prefer dry soils, some like acid conditions or waterlogged ground, some can cope with sand or salt, many more require lime in the soil. The character of the land can be defined by the plants it supports—so a birch wood differs from a hay meadow, a reedbed or a heather moor.

In the language of popular ecology each of these plant groupings is called a habitat, and each habitat becomes the chosen home for a characteristic combination of insects, birds and mammals which will not be found elsewhere.

A habitat does not spring up overnight. It takes decades for the margins of a lake to become a marsh, centuries for scrub to become an oakwood and thousands of years for a sphagnum bog to grow into a mature peatland. This slow growth and development involves the ecological processes of 'colonization' and 'succession'. The colonization of Ireland and its habitats, then, is the real subject of *Nature In Its Place*.

In order to acquaint the more inexperienced reader with these processes at their most stark and active, I have begun the book in the rawest of all habitats, the city. In Chapter Two we go to Cape Clear, a small offshore island where the laws that regulate the colonization of any piece of land can be easily illustrated. These laws of climate, size, topography and the like apply equally to the whole island of Ireland and Chapter Two also explains how Ireland has acquired its contemporary fauna. Chapter Three looks at a sand-dune system and the steps by which a habitat can develop from scratch—how heath and wood grow out of bare sand. Chapter Four is about the development of upland life from mountaintop to foothill—the effects of altitude on colonization—while Chapter Five explores the structure of a mature Irish woodland. Chapter Six is about grassland and the flowering limestone wilderness of the Burren, a place where an unusual variety of ecological influences combine to produce a unique mixture of plants. Finally, Chapter Seven examines Irish wetlands and the orders of life in a typical river.

These chapters follow the line taken by a series of eight half-hour television films that my co-producer, Dr Patricia Phillips, and I completed in 1987 for the Irish national television station, Radio Telefís Éireann. The aim of the series, also called 'Nature In Its Place', has been to explain the natural history of Ireland through eight representative habitats. (For the convenience of the book the farmland story has here been absorbed into other chapters.) Although the book attempts to go far beyond the necessary limitations of the film scripts, it benefits, I hope, from concentrating on specific locations. These can become useful case histories which expound the principles of ecology beyond the boundaries of Ireland.

No comprehensive natural history of Ireland has appeared since the outstanding botanist Robert Lloyd Praeger published his in 1950. I cannot claim to be filling that gap but I hope *Nature In Its Place* is a step in the right direction. I have tried to provide an accessible bridge between the increasingly scientific discipline of ecology and the interested general reader. I have tried to write 'up' rather than 'down' to children, explaining rather than avoiding technical language. And I have tried to give naturalists who specialize in one field of study enough material to become interested in others. In particular, I am anxious that the growing army of birdwatchers in Ireland should learn something about the plants that their birds live amongst and the insects they feed on. For it may be more rewarding to appreciate the whole web of life by which Irish habitats are sustained than to concentrate strictly on one thread.

This is at heart a scientific book. But science need not involve merely the cold wish to know. The best scientific curiosity is inspired by a love of nature and a broadening sense of the world. I believe it is as important to evoke the charm of the Irish landscape as it is to describe its vital statistics. This brings us to the issue of conservation in a changing, industrializing society. I have hardly mentioned conservation in this book. This is because in the past and in my own limited fashion, I have used energy, like other contemporary naturalists, to put the political arguments across and have tended to neglect the lyrical or simply informative approach. Now, by helping people to understand more about the nature of Ireland, I hope I will have made the need to conserve it self-evident.

Stephen Mills, 1987

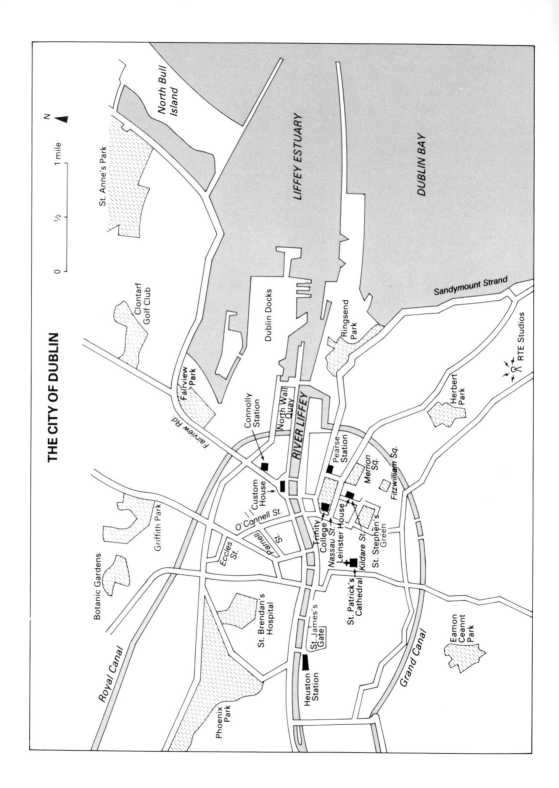

THE CITY OF DUBLIN

N

0   ½   1 mile

St. Anne's Park

North Bull
Island

LIFFEY ESTUARY

DUBLIN BAY

Clontarf
Golf Club

Dublin Docks

Sandymount Strand

Fairview Park

Ringsend
Park

Fairview Rd

Connolly
Station

North Wall Quay

RIVER LIFFEY

RTE Studios

Herbert
Park

Royal Canal

Griffith Park

O'Connell St.

Custom
House

Pearse
Station

Merrion
Sq.

Fitzwilliam Sq.

Botanic Gardens

Eccles St.

Parnell St.

Trinity
College

Nassau St.

Leinster House

Kildare St.

St. Stephen's
Green

St. Brendan's Hospital

St. James's
Gate

St. Patrick's
Cathedral

Phoenix Park

Heuston
Station

Grand Canal

Eamon
Ceannt
Park

1
The Other Dubliners

It may seem strange to begin the story of Ireland's natural history in the middle of the city, but this is a book about Irish habitats—about the places in which plants and animals live—and in particular about how those places are colonized.

When we look at a piece of woodland or a stretch of bog it is easy to assume that it came into the world fully developed, that it has always looked much the way it does today and that its wildlife was delivered one morning in pre-history as a job lot. The only thing that will change it, we might think, is a climatic catastrophe or the arrival of a chain saw or a turf-cutter.

But this, of course, is not the case. Habitats are changing all the time. Very slowly, the edges of lakes are turning into fens, sand dunes are developing into heaths and heaths into woodland.

At any given moment we can freeze this activity and describe what we see, but to really understand a habitat we need to appreciate its living history and to be aware of the ceaseless process of colonization.

Nowhere is this process more active than in the city. At first glance, the concrete landscape seems a hostile environment for wildlife. The clamouring streets are arid and unforgiving, buildings and people crowd each other and green spaces are overlain by fumes and city dust. It is a frightening and unstable place where old homes are flattened in a fortnight, where new roads are thrust into being and flooded with sudden traffic and where bare-faced office blocks spring up like mushrooms.

And yet there is hardly a square yard of this modern, human bustle that is not shared by a plant or an insect, a bird or a mammal. In wastegrounds and building sites, on pavements and in gutters, in gardens and on rooftops the 'Other Dubliners' are busy establishing their own communities.

The strategies that species employ for invading the city and consolidating their hold upon it, the way plants spread across a rubbish tip and the way insects and birds arrive once the plants have taken root, are comparable to the methods used to colonize any habitat. The difference is that in the city we don't expect to find swathes of delicate orchids by the main railway line and we are surprised to see bright-coloured oystercatchers lining up on the playing fields. When butterflies flutter around dusky tenements and foxes nose around the dustbins even the most confirmed non-naturalist and city-dweller grows curious. And because the presence of so much wildlife in town is unexpected, its behaviour tends to be more memorable.

There is, however, another reason for beginning this study of the strategies of habitat colonization in the city, and in Dublin in particular, and that is the simple fact that Dublin is familiar to so many people in Ireland. Its population has trebled in the last twenty years and now nearly a third of Ireland's people live in and around the capital. It is helpful to view unfamiliar concepts, like the development of animal communities, in the context of a familiar type of location. For some country people, furthermore, coming to the city has not been easy. It has meant learning a new way of life, coping with noise, with seamless traffic, with high-rise existence. There can be few of us who do not feel some pull of fellow-feeling when we notice a wildflower marooned on a city wall or a bird singing against a volley of car horns. It may be that a little sympathy will also help us to understand more about plants and animals and their pioneering efforts.

This push to colonize the urban environment is not, of course, an entirely twentieth-century phenomenon. The first study of the city's flora *Synopsis Stirpium Hibernicarum*, was written way back in 1726 by a clergyman called Caleb Threlkeld. It is reputed to have appeared on the 27th of October, the day before Threlkeld's neighbour, Jonathan Swift, published *Gulliver's Travels*. Swift poked merciless fun at scientific endeavour, but science has endured and Threlkeld's observations are useful because they give us a reference point. They show how plants have come and gone in Dublin as the city has changed, how maritime plants and some of the old weeds of cultivation, for instance, have declined and how plants of dry, stony ground have increased with the spread of concrete. The influence of Dublin's citizenry has changed as well. Threlkeld's most celebrated record refers to 'moss growing on a dead man's skull'. He describes it as 'frequent in Ireland where the poor people who are naturally hospitable, being misled by restless companions, rush into war foolishly thinking to throw off the blessings of the English government. I took some from skulls upon the Custom-House Quay, imported in large butts from Aghrim.'

Today, all of Ireland's cities have things less morbid but equally interesting to claim the naturalist's attention. Cork has its herons that line the River Lee, Galway has its salmon leaps, Belfast and Derry have their estuaries and the little town of Dunmore East in County Waterford has lamp-posts that once held the nests of kittiwakes. But Dublin must hold pride of place. It is the city of Joyce and O'Casey, of canals and rivers, of pubs and bridges, of Georgian backwaters and brash developments.

And for me it is also the city of buddleja and red valerian, of hogweed and ragwort and courageous arctic terns. When I walk up the straight half mile of O'Connell Street it is not only politics but the busy winter roost of hundreds of pied wagtails that I think about, and on Sandymount Strand I am looking for ringed plovers as well as literary allusions.

Filming wildlife in Dublin is always a revelation. We found long-eared owls nesting along the main avenue of St Anne's Park. We were shown the lawn of an elegant house in the southern suburb of Foxrock which had been excavated by badgers. We had a line of car drivers searching the sky over the present-day Custom's House, as we tried to film a passing peregrine falcon. We located three sparrowhawk's nests. And three little boys who wanted to hit our camera with sticks went away wide-eyed after looking at the magnified world of an ichneumon fly through the macro lens.

Arriving in the City

It was little more than twenty years ago that cattle were still herded on the hoof through the north of the city, on their way to the North Wall Quay and the export market. They brought the countryside with them in their stomachs and they left samples of it all along the old North Circular Road. The seeds of numerous pasture plants like greater plantain (*Plantago major*) and ribwort plantain (*Plantago lanceolata*), the occasional red bartsia (*Odontites verna*) and the ubiquitous white clover (*Trifolium repens*) might all have come to Dublin on four legs.

Of course, like any city, Dublin is only a skin which men have grafted across the surface of the natural landscape. As the concrete has spread and hardened the original habitats have diminished yet some of the plants they supported can still be found. Little patches of scarlet pimpernel (*Anagallis arvensis*) that once must have carpeted the edges of ancient rural fields, still turn up occasionally in city wastegrounds. Plants of the deep forest, like wood avens (*Geum urbanum*), and woodruff (*Galium odoratum*), ground ivy (*Glechoma hederacea*), tutsan (*Hypericum androsaemum*) and herb robert (*Geranium robertianum*) still cling to traditional sites—now gardens or the grounds of institutions like St Brendan's Hospital—where old maps show long-lost woodlands once stood.

These scraps of native wildlife are continually reinforced. Roadside verges and hedgerows provide avenues of greenery along which animals and plants can make their way into town. The white-clustered flowers of cow parsley (*Anthriscus sylvestris*), and hogweed (*Heracleum sphondylium*) follow this route, providing feeding stations for their insect attendants, like the bright red soldier beetles (*Rhagonycha fulva*) that never seem to leave them.

The banks of Dublin's River Liffey, and of the Royal Canal which forms the inner city boundary to the north and of the Grand Canal which marks the southern limit, are a path for rich, pale meadowsweet (*Filipendula ulmaria*) and the lilac-coloured crosses of lady's-smock (*Cardamine pratensis*), for yellow flag (*Iris pseudacorus*) and the pink umbellifer, wild angelica (*Angelica sylvestris*). The water, too, brings aquatic plants like great water plantain (*Alisma plantago-aquatica*) and arrowhead (*Sagittaria sagittifolia*), with its extraordinary arrow-shaped leaves, into the heart of the city, while the decline of water-borne traffic has allowed the spread of the various pondweeds (*Potamogeton spp*).

The city, like any 'new colony', is a melting-pot. It contains an unpredictable mixture of wildlife species that may have come in from all over the world to try their hand at town living. At least 35 per cent of the plants now growing wild in Dublin are not native to Ireland. In 1944, a Guinness employee conducted a botanical survey around the company's premises at St James's Gate. Among the 200 plant species he recorded were numerous exotics: there was tall melilot (*Melilotus altissima*) from Europe, tall rocket (*Sisymbrium altissimum*) perhaps from North Africa and eastern rocket (*Sisymbrium orientale*) from the Near East. Many of these foreigners had probably arrived on board ship, in grain consignments bound for the brewery.

Because there is so much traffic and so much international trade the city is being colonized like this all the time. In 1980, a botanist first spotted a Peruvian weed, the white and yellow flowered gallant soldier (*Galinsoga ciliata*) which had lodged itself in a flower pot in Kildare Street. The next year there were nine and by 1982 the little South American ghetto had spread to Nassau Street nearby!

Many such immigrants—both those from abroad and those from elsewhere in Ireland—must come and go through Dublin without trace. Some, however, find urban conditions particularly suitable. The procumbent pearlwort (*Sagina procumbens*), for instance, which is found in all sorts of stark locations in Ireland, is something of a masochist. Its creeping threads and tiny yellow flowers seem actually to enjoy being stepped on and it is one of the few plants that thrives in the cracks of the pavements.

Once a plant has become established in the city it may act as a stepping-stone on which other organisms, particularly any that feed on it, can get to town as well. One of the most interesting examples of a plant that has made a long perambulation to reach Dublin, and has extended the range of at least one insect once it got there, is Oxford ragwort (*Senecio squalidus*). Oxford ragwort has yellow dandelion-like flowers, like the common field ragwort (*Senecio jacobaea*) but its leaves have a narrower, more stringy look. It comes from southern Europe where it grows on warm, dry ground, and it has arrived in Dublin in a particularly roundabout fashion. The first British specimens were found growing in Oxford in 1794, having escaped, it is assumed, from the university's Botanical Gardens. When the railways were built it began to spread, its seeds blown along as free passengers in the slip-streams of the trains. By 1867 it was in London, and soon after that had spread all over England. From there it must have come by boat to Cork, its first port of call in Ireland, and by 1960 had travelled up the line in small numbers to the capital. Now, however, it is common in Dublin. Since, in places like Sicily, it flourishes on volcanic ash, it is comfortably at home on the barren streets, lodged in the corners between pavements and buildings. It so happens that the cinnabar moth (*Tyria jacobaeae*), a large common bright red moth, produces larvae that will only eat ragwort. But it doesn't have to be genuine Irish ragwort. Because the Oxford ragwort is such a successful colonizer, even in the hostile inner city, the cinnabar has been encouraged to become a town-dweller as well, and its striking orange-and-black-striped caterpillars can now be found crawling down Joyce's beloved Eccles Street.

The Oxford ragwort, the hawkweed (*Hieracium gougetianum*) that has somehow turned up from the Pyrenees, and Dublin's only bulrush (*Typha latifolia*) which for years grew twenty feet up in a railway water-butt outside Pearse Station, have all arrived by accident. But there is another, large group of plants which have been brought to Dublin deliberately by its citizens. In the early days these were the medicinal herbs, like feverfew (*Tanacetum parthenium*) and wormwood (*Artemisia absinthium*). Now they include burgeoning numbers of escaped garden plants. Some of these have made a spectacular success of city living. The large, heart-shaped leaves and starry white flowers of Japanese knotweed (*Reynoutria japonica*) are found in most wastegrounds, snapdragons (*Antirrhinum majus*) can crop up on almost any pile of rubble and red valerian (*Centranthus ruber*) gives a scarlet crest of colour to wall tops all over the inner city, along the North Circular Road, south to Trinity College and Fitzwilliam Square, and on out past Donnybrook.

There is one naturalised garden plant, however, that has made a greater contribution to city wildlife than any other. That is buddleja (*Buddleja davidii*). Buddleja was brought from western China around 1890. In its early stages of growth it doesn't compete well with grasses, but in the city on pavements and walls where little else grows, it does extraordinarily well. It sprouts from the tops of derelict buildings and, clinging halfway down houses, draws water from gutters and drainpipes. It thrusts up out of basement window-wells and squeezes its way along the edges of billboards, nicely obscuring the pictures of Coca-Cola and inappropriate German cars. What a wonderful plant! Best of all, it is beloved of butterflies. Its unmistakable fingers of purple flowers actually consist of hundreds of tiny drinking-cups filled to the brim with nectar.

The caterpillars of several of our most colourful butterflies— resident species like the tortoiseshell (*Aglais urticae*), the peacock (*Inachis io*) and the migrant breeder the red admiral (*Vanessa atalanta*)—feed on the common nettle (*Urtica dioica*). Since these grow side by side with buddleja all over the city's waste areas, the combination provides the ideal food service. When the adult butterflies emerge in late summer they don't have to hunt the streets in search of food. All they have to do is fly up and cluster, three or four at a time, on the buddleja flowers and drink up the sweet oriental juices!

Getting Along with Man

Every habitat has what we might call a 'dominant characteristic', which shapes the lives of its resident plants and animals. If you don't get along with it then you won't be able to join the community supported by that particular habitat. In the mountains, the dominant characteristic is altitude, and the consequent cold and exposure it brings. On the sand dunes it is the rapid progress of the soil from infancy to maturity. In an oak forest it is the oak tree itself and in the city it is man.

Most of the creatures that we find in Dublin either derive some benefit from their contact with humans or they have at least adapted their lifestyles so that they can live alongside us and share our space. The different relation- ships they form with us can be thought of as different strategies for survival, comparable, for instance, with the different methods seaside plants have evolved for coping with salt, or the various ways in which bog-dwellers adapt to acidity!

Let's look at some examples. In rusty crevices on the green painted metal railings of Fairview Park, shaken by the buses as they rattle down Fairview Road, you can often find the little yellow pupae of two-spot ladybirds (*Adalia bipunctata*). In Britain the two-spot tends to be an animal of woods and gardens, laying its eggs in cracks in the bark of trees and pupating on their leaves. In Ireland, however, where woodland is scarce, it is mainly an urban inhabitant. The larger seven-spot (*Coccinella 7-punctata*) and the yellowish ten-spot (*Adalia 10-punctata*) ladybirds are also common in Dublin and it may be that their diets are actually improved by city life. Ladybirds derive their name from medieval times when they were associated with the Virgin Mary and called 'Beetle of Our Lady', but they are not particularly meek and mild. They are tough little meat eaters, and their favourite food consists of aphids (*Aphidoidea*), which they stalk among the roses and shrubs of the city parks. Scientists have recently discovered that those aphids which eat plants affected by pollution grow much bigger than their clean-air brethren. We don't know why, though it may be connected to the high nitrogenous content of exhaust fumes. In any case, Dublin's ladybirds can always be sure of a well-stuffed aphid larder.

This is one of the few instances where pollution can be said to benefit a species. By contrast lichens require a pollution-free atmosphere and of the twenty-one species found near Dublin only four survive in the inner city. Between these two extremes sit the rest of Dublin's wildlife, either indifferent to pollution or, like us, willing to tolerate it for the sake of other benefits.

Ladybirds come to Dublin because their opportunities for feeding are enhanced by man. That, if you like, is City Strategy Number One. City Strategy Number Two is to find, in some aspect of the town, a manmade replica of your own natural habitat. The swifts (*Apus apus*) that nest in the high eaves of Trinity College's old library cannot be said to be tame or particularly man-orientated. In fact when they arrive suddenly in mid-May, wheeling and screaming and hurtling among the house-tops on their long black wings, they seem to bring a spirit of intense wildness to the town. And they take it away with them when, just as suddenly, one day in late summer they are gone from the Dublin skies, speeding back to South Africa. These wilderness birds are made for the air. They feed on the wing; they preen on the wing; they can roost on the wing, ascending at night in large flocks to warm air layers thousands of feet up; they can even mate on the wing. Yet right across Europe and northern Asia they have all given up their old nesting sites on sea cliffs, in caves and in hollow trees, and have moved to town, preferring the superior sort of cavity to be found in tall city buildings.

House martins (*Delichon urbica*) have developed a similar taste in architecture, though they go for more suburban surroundings, sticking their mud-cup nests under the outside eaves of private houses. One of the neatest examples of City Strategy Number Two, however, exists in the north of the city along one of the main railway lines, just west of the poetically named Cross Guns Bridge. There the trains cut through the remains of what may once have been an old esker. The rock is limey and the steep embankment provides good drainage and plenty of shelter. In this warm haven an attractive community of typical limestone plants has grown up. In June, you can lie there in the quaking grass (*Briza media*) and kidney vetch (*Anthyllis vulneraria*), with your view framed by pyramidal orchids (*Anacamptis pyramidalis*), fragrant orchids (*Gymnadenia conopsea*) and spotted orchids (*Dactylorhiza fuchsii*), while the goods trains from Connolly station rumble past five yards away.

City Strategy Number Three is to keep on coming back to the same old location that your ancestors lived in, simply adapting to whatever changes men have made to it. Dublin is a port, constructed on land that was once part of a continuous coastline of sand dunes and mudflats. Every year arctic terns (*Sterna paradisaea*) return from far down in the southern hemisphere to enjoy the privilege of fishing in the mouth of the Liffey. But now they find that their traditional nesting-sites have become part of a fast-growing dockland. They have to make do with little scraps of land left undeveloped and their colonies move from year to year. In the season before we began filming in Dublin, a group of terns nested in the coal stocks piled outside Ringsend Power Station. In the year we were there a colony of about thirty pairs had established itself on a large mound of builder's gravel, and as the parents screeched and squawked, rushing to incubate their eggs and rear their chicks, the bulldozers beneath them gnawed day by day into their makeshift home.

This whole cacophonous nursery was a miracle of survival. Lorries thundered back and forth carting the gravel across to the new pier that was being built. Down among the deep ruts that they ploughed into the ground was another colony, this one of common terns (*Sterna hirundo*)—very like arctic terns but with longer legs and black tips to their scarlet beaks. Some of the lorry drivers had erected barriers of barrels to make sure they didn't drive over the nests, while the young terns already well grown, hid motionless under bricks, behind tin cans and even in plastic bags! Nearby a pair of ringed plovers (*Charadrius hiaticula*) sat on eggs. In a tuft of docks a skylark (*Alauda*

arvensis) was feeding her young and up above some of the arctic terns took time off to ride across the docks on the lugubrious loading cranes.

City Strategy Number Four—if it can be called that—is the path to extinction. It involves staying in the same old place and not adapting. To some extent this applies to Dublin's red squirrels (*Sciurus vulgaris*). The native red squirrels of Ireland are believed to have died out some time after 1662—perhaps partly because of overhunting for their fur. From 1815 onwards they were extensively reintroduced and within 100 years they were back in reasonable numbers in all thirty-two counties. But there are not many left in the capital. They cling to the few remaining stands of old native oaks and introduced beech trees in places like St Anne's Park. They are too shy to benefit from man and not shy enough to evade his pets. They are particularly vulnerable when they try to forage away from their trees during hard winter weather. Almost the whole colony that once graced the Glasnevin Botanic Gardens was wiped out a few winters ago when, one after the other, they were caught by cats as they visited local dustbins.

To be a success in the city you have to be aggressive, adaptable or at least lucky. Ireland's red squirrels don't appear to have had any of these qualities, but the last group of urban strategists are blessed with all three.

The Scavengers

There is one group of creatures that seems to work on the principle that if you can't beat man you may as well join him. These are the scavengers and theirs is the City Strategy *par excellence*.

The mess, the litter and the refuse we create is a headache for us, but for several animals it's an easy meal-ticket. Every summer Dublin children splash in and out of the Grand Canal, shinning up and down the steps of the locks and ducking themselves in the turgid pools unaware that they are sharing the facilities. For, in the evening, when everyone has gone home, out come the rats to finish off the bits of sandwiches and defecate in the water.

Our relationship with rats is chronicled in the long history of disease. They have always managed to collect their tithe of harvests and winter stores, helping to spread typhoid and bubonic plague as they did so. Even the most ardent naturalist tends to be a little cool about rats. We have hunted them, trapped them and poisoned them, but we have failed to eradicate them and wherever we go, they go too.

But this has not always been the case. The rat of the canals and of the Dublin sewers and back-streets—the rat of all European cities—is the brown rat (*Rattus norvegicus*). It originally belonged in China and Siberia, and did not arrive in Ireland until the early eighteenth century. Before that, we only had the black rat (*Rattus rattus*), a smaller, 'prettier' animal, with neater fur —much darker on the back and paler underneath—and a longer tail. It was

the black rat whose own private flea, *Xenopsylla cheopis*, carried the Black Death. The first record of black rats in Ireland was made by Giraldus Cambrensis a Welsh ecclesiastic in the entourage of King Henry II who, as tutor to Prince John visited the country in 1185. He wrote a somewhat fanciful account of the place called *Topographica Hibernica* in which, among other things, he listed its fauna. The black rat came from Indo-Malaya, and was the original seafaring rat common on ships and in ports. On dry land, however, it has not competed successfully with its heftier, more aggressive cousin, and it now only survives in Ireland in transient, harbour populations.

There are several reasons why brown rats are such effective scavengers. Firstly, they will eat almost anything, meat or vegetable, cooked or un-cooked. Secondly, they are athletic, and small enough to keep out of the way when necessary. Thirdly, like most rodents, they have a prodigious ability to breed. Females are sexually mature eighty days after birth, when they are still only a third of their adult weight. (Black rats mature a little later which may be a clue to why they lost the battle for space to the brown.) They can produce up to five litters of six or eight young each year and in an average population a third of the females will be pregnant at any given season.

But brown rats have one additional mysterious quality which they share with the other imported 'pests', the black rat and the common house mouse (*Mus musculus*), which came from Asia. It is that indefinable 'genetic courage' which first enabled their ancestors to travel with their food supply, to exploit a ship as a habitat, and to function effectively in unfamiliar circumstances. In humans we would probably label this sort of adaptability as 'intelligence'.

Another adaptable creature has been making itself heard in Dublin recently. Herring gulls (*Larus argentatus*) have moved in from their seaside colonies and are beginning to nest on the roofs of houses in the north of the city. They like nice new houses, with a bit of flat roof space around the chimney pot. Importing their own decor, usually a splendid pile of twigs, they find a large colour-television aerial is just the place for keeping an eye on the neighbours!

Having a family of herring gulls upstairs is fine if you want your roof whitewashed but at the nest we filmed, the patient householder had finally cracked when she couldn't use her washing line any more. That year she had erected a frame of chicken-wire right over the chimney area. Undeterred, the accommodating gulls had built a 'high rise' sort of nest, squeezed up against the side of the frame. Furthermore, quick to see an advantage in any situation, the parents posted the chicks in behind the wire for safety during the first few days after they hatched!

And where do these new suburban gulls go for dinner? Not to the sea, but away down towards Tallaght, to the city dump. There they join thousands of other gulls, as well as rooks (*Corvus frugilegus*), jackdaws (*Corvus monedula*) and house sparrows (*Passer domesticus*) in the great garbage game. These are all skilled operators. They seem to know whenever a big load of rubbish has arrived. They certainly know exactly how long they can go on feeding before skipping aside to avoid the thrashing treads of the bulldozers. And they are also surprisingly adept at dealing with supermarket packaging. We filmed

one team of gulls opening a packet of bread and plunging their heads right
to the bottom of the plastic bag to get every last scrap.

This ability to find new man-made nesting-sites, to feed on dumps and to
roost and breed on inland reservoirs is significant. It has helped the herring
gull and its smaller and even more adept relative the black-headed gull (*Larus
ridibundus*), to increase the gull population of Ireland.

There is one more Dublin scavenger worthy of a mention. Those ducks
you see floating around like fluffy toys on the waters of St Stephen's Green
and the parks may not be as tame as they look. Many of them are perfectly
wild mallards (*Anas platyrhynchos*) 'in disguise'. They are crafty too in their
own way because, unlike the rats and the gulls, they have charmed us into
co-operating with their scavenging habits. Who, after all, does not enjoy
feeding the ducks?

Mallards breed in grassy nooks all round the city. One of them became
something of a legend a few years ago when she hatched out a nestful of
chicks in the garden of Leinster House. She marched them off towards the
Green along Kildare Street in broad daylight, and the Guards had to stop the
traffic for them.

The ducks aren't the only water-birds to benefit from the generosity of
Dublin's park visitors. We enjoyed filming the antics of a mother moorhen
(*Gallinula chloropus*) in Herbert Park. She lived on an island and liked sliced
white bread. Whenever a pile had accumulated nearby she used to sneak out
of the bushes, creep ever so warily up to it and haul slice after slice back
under cover to share with her chicks.

Being a Weed

Plants can't scavenge but they can become weeds. The city landscape is
always changing. Buildings become derelict, sites are cleared, new office
blocks are raised. Fallow ground appears and disappears continuously all
across Dublin, providing opportunities for plants that are quick off the mark.
These fast movers are the urban weeds, the vegetable squatters that take over
after the demolition squads and move on ahead of the building contractors.

Weeds are a creation of mankind. Like the rats that have learned to feed
off us, they have evolved in direct response to our activities. Botanists
identify two types of weed: the 'ruderals' which grow on waste areas and
roadsides and the 'agrestals', unwanted plants of cultivated ground. Most of
them belong to families of plants that grow naturally on land which is open
and unstable—near the shore, on cliffs and river banks or in the furrows and
scrapes made by wild animals.

So, already programmed to cope with difficult or ephemeral conditions,
the successful weeds have undergone further genetic adaptation. Through
the process of natural selection, generation after generation, they have

'learned' to like being cut or uprooted, tilled, grazed or burned. They have found ways of flourishing in the face of catastrophe and benefiting even from our efforts to eradicate them.

The typical short-term Dublin wasteground is not a very friendly looking place. Strung round with barbed wire, it will usually have a dry gravelly surface, an earthmound or two, a portion of late-lamented motor-car and plenty of litter. Its flora will be predictable: nearly always the same group of plants which, between them, exhibit an impressive variety of highly developed 'wasteground' strategies—the ultimate in 'weedism'.

Much of its flora will be the quickest of annuals. These are plants like the yellow-flowered groundsel (*Senecio vulgaris*), the straggling white chickweed (*Stellaria media*) or the upright shepherd's purse (*Capsella bursa-pastoris*) which can be a seed one day, germinate the next day, and be mature to the point of flowering a couple of weeks after that. Shepherd's purse produces thousands of seeds. In good, wet, germinating weather, these get sticky and so are easily distributed on the bottom of shoes, or on dogs' tails. They can grow fast enough to exploit a clement period in winter as well as growing throughout the summer and, by getting through three or four generations, a single plant can give rise to 1000 million seedlings in one year!

Then there are the plants, like curled dock (*Rumex crispus*) whose seeds can remain in the soil for long periods, perhaps even from one era of dereliction to another, awaiting the right conditions for growth. One experiment showed that nearly one in ten dock seeds could stay immured like this for seventy years.

A third wasteground strategy is to produce seeds that are programmed to germinate at different times or, cleverer still, under slightly different environmental circumstances. Again, to some extent the shepherd's purse is an example of this. Its tiny round golden seeds are kept safe in the triangular 'purses' or seed cases that dangle on threads from the stem. They ripen at staggered intervals thus ensuring that, when the bulldozer arrives, or the spade is wielded, the plant's output will not all be destroyed at once.

The fourth order of 'weedism' contains plants that can grow up again from fragments of their original roots, even when they have been cut into small pieces. Bindweed (*Calystegia sepium*), creeping thistle (*Cirsium arvense*), perennial sow-thistle (*Sonchus arvensis*) and the docks are all endowed with this ability. This means that neither the digger, the cultivator nor the plough will easily eradicate them.

Next comes wind power. In a city like Dublin, with its untidy corners and its small backyards, the ability to make your way into any number of tight spaces can be extremely useful. Wind is the ideal vehicle and the obvious passengers are the floating seeds of dandelions, thistles and groundsel, all members of the *compositae* family. Equally important, however, are the willowherbs. Rosebay willowherb (*Chamaenerion angustifolium*) is a beautiful plant. It is tall and imposing, with large mauve-pink flowers which are intricately clustered with long stamens and are very attractive to bees. It is one of the few Dublin flowers that can grow rapidly on unweathered ashes, so it often appears on the sites of bonfires, or growing up out of burnt-out cars. Its seeds, like those of its smaller relative the broad-leaved willowherb (*Epilobium montanum*), become easily airborne, buoyed up by their long, feathery hairs.

Once in position, up on a wall or in a patch of gravel, the willowherbs can spread underground very effectively, sending up new shoots from beneath, wherever they can find a favourable spot. Working on the principle that, having located a good piece of waste ground one ought to stay there, this is a good alternative to their hazardous wind method of propagation. Brambles (*Rubus fruticosus*), of course, do something similar, but since they travel above ground they can even spread over concrete. They worm their tentacles across the smoothest surfaces, only rooting when they come to a crack with a bit of soil in it.

A certain flexibility of shape, size and form is another handy feature for 'squatter' plants to have. The dandelion (*Taraxacum officinale*), for example, can spread out its leaves in a broad rosette on poor ground where there is little competition. On better soil, however, it will even fight with the grasses, making its leaves stand up vertically so they can still reach the light. Similarly, the smooth sow-thistle (*Sonchus oleraceus*) can produce a couple of flowerheads or a whole bushel of them, depending on whether it is growing in a bleak location, like the top of a wall, or in comparative luxury, in the corner of a park rose garden.

One last point, but perhaps the most revealing, is that weeds tend to be genetically dynamic: they seem to have been able to respond to environmental changes more swiftly than other plants. One reason is that many of them are adept at both methods of seed production: self-pollination and cross-fertilization. To appreciate the benefits of this we need to take a last look at the shepherd's purse. Most of the time its tiny white flowers pollinate themselves before they even open. Self-pollination preserves the characteristics of the parent plant, and this is obviously valuable in a species which is so successful at colonizing the hostile city environment. Self-pollination is also an effective short-cut, helping the plant to reproduce as fast as possible in its transient locations. Nevertheless, although the flowers of shepherd's purse are rarely visited by insects, they do contain nectar, and there is evidence that every few generations the plants receive a dose of cross-fertilization. This ensures that their gene bank remains sufficiently varied to keep pace with any widespread changes that may occur in the environment.

Dublin's weeds are typical pioneers. They have the vigour, the adaptability and the brazen audacity to make the first move onto bare ground and to get in and out while the going's good. All habitats, be they mountaintops, sand dunes or bogs, have their pioneer species. But pioneers are only the first wave of colonizers on any piece of land. Given time—and in some parts of the city there are enduring green spaces—more permanent communities develop.

The Growing Community

Where waste ground is left undisturbed for several years, a different class of tenant takes up residency. The gravelly soil is gradually enriched by the plant matter left as short-lived weeds die away each year. Perennial plants begin to take over. These are plants that extend their life-cycles beyond the confines of a season but require the security of a more permanent home. Although they may grow more slowly, once established they will inevitably shade out most of the annual weeds. For their strategy is to draw on stores of food, or to build on advances in growth, made in previous years.

The long-term wasteground begins to take on a settled look. It has tall shrubberies of buddleja and the pale-leaved mugwort (*Artemisia vulgaris*) that Dublin's viking invaders liked to use to flavour their stews. It may have jungles of Japanese knotweed and the first saplings of sycamore (*Acer pseudoplatanus*) that have sown themselves from their 'advance attack' helicopter seeds. Around the edge, where people walk and litter is thrown, there will be nettles and willowherbs, dandelions and ragworts, giving way to swathes of perennial hogweed.

For other organisms, for insects, birds, even for mammals, this is becoming a reliable habitat around which a more mature food chain can develop. On a single summer's day it is possible to see what an ordered diversity of invertebrates just a few sprigs of hogweed will help to support. Hogweed is a large white umbellifer which means that it has hundreds of small flowers, clustered together on separate, slightly domed heads. Apart from the ubiquitous soldier-beetles that seem to do nothing but mate and drink, the nectar in the flowers attracts honey bees, blue-bottles (*Calliphora*) and sometimes dozens of hoverflies at once. The leaves will be chewed by aphids and one or two of the flowerheads will be pulled together and spun into a nursery for *Geometridae* moth larvae. The greenish caterpillars of the white-spotted pug (*Eupithecia tripunctaria*), a common nondescript

brownish little moth, are very keen on munching hogweed leaf-stems. All
these hungry feeders attract other predatory invertebrates. Ladybirds and
long-legged stilt flies (*Trepidaria spp*) arrive to hunt the aphids. Orb-spinning
spiders like the garden spider (*Meta spp*) sling their webs between the stems
hoping that a bluebottle or a hoverfly will drop in for dinner, and Ichneumon
flies come to look for moth caterpillars. Ichneumons (*Ichneumonidae*) don't
eat caterpillars, they lay their eggs in them, injecting them into place with
their long pointed abdominal 'ovipositors'. When the Ichneumon larvae
hatch, they eat their way out of their unfortunate hosts leaving only empty
husks behind.

Down on the ground beneath, long nosed weevils (*Curculionidae*) feed on
the grass stems, quick, black-bodied ground beetles (*Carabidae*) hunt for
small earthworms and little slugs and harvestmen like *Mitopus morio* wait to
pounce on passing mites (*Acarina spp*). Harvestmen are like spiders, but they
have tiny round bodies and extremely long legs which they can drop off and
replace in the event of a struggle.

With so much permanent vegetation there's plenty of food and shelter for
garden snails (*helix aspersa*) and for the black slug (*Arion ater*). The black slug
is an amusing personality. He is big and dark brown and will eat almost
anything he finds on waste ground, even cardboard boxes. When he sees
something he doesn't like he squeezes himself up into a damp ball of jelly
and wobbles slowly from side to side. This is what he does if he meets a
hedgehog (*Erinaceus europaeus*), not that it helps much because the hedgehog
will eat him anyway.

Most of the older Dublin waste grounds are bounded by half-derelict
walls. A crack in the mortar or a missing brick can become a nest-site for
blue tits (*Parus caeruleus*) for whom moth caterpillars and harvestmen are
pure ambrosia. Other birds, blackbirds (*Turdus merula*), robins (*Erithacus
rubecula*) even the occasional spotted flycatcher (*Muscicapa striata*) find the
wherewithal to play a respectable part in the wasteground society and so,
step by step, the 'Other Dubliners' have become an integral part of the city.

This large, busy, unofficial Dublin community is also sustained by more managed environments—by the green spaces provided by gardens, churchyards, parks and playing fields. While supporting a broadly similar line of species each of these facilities makes its own special contribution to the city's wildlife. Churchyards, for instance, are wonderful places for woodlice. Lift any stone and you will find the large grey *Oniscus asellus*. It lives under stones because it must remain damp. Like all woodlice it is a crustacean, the only 'marine' animal in Ireland that lives on dry land, and it cannot breathe unless its skin is covered with a film of moisture. Woodlice will eat both meat and wood which is why in some places they are known as 'coffin-cutters'. *Oniscus* likes acid conditions and some naturalists have humorously dubbed it the Catholic woodlouse, since it is particularly common around the granite stonework of Catholic churches. As you might expect, a Protestant woodlouse also manages to live respectably in Dublin! It is the small, pink *Androniscus dentiger*, which requires lime-rich soils and frequents Protestant churchyards—probably because of the whitewash once used so liberally round the buildings and pathways.

Private gardens, of course, combine in an infinite patchwork of greenery providing an important reservoir for plant and animal species through the city. They take on an extra significance, however, where they are owned by someone who likes birds. A well-stocked bird-table during winter will feed not only the one or two birds that the householder thinks he has in his garden but literally hundreds of different individuals. Ornithologists in Britain have proved this by catching and ring-marking birds as they come to the tables. The record is held by a suburban garden in Hertfordshire which hosted 152 different blue tits in a single day! In at least one case, that of the greenfinch (*Carduelis chloris*), the provision of winter food, and nuts in particular, seems to have led to a marked increase in the species' population right across Britain and eastern Ireland.

Gardens, churchyards and wastegrounds all help to draw wildlife deep into the heart of the city, but it is the parks that provide the wide spaces, the woodland groves, the shrubberies and the domesticated meadowlands from which species can take the final step into high-density living. They form the all-important buffer zone, the bridge between countryside and town.

Dublin is well endowed with parks. Although the city's inner centre only has three substantial areas of greenery—St Stephen's Green, St Brendan's Hospital and the grounds of Trinity College—its northern rim is framed by an almost continuous expanse of parkland. There is St Anne's Park, Clontarf golf course, Fairview Park, Griffith Park, the Botanic Gardens and in the north-east of town, the four square miles of Phoenix Park, the largest enclosed park in western Europe. South of the Liffey there are three large golf courses within two and a' half miles of the centre and numerous open spaces like Herbert Park and Eamon Ceannt Park.

The parks are where most of Dublin's small birds live and where the predators hunt and breed. One of their richest assets is the soil. Scientists have estimated that the top nine inches of an acre of wild grassland can harbour, on average, some three hundred million individual invertebrates. The parks lack the variety of grasses and are too well trimmed and tidied to support such teeming, invisible populations. Nevertheless, they offer an essential fast-food service to anyone willing to stick a beak into the soil. Blackbirds, robins, song thrushes (*Turdus philomelos*), mistle thrushes (*Turdus viscivorus*), dunnocks (*Prunella modularis*), magpies (*Pica pica*) and the winter

flocks of northern fieldfares (*Turdus pilaris*) all enjoy the park facilities. Near the sea as they are, Dublin's parks have some less typical visitors as well. On late summer days, when the municipal mowers are out cutting the lawns, oystercatchers (*Haematopus ostralegus*) come in from the shore. They stalk purposefully just behind the machines, using their ungainly long red beaks to snatch up the froghoppers and other invertebrates as they are evicted from their grass homes. While on misty autumn mornings the parklands echo to the sad cries of curlews (*Numenius arquata*), striding over the damp turf and helping themselves to deep-tunnelled worms until the first walkers and their dogs put them to flight.

1 *Top* Pyramidal orchids.
2 *Bottom* A long-term wasteground crowded with buddleja and Oxford ragwort.

Colonizing the city is like colonizing any habitat. It takes time. The selection of successful species depends on prevailing conditions—on opportunities and the ability of certain organisms to perceive them as such. It is rarely a haphazard process. Rather, it follows the more or less predictable course that rules the growth of natural communities. Slowly, opportunistically, with the success of one species often dependent on the presence or absence of another, this is how the whole of Ireland has been colonized by its wildlife.

3 *Left* Large-flowered butterwort on a damp peat bank in Kerry.

2
This Island: Cape Clear, and the Post-Glacial Colonization of Ireland

It is midsummer on the Atlantic island of Cape Clear. Here, five miles off the south-westernmost tip of Ireland, the seabirds are back from their winter-feeding quarters among the shoals of sprats far offshore. They have recolonized the island's rocky coastline as they do each year, and the throaty squawking of the auks and the high cries of the gulls can be heard along the ledges of the cliffs.

Razorbills (*Alca torda*), black-bodied and white-breasted like little penguins, with beaks as heavy and sharp as flintstone, line the sparkling rocks to court one another. They bow and nuzzle and touch bills and then, one by one, they drop away like stones to glide down to the sea far below. Beyond them, south by south-west, beyond the lighthouse rock of Fastnet—the very last pinnacle of the table of dry land on which Ireland rests—there is nothing but ocean, wide ocean all the way to the Antarctica.

To the birds and the fishermen of Cape Clear the teeming sea means food. In the summer it also means the constant offshore passage of distant shearwaters (*Procellariidae*), the strange, dark, slender birds who spend almost their entire lives on the wing, skimming the water, quartering the oceans back and forth. The sea brings temporary visitors to the island like the hefty grey seals (*Halichoerus grypus*) that land to dry in the sunshine and occasionally it rewards the patient watcher with more exotic sights. Great barrelling shapes, sharp-finned and powerful, are there and gone from the surface in a moment. These are the schools of whales and dolphins—of piebald killer whales (*Orcinus orca*), of grey, round-nosed Risso's dolphins (*Grampus griseus*) or quick, leaping porpoises (*Phocoena phocoena*)—that, unknown to most people, are travelling these waters throughout the summer.

But most of all, the sea means isolation. The narrow bank of water that separates Cape Clear from Ireland and then stretches away southwards for thousands of miles is a palpable barrier. It inhibits the free and easy exchange of birds, insects, flowers, and especially of mammals, between the mainland

and the island. This makes it more difficult for a given species to establish itself on Cape Clear since the island's colonizers may not receive a constant stream of reinforcements from Ireland or Europe. Consequently, only those for whom conditions on Cape Clear are particularly favourable are likely to succeed.

One of the most significant 'conditions' is the nature of the island's topography—its habitats. Take the cliffs and their seabirds, for example. They provide an interesting illustration of how the structure of a habitat restricts the number and variety of species it can support. When you look at a cliff-wall colony of seabirds like the small scattered colonies you find round the southern and western inlets of Cape Clear, the chatterings, the dotted nests, the comings and goings of the birds may look casual and haphazard. In fact, they are not. Each prospective inhabitant approaches the chosen piece of seaside real estate with a different requirement in mind.

Razorbills look for holes and cracks near the clifftops, often squeezing between crevices in the sloping slabs of the rocks to nest out of view in the secret cavities underneath. Guillemots (*Uria aalge*), on the other hand, prefer flat ledges lower down, open to the elements and usually facing out to sea. Guillemots look very like razorbills—both belong to the auk family—but the dark top-side of their plumage has a brownish hue rather than being glossy black. They also have slender pointed beaks, quite different from the chisel-edged beak of the razorbill with its striking vertical white stripe.

Guillemots don't build nests. Each pair lays a single, large egg on the bare rock. It can be green, blue, brown or creamy white, mottled and lined with extravagant chocolate brown decorations. But whatever their colour, all guillemots' eggs have one thing in common: they are always very pointed at one end and broad at the other. This is a life-saving design for it ensures that if an egg receives a knock it is more likely to revolve gently like a weighted spinning-top, rather than roll off the breeding ledge.

This is a specific adaptation to a habitat and its value is obvious considering the way guillemots cram themselves together on their platforms. They usually keep the peace through elaborate bowing rituals. Whenever a bird returns to the colony he 'doffs his cap' to his neighbours in a pantomime of politeness. But if a careless individual lands in the wrong place, pandemonium breaks out as he struggles over angry bodies back to his proper station, running the fierce gauntlet of stabbing beaks. An egg that rolled would never survive!

But why do guillemots live in these hectic ghettos? The answer, of course, is for protection. In such exposed locations, isolated nests would soon fall victim to the elements or to the gangs of predatory gulls that patrol the cliffs. By modifying the shape of their eggs and by developing their rituals and their propensity for colonial life, guillemots have evolved the best way of using sites which, to other birds, would seem inhospitable. These sites are common around Ireland's rocky coastline so guillemots have become the most numerous species of auk.

The biology of the guillemot has become so dependent on the stimulus of numbers, that unless they are in an ample crowd, on a ledge large enough to hold them, they cannot breed at all. Again, this is conspicuous on Cape Clear. The available ledges, and therefore the colonies there, are small. They rarely hold more than 40 pairs, and most years only half a dozen chicks will fledge from each platform. In the larger colonies, further round on the Kerry coast, for instance, a sample of the same number of parents, embedded in a much bigger crowd, would usually produce four times as many young.

An even more extreme attachment to colony nesting is exhibited by gannets (*Sula bassana*). Gannets are the magnificent white birds you see plunging like black-tipped arrow-heads from impossible heights into the sea as they follow the mackerel round the coasts. 70 per cent of the world's population of gannets breeds off the shores of Britain and Ireland—but only in eighteen known locations. The largest colony, up in St Kilda, with 59,000 pairs, has been known since the year 900 and new colonies are only established with the greatest reluctance. Ireland has one 'new' gannetry, on the island of Great Saltee off the south Wexford coast. Since the first nest in 1929 it has grown to 700 pairs, but it took thirty years for numbers to reach double figures. There are gannets on the Bull off West Cork and a colony of 21,000 pairs, the fifth largest in the world, on the rock of Little Skellig off County Kerry. There are no other Irish gannetries. Although gannets fish every day in the blue bays of Cape Clear, the island lacks the mystery gannet ingredient and no gannets nest there.

Among the seabirds that Cape Clear does manage to accommodate are just a handful of puffins (*Fratercula arctica*). Puffins are endearingly comical birds recognisable to almost everyone. They have large multi-coloured clown's beaks in which a stack of small fish can be carried home to the nest. They like steep, sandy slopes above the rocks, with enough depth of soil to burrow into, since they lay their single eggs at the ends of tunnels at least 1.5 metres long. The grassy headlands on Cape Clear are mostly flat-topped. Suitable slopes are scarce which is why puffins are not common on the island.

Black guillemots (*Cepphus grylle*)—all black except for a neat white square on the wing and startlingly red legs—like razorbills go for crevices but usually much lower down, nearer the waterline. They are rather secretive and solitary, nesting in ones and twos in sheltered inlets, particularly along the northern shore of the island which is more indented.

Then there are shags (*Phalacrocorax aristotelis*), small, all-black cormorants with a greenish sheen to their plumage and bright green gimlet eyes. They choose individual, nest-sized ledges, again often high up on rocky inlets where they are sheltered from the wind. They build sometimes mountainous barricades of twigs to keep their eggs and chicks safe. Among shags, twigs are something of a status symbol, for research has shown that, on average, the most successful nests are the biggest ones.

No shoreline is complete without its gull colony. Gulls prefer less precipitous locations, either on the gentler slopes where the last tongues of the rockscapes feel their way into the sea, or on outcrops and deserted grassy islands offshore. The ideal set-up for a herring gull is more of an estate than a nest-site! It must have a firm, flat foundation for the grass cup of the nest and a raised look-out station nearby from where the parents can keep watch. It also needs numerous nooks and crannies where the beautiful fluffy chicks can spend long hours keeping very still, waiting in safety for food and for their feathers to grow. The discerning herring gull will not be content with just any old rock, and a respectable herring gull suburb of say 100 pairs can easily cover several acres of land.

Finally we come to the fulmar (*Fulmarus glacialis*) which, wings rigid like a miniature albatross, can glide and float motionless all day in the air currents along the cliff-faces. The fulmar is a phenomenon. A hundred years ago there were none at all round the coasts of Ireland or Britain, and now there's hardly a rock face without them. The reason for the astonishing expansion of the fulmar's range—they were previously confined to Iceland and St Kilda —remains a mystery. Explanations have been put forward relating to changes in climate and sea temperature, and to the development of the deep-sea fishing fleets that have left a food trail of fish offal across the North Atlantic.

The fulmar exhibits one characteristic which is particularly relevant to our discussion of habitat use. It will nest anywhere on the cliffs: high or low, in sandy scapes or rocky holes, on exposed ledges or protected inlets. It is now probably the most widespread and one of the most numerous of our seabirds, a fact which owes much to its flexibility in selecting nest-sites. The message, then, seems to be that if you don't need just one type of habitat you'll end up more common than your competitors.

The fulmar is the exception that proves the rule that different species of seabird, and indeed different species of most organisms, make very distinct demands on their habitats, and their populations in any locality will depend upon the extent to which those demands are met. It is not enough to say that a bird requires a 'cliff'. As we have seen, most birds require a particular type of cliff and a particular place on it. So a habitat—a 'cliff' or a 'wood' or a 'bog'—does not only represent a generalized piece of topography, it is also an assemblage of specific niches (high holes, low holes, large ledges, small nooks) which are occupied in a variety of ways. The provision of variety is very important in deciding the composition of the fauna or the flora of any area. This is reflected in the natural history of the whole of Ireland, as much as it is in that of Cape Clear.

Returning to our cliff birds, we have seen that they exploit vertical rather than horizontal space. Furthermore, they do not depend on the limited resources of the land. They feed at sea, only using the cliffs as a sort of commuters' dormitory town. Consequently, nature can pack plenty of them onto a small island and Cape Clear supports far more sea birds than land birds.

The same is true of Ireland. It too is a comparatively small land mass. But it has a long and varied coastline offering birds a wide range of rock types, of shoreline topography and niches, as well as the convenience of sufficient fish stocks. The result is that Ireland contains the full complement of all twenty-two species of seabird (excluding the boreal skuas)—petrels, auks, gulls and terns—that breed off the much more extensive shores of Britain. The mixed colonies on the charming Saltee Islands, on the breath-taking Cliffs of Moher in County Clare or round the steep shores of Rathlin Island off the north Antrim coast are as impressive as any in the region.

In all other fields, however, Ireland is deficient in species when compared with Britain. Again, we can understand this by looking at some of the restrictions imposed on animals and plants that try to live on Cape Clear.

An Island's Wildlife Economy

When the fierce Atlantic storms break in off the sea, when the gales seem to raze the headlands and bend the cottage chimneys and the salt spray flies high above the rocks, this small hummock of stony ground can be a bleak and bitter refuge. Dismal oystercatchers, their beaks under their wings, huddle in blind, tilted lines along the shore. The cliff-top pastures are lost in racing mists and the bright white houses fade, turning drenched and grey. Only those who must, wrapped in oil skins, with collars up and heads down, struggle from door to door against the soaking thrust of the wind.

If you are on Cape Clear when such a storm strikes, you can easily appreciate that no colonizer, neither human nor animal, can have more than a precarious hold on such a place. For people, such a small island, with indifferent soil and far from markets, is not a land to get rich on. For as long as the sea provisioned them the islanders, like the seabirds, could survive, working their small-holdings for oats, barley, hay and cattle and plying their drift-net boats for mackerel and herring. But the economics of fishing have changed. Deep-sea trawling fleets have been consolidated into a handful of major ports, and the local offshore industry has collapsed. Cape Clear, which in 1920 had forty-three fishing boats employing over 200 men, now has almost no fleet at all.

One hundred years ago a thousand people could eke out a living on Cape Clear. Since then death and emigration have reduced the number of permanent residents to its current level of about 150. Disappointment, dereliction, departure: the signs are everywhere. Cottages, fondly built and husbanded stone by stone, are now in ruins, unroofed and returning to the ground. Fields that were once tended by hand are now waist-high in bracken (*Pteridium aquilinum*), that invader of men's works which the island now wears like a badge of desertion.

This is not to say that Cape Clear is depressing. Its pastoral beauty is idyllic. Tiny green pastures, latticed with stone walls, stretch down on the northern side right to the smooth sea's edge. There is the little thirteenth-century church of St Kieran standing among its quiet graves, looking down on the winking harbour of Trawkieran. There are also the stark and lonely ruins of Dunanore—the 'Golden Fort' of the O'Driscolls—which was split by British cannon in the sixteen hundreds. There are the laughing cries of the herring gulls, the rich scent of summer flowers, and the tenacity of the people—all inspiring symbols of the island's distinct character.

Nevertheless there is a great gulf of experience separating the many people who visit Cape Clear—the day trippers, the naturalists, the students who come to practise the Irish language in this one of its surviving heartlands—and the resident islanders. The tribulations of the exposed and isolated island people can be compared with the tribulations faced by plants and animals on Cape Clear. For the wildlife 'economy' is limited by similar factors, by the climate, the soil and the island's size—all factors which restrict the number of habitats available.

Cape Clear is only three miles long and covers little more than 1,500 acres. Its soils, lying on old red sandstone, are mostly acidic and its climate, if temperate, can be wild. The wind carries salt right across the island, 'burning' the vegetation wherever it is not deliberately sheltered. Out on the headlands on the windward side almost the only plant that will grow is thrift (*Armeria maritima*). It has long tap roots that can reach deep-seated supplies of unsalty water and it can excrete salt through its leaves. This salt tolerance gives it an advantage along exposed shores and, in the absence of all competition, its bright pink, papery flowers appear in June on Cape Clear in fantastic profusion. As a defence against the wind, thrift grows in tight clumps, like pin-cushions. Taller plants, however, have no such defences against salt and wind and there are almost no trees on Cape Clear. Apart from the hedges of fuchsia (*Fuchsia magellanica*) and, more successful, of red-flowered escallonia (*Escallonia macrantha*) which the islanders have managed to nurse along near their houses, the only trees on the Cape are a few gaunt hawthorns (*Crataegus monogyna*) and a couple of gnarled sycamores. Because of the scarcity of trees, woodland and hedgerow birds like great tits (*Parus major*), blue tits, coal tits (*Parus ater*) and blackcaps (*Sylvia atricapilla*), which are among the commonest of all birds elsewhere in Ireland, hardly ever breed on Cape Clear. Woodland is not the only habitat missing from Cape Clear. Its soil and topography ensure that it has no lime-rich grasslands, no fens, no rivers, no sand dunes and no uplands or mountain tops. In fact, the island only has sea cliffs, submaritime heaths, three bogs, one small lake and its old-fashioned fields. This composition of habitats is mirrored precisely by Cape Clear's flora—very few lime-loving plants but plenty of aquatics, no upland flowers but a surprising number of plants associated with cultivation.

Among these are the yellow rattle (*Rhinanthus minor*), fat hen (*Chenopodium album*), and the rare yellow bartsia (*Parentucellia viscosa*). Their presence indicates the one point where the human experience on the island diverges from that of the natural colonizers. For the very isolation and relative poverty which has slowed the pace of agriculture here, has limited the use of fertilizers and herbicides and therefore increased the chances of survival for the traditional meadow weeds.

Isolation, the third factor alongside climate and topography affecting the number of species on any island, has had its most obvious influence on Cape Clear's mammals. Although Cape Clear was cut off from the mainland relatively recently, probably just a few million years ago, this happened long before any of today's mammals could have reached it. For the mammals we see in Ireland now could not have survived the harshest periods of the Ice Age and must have arrived during the last 10,000 years. So, apart from bats that can fly, mammals have either had to swim to Cape Clear, as the grey seals and the otters (*Lutra lutra*) do, or be transported by man. Rabbits (*Oryctolagus cuniculus*), brown rats, wood mice (*Apodemus sylvaticus*), house mice and probably the island's pigmy shrews (*Sorex minutus*), have come this way. Of Ireland's other mammals—foxes (*Vulpes vulpes*) and badgers (*Meles meles*), stoats (*Mustela erminea*) and hedgehogs, pine martens (*Martes martes*), squirrels and deer—there is not a trace.

Finally we come to the matter of size. There is a general rule that the smaller an island is, the fewer species it can harbour. This is because most species require ready access to a wide 'gene pool', that varied assortment of individuals from which healthy breeders can be drawn. A small island lacks the resources—the space, the food, the habitats—to sustain large gene pools of many species.

One indication of the degree to which space is at a premium on Cape Clear is the avidity with which animals and plants exploit its tangled pattern of stone walls. Most of the island's small breeding birds, robins, wrens (*Troglodytes troglodytes*), blackbirds, song thrushes, occasional mistle thrushes, dunnocks and pied wagtails (*Motacilla alba*)—all species which might prefer trees, bushes or ivy-clad tree trunks—have learned to nest in holes in the walls. At the same time, plants have run riot, finding that each wall provides at least three different types of habitat. Moist, sheltered wall-bottoms become crowded with ferns, their dry vertical sides hairy with lichens, particularly species of *Ramalina* and every waterless joint has its pennywort (*Umbilicus rupestris*). This is a typical *Zerophyte*—a plant of arid locations—whose fleshy, coin-shaped leaves, succulent water-storing stem, and finger of pale-greenish flower-bells, are one of the dominant sights of the island. Finally the damper,

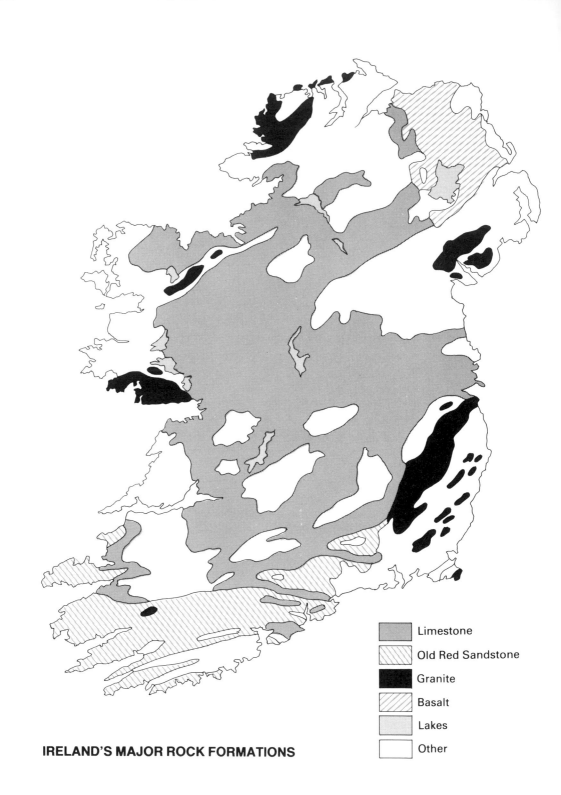

IRELAND'S MAJOR ROCK FORMATIONS

Limestone

Old Red Sandstone

Granite

Basalt

Lakes

Other

but exposed tops of the walls are inches thick in stonecrops (*Sedum album*) and scattered with the blue heads of scabious (*Jasione montana*).

In fact, whenever a farmer adds a new pile of stones to the edge of a field, the real surface-area of the island available to wildlife is increased, thus expanding the island's resources and enlarging the gene pools of those species that can take advantage of such efforts.

These factors that have limited the colonization of Cape Clear apply equally to that larger island which is Ireland. Ireland, too, is cut off from the 'mainland', from the gene pools of Britain and Europe. It endures the same oceanic climate, which has fixed the broad nature of its fauna and flora. Similarly, Ireland's size, soils and temperatures have limited the variety of homes, or habitats, it has been able to offer the creatures that, over many thousands of years, have come its way.

Like Cape Clear, the island of Ireland has not gained its species by lottery or by luck. Its relative isolation, its geological and climatic history and the structure of its habitats as they were once and are now, have all played their parts in the process of its colonization.

Ireland's Geological Bones

Let us imagine that we are a new species of bird, flying over Ireland and prospecting for a home. What would we see? In the first place, it could not escape our notice that Ireland is rather like a diamond-shaped saucer. Its perimeter is rimmed almost all the way round with hills and mountains. If we followed this ring of summits, counting those that climbed over 500 metres, we would find that out of about 176, all but half a dozen are within thirty miles of the sea. Inland, inside the rim, the land angles gently down to a wide, low-lying plain.

This has an interesting effect on the country's drainage patterns. Put simply, Ireland has two types of river: those that rush precipitously down the short, seaward slopes to the shore, and those that meander from the landward side of the watersheds, filling broad lakes, combining from a myriad network of tributaries, and finding the most lengthy and circuitous routes to the sea.

If we stopped for a while, for a year say, just to get the feel of the place, we would be rained on for at least 170 days. If we chose Connemara or Kerry we would get wet on two days out of three. In fact, unless we kept our head up we would drown, for there are plenty of places out west that receive over two metres of rain a year!

So much water draining into the wide, shallow bowl of Ireland gives us a land of streams, rivers and lakes, of fens and bogs, water meadows and rich grasslands, surrounded by damp hills—an exposed Atlantic island, standing on its own shallow coastal shelf, fringed with steep cliffs and fine, sandy beaches where life on dry land begins. If our prospecting bird requires aquatic or shoreline conditions he will settle down to a contented life. If he prefers trees, however, he will be disappointed, for Ireland has very little of its ancient woodland left.

The disappearance of the forests—and the spread of bogs and pastures— has occurred since the arrival of man eight or nine thousand years ago. The history of the rest of the landscape is, of course, on an altogether different timescale. The 'body' of Ireland, its basic shape, relief, and size, has probably been roughly constant for the last twenty million years. Its 'bones', the skeletal rocks beneath, are far, far older. Its 'skin', its dominant soils, and the 'scars' of its rivers and its mountain faces, date from the beginning of the Ice Age, less than a million years ago, and its 'clothes', the country's vegetation and its fauna, have mostly been donned in the last 10,000 years.

Geologists have classified the ages of rocks according to the evolutionary status of the fossils they contain. Older rocks, for example, contain only the remains of the most primitive organisms. The most ancient rocks to have preserved large numbers of fossils are about 600 million years old. In our region such rocks were first found across the Irish Sea in Wales and were called 'cambrian', after the Roman name for Wales. Even older rocks, whose existence stretches back over thousands of millions of years, pre-date the dawn of life itself, contain no fossils and have been classed simply as 'pre-cambrian'. Modern science has developed more accurate technologies for dating objects, most notably radio-metric dating. Some rocks, particularly igneous rocks, and organic matter less than 40,000 years old, contain traces of radioactive materials. Depending on their nature (Potassium-Argon 50 in rock, carbon 14 in organisms), these deplete at a predictable rate. So by measuring to the finest degree the amount left in a given object scientists can calculate its age. Nevertheless, geologists still use the broad, fossil-based names to describe the major rock-forming epochs.

The oldest rocks in Ireland, 2,000 million years old, have been found, in the far south-east, at Kilmore Quay and Rosslare in County Wexford. These were part of a continuous pre-cambrian shelf, which now only reappears in the far north-west, in Donegal and County Mayo. 700 million years ago the shelf was covered by a vast sea, where life was just beginning to form, and which lay from Scandinavia, over northern Britain and Ireland and merged with the Atlantic. From the land masses to the north-west and south-east of this sea sediments of clay and sand were washed down and deposited, thousands of metres thick, on the sea bottom. The lowest layers, pressed by the great weight lying over them, grew hot. The clay turned into shale and the sand became sandstone, both of which are still common in the central depression of Ireland's saucer.

About 400 million years ago the land began to rise. This was the beginning of the 'Caledonian Upheaval' which produced the Highlands of Scotland.

The shelf buckled and probably the first parts of Ireland to appear above sea level were the new-created hills of pre-cambrian rocks in those north-west and south-east corners. The heat of the upheaval produced the first granites of the Wicklow and Newry mountains, and so the rim of the saucer was already half complete. The whole plateau kept on rising until it was all above the sea. The central depression now filled with new debris, eroded from the hills. Rich in iron, this compressed into 'old red sandstone', the main rock of the south-west.

Subsequently, the area which is now Ireland was to be flooded by at least two more seas and each alternating period of water or dry land added something to the skeleton of the island we have now. Around 350 million years ago all but the highest ground was submerged under a new, warm, tropical sea, full of marine life, which left the rich legacy of carboniferous limestone enjoyed by the central and western lowlands. Then came a further upheaval, centred down in Brittany some 270 million years ago, and called the Armorican upheaval—again after the Roman name for the region. This raised up the old red sandstone hills of west Cork and Kerry. It was followed by the age of the dinosaurs, bringing another influx of ocean when chalk, most of which has disappeared from Ireland, was deposited. Finally we have a period of volcanoes, which created the magnificent mountains of Mourne in County Down 60 million years ago, and then, at the twenty-five million year point, a gradual cooling off, when the land mass of Ireland stabilized and the Great Age of Ice loomed.

Ireland's Ice Age: The Rise and Fall of a 'Glacial' Fauna

We have come to take the Ice Age for granted. The corries and tors (the hollows and spikes) carved by frost and ice from the faces of our mountains, the 'eskers', the raised fossilized courses of sub-glacial rivers preserved as ridges across the Irish lowlands, the whale-backed piles of boulder clay we call drumlins and the scattered boulders or moraines left as the ice retreated, are all now the stuff of basic geography lessons. Yet it was little more than a hundred years ago that geologists first realized that these were features of a glacial past.

The Ice Age had an enormous influence on the landscape of Ireland, sculpting its relief and distributing eroded drift soils throughout the lowlands. But in the context of the colonization of the country by plants and animals the Ice Age has one particularly interesting aspect. It confirms that a whole ecosystem could establish itself, develop to a climax and then be wiped from the face of the land, all within the short space of a few thousand, sometimes a few hundred years.

Just as mammals deposit their bones so plants leave their own distinct signatures in the soil in the form of the characteristic pollen each species produces. Consequently scientists can bore down to a selected layer of soil, age it where possible by radio-metric dating and then identify most of the plants it contains. Evidence from a boring near Gort in County Clare, and another at Kilbeg in Waterford, dating from about 200,000 years ago, shows the presence of freezing tundra-type vegetation giving way to dwarf birch (*Betula nana*), common birch (*Betula pubescens*), then juniper (*Juniperus*), pine (*Pinus sylvestris*) and willow (*Salix*). These were replaced by temperate climax forests of oak (*Quercus*), with alder (*Alnus*), hazel (*Corylus avellana*), ash (*Fraxinus excelsior*), holly (*Ilex aquifolium*) and yew (*Taxus baccata*). Next, the arrival of fir and spruce implies a soil degrading into acidity, while the presence of rhododendron is also a witness of comparative warmth. Finally, pine, birch and juniper return, then vanish and tundra spreads back to hold the region once more in its icy grasp.

This ancient rise and decline of familiar vegetation during what we think of as the Ice Age is evidence of a warm spell sandwiched between two long, cold periods. It is called the 'Gortian warm phase' in Ireland and it typifies the inconstant moods of the late Pleistocene, the last epoch before modern time. Geologists have analysed sites all over Ireland and have built up a jig-saw impression of the Ice Age as a long era of permafrost and tundra, plunging sometimes into ice-forming cold when glaciers advanced, and easing up into warmer periods when vegetation returned.

Geologists in Ireland have produced evidence that, in the midst of the last great cold period, the 'Midlandian cold', there were at least two warm stages which supported an interesting fauna. The femur of a woolly mammoth (*Elephas primigenius*) found in a cave at Castlepook in County Cork has been dated as 33,500 years old. Other bones in the cave of a similar age included the only remains of spotted hyena (*Crocuta crocuta*) ever found in Ireland. The fauna at the time was mainly northern in character, with wolf (*Canis lupus*), brown bear (*Ursus arctos*), reindeer (*Rangifer tarandus*), arctic fox (*Alopex lagopus*), mountain hare (*Lepus timidus*) and Norwegian lemmings (*Lemmus lemmus*). It also included the giant deer (*Megaloceros giganteus*) which is perhaps the most famous of all Irish mammals. Remains of the giant deer, and in particular its magnificent antlers—three metres wide and weighing thirty kilos—have been well preserved in Irish bogs. Consequently, many museum specimens come from this country and it is sometimes mistakenly called the Irish deer, although the animal was common all across western Europe. Its presence indicates a vegetation of lush grasslands and open, scattered woodlands of birch and willow.

But again, this was not to last. Examination of moraine deposits as far south as Ballylanders in County Limerick, shows a new advance of ice beginning about 26,000 years ago. The grass, the deer and the other mammals were swept away, and mammoths and hyenas were never to return. Thirteen thousand years later, however, the giant deer were back, along with reindeer

and many of the rest. The first signs of this new improvement in climate were found in a basin of land between drumlins at Woodgrange in County Down, and it is known to geologists as the 'Woodgrange interstadial' or warm phase.

What finally killed off the giant deer? In fact, of all those mammals probably only the wolf, the bear and a subspecies of the arctic hare reappeared in the post-glacial fauna of Ireland. So what happened to them all? The answer appears to have been unearthed at Lough Nahanagan, a corrie lake up in the Wicklow mountains. There, the band of temperate grasses from the last era of the giant deer was overlain by a new layer of arctic plants and above them was found evidence of one last glacier. It appears that what we call the Ice Age (though we may still be in it) ended with a final terrible swipe at life in Ireland. During the 500 years between 10,500 and 10,000 years ago, a period of intense cold struck. It was not long enough to form more than a few isolated ice caps, like the one in Wicklow, but it was probably cold enough to impose permafrost right across the country.

It is generally accepted that parts of Cork and Kerry were never covered by ice. It has often been assumed too that some southern plants growing naturally in Ireland are relics from the warm interstadials, and that at least Ireland's arctic flowers have been left behind by the glaciers. Some experts, however, are now wondering whether anything could have survived the last fierce cold snap.

Before its final extinction the giant deer, as we have seen, managed to make its way back into Ireland several times even after it had been completely expunged from the country. Similarly, it may be that our modern, post-glacial flora and fauna returned to colonize what was almost a clean slate.

Geologists have decreed that the Ice Age, and the Pleistocene epoch, ended about 10,000 years ago. True glaciers no longer exist in Ireland, they have retreated to the tops of the world's highest mountain ranges, to the lands far above the Arctic Circle and to the poles. Optimistically (for there are signs that our part of the world was at its warmest 6000 years ago and has been getting cooler ever since), we regard this as a new era, the Holocene.

The composition of Irish nature now is influenced less by what did or did not survive the Ice Age than by what could or could not get here afterwards. As the world's ice melted and the sea levels rose, Ireland became once more an island. The limiting factor on colonization ever since—just as we found it to be on Cape Clear—has been isolation.

Why Ireland Has Fewer Species Than Britain

Everyone knows the legend that St Patrick banished snakes from Ireland, but this would have been a miracle indeed since there weren't any snakes here in the first place. Indeed there are numerous animals and plants that are found nearby in Britain but are excluded from Ireland. Compared with Britain, Ireland has half the number of land mammals (twenty-eight out of fifty-five), and less than half the species of resident butterflies (twenty-nine out of sixty). It has fewer breeding birds (167 out of 229), only four amphibians and reptiles (or five if you count the very recently introduced slow worm, *anguis fragilis*) out of twelve native to Britain, and a more limited flora (940-odd flowering plants as opposed to around 1,400).

If we were to believe the mythology we would have to accept that St Patrick has been rather choosy about who can live in Ireland. There are several reasons for Ireland's short-fall in species. They are all connected to its status as an island and they are similar to the limiting factors which affect the natural history of Cape Clear. Firstly, Ireland is much smaller than Britain. To be precise, it covers 83,042 square kilometres, whereas Britain spreads over 230,607. Smaller size means a smaller gene pool so species that are anyway rare in north-west Europe are less likely to survive. Golden eagles (*Aquila chrysaetos*), for example, have become extinct in Ireland as their overall numbers have dropped. Remember, too, that Britain in its turn has only about a third of the species of mammals found in western Europe and has lost several of them including wolves, boars, bears and beavers (*Castor fiber*) in historical times. Ireland has also less variety of habitats. Its mountain ranges, for example, are neither so high nor so extensive. Consequently, alpine birds found in areas like the Cairngorms in Scotland, the ptarmigan (*Lagopus mutus*) and the dotterel (*Eudromias morinellus*), and a whole group of rare mountain flowers including a lady's-mantle (*Alchemilla glomurans*), alpine bartsia (*Bartsia alpina*), the mountain hawkweed (*Hieracium alpinum*), alpine sandwort (*Minuartia rubella*) and Highland saxifrage (*Saxifraga rivularis*) are absent from Ireland.

Ireland's mild but wet oceanic climate has also inhibited the advance of some species, particularly those that in Britain were already at the western or north-western fringe of their natural range. There are a number of birds, for instance, found in the south-east of England whose populations have never had the vigour to press further out in the direction of Ireland. Many of these, like the dartford warbler (*Sylvia undata*), the savi's warbler (*Locustella luscinioides*), the stone curlew (*Burhinus oedicnemus*), even the nightingale (*Luscinia megarhynchos*) and the woodlark (*Lullula arborea*) are insect-eaters that benefit from sunshine and are more common in southern Europe, or like the hobby (*Falco subbuteo*) and the red-backed shrike (*Lanius collurio*), they eat both insects and the birds that feed on them.

Then there is the question of Ireland's trees. The pollen record shows that as the ground warmed up after the end of the Ice Age 10,000 years ago, trees spread back across Ireland in an orderly succession, rather as they had done during the Gortian warm phase. First came juniper, followed by willow and birch. After 750 years, around 9,250 years ago, hazel and pine took over.

These were replaced as climax trees between 8,000 and 7,000 years ago by oak and elm. At the end of that period, pine declined very rapidly and alder appeared, implying a rise in temperature and rainfall. But the most cataclysmic change occurred 5,500 years ago when elm almost vanished right across northern Europe. Disease or a worsening of climate have been posited as explanations. The elm's decline, however, was accompanied by a sudden rise in weeds of cultivation, like docks, nettles and plantains; archaeologists interpret this as the moment when neolithic agriculture took off.

It is hard to imagine how neolithic man could have had such a sudden and devastating impact. He may have burned and slashed his way through the woods but the most convincing archaeological account involves the most labour-saving method. It has him cutting rings round the bark of the trees and leaving them to die while he grazed his animals and sowed his seeds between the trees as the light came streaming through the dead and leafless canopy.

Whatever the technique, the pollen record shows that 3,700 years later, by the year AD300, elm and ash were gone, hazel scrub was common and the grand ancient forests had diminished to small islands of woodland. Many of these were cleared in Tudor times and Ireland was left with the lowest tree-cover in Europe.

The loss of the forests has had a mixed effect. Ireland has probably retained most of its post-glacial woodland plants. They can still be found growing in hedgerows and in shady spots in treeless areas like the cavities out on the limestone of the Burren in County Clare. Birds, on the other hand, suffered dramatically. There are no breeding woodpeckers in Ireland, though we know from remains found in a cave in County Clare that at least one, the great spotted woodpecker (*Dendrocopos major*) was here several thousand years ago. There are no marsh tits (*Parus palustris*), no willow tits (*Parus montanus*), no crested tits (*Parus cristatus*), no tree pipits (*Anthus trivialis*), no hawfinches (*Coccothraustes coccothraustes*), no pied flycatchers (*Ficedula hypoleuca*) and no tawny owls (*Strix aluco*). These are all significant woodland birds in Britain.

Small size, the small variety of habitats, climate and history, have all played their part in limiting the number of species that Ireland can support today. The impact of these factors, however, has been exacerbated most of all by relative isolation, and isolation has had its profoundest effect on Ireland's quota of land mammals, reptiles and amphibians, the organisms that cannot travel by air.

Isolation, Ireland's Mammals and the Land-Bridge Theory

A mammal is judged to be a native species on the basis of archaeological evidence. If its bones are found in reasonable numbers at one or more mesolithic sites, say 7,000–9,000 years old, then this is taken as proof that the species was already established in Ireland at the time of man's earliest colonization.

Using this criterion, scientists have concluded that most of Ireland's contemporary mammals are not, in fact, native to the island. Leaving aside the seven species of bat that fly and the grey seals, common seals (*Phoca vitulina*) and whales that belong in the sea, it seems that man had a hand in the introduction of at least twelve of our twenty-one land mammals.

Some were brought here deliberately and we have records of their first arrival. These include the grey squirrel (*Sciurus carolinensis*), the rabbit, the brown hare (*Lepus capensis*), the fallow deer (*Cervus dama*), the sika (*Cervus nipon*) and the American mink (*Mustela vison*). It is generally accepted that the common rodents, the brown rat, the black rat and the house mouse were early stow-aways. The bank vole (*Clethrionomys glareolus*) is a mystery. It was first discovered in Kerry in 1964 during a live-trapping survey and it appears to have spread to counties Cork, Clare and Limerick since then. No one knows how it got to western Ireland – presumably, like its relatives, by boat since it certainly hasn't been sitting there since the Ice Age! The hedgehog was introduced probably in the late Middle Ages as a source of food.

The red squirrel is a 'native', but it died out and had to be reintroduced. There is even a question-mark over the red deer (*Cervus elaphus*). Most scientists believe the Kerry herd in Killarney is native, and genetically they appear to be a distinct race. Nevertheless, some sceptics have suggested that they just might have been shipped over by early man. The reasoning is that for an animal that would surely have been a major source of food, red deer remains around mesolithic habitations are surprisingly scarce, implying that they might have only just arrived at that time.

This means that only eight, or at the most nine of our present-day mammals can hold up their heads in any company and claim to be Irish. They are the fox, the badger, the stoat, the pine marten, the otter, the Irish hare (*Lepus timidus*), probably the red deer and the formidable pigmy shrew. A recent excavation of a mesolithic site near Clondalkin in Dublin has now confirmed the native status of the wood mouse as well.

Apart from the mammals we still have, there were several others that also returned to Ireland after the Ice Age but which have since become extinct. These have to be regarded as members of our 'modern' native fauna. The most important to humans was the wild boar (*Sus scrofa*), which was the staple diet of later mesolithic man. Others included the bear, the wild cat (*Felis silvestris*), and the last to disappear, the wolf.

Tenuous documentation of this list is provided, incidentally, by Ireland's 'first naturalist', an obscure monk called Augustin. In 655 he wrote a treatise *Liber de mirabilis Sanctae Scripturae*, and because his name was confused with that of the 'real' St Augustine of Hippo the book was preserved. In it he equates our concept of native, in effect, with the hand of God: 'For who else, indeed,' he said, 'might have brought wolves, deer and wild boars, and foxes, badgers and little hares and little squirrels to Ireland?'

The next question – assuming that God remained neutral – is how did these mammals get here and why are there, for instance, stoats but no weasels (*Mustela nivalis*) and pigmy shrews but no common shrews (*Sorex araneus*)? We believe that England remained attached to the continent along part of the English Channel for some time after the end of the Ice Age and that early recolonizing species made their way back into Britain along that route. It is also suspected that a similar connection survived, though for a shorter time, between Britain and Ireland. So all mammals and reptiles would have had to cross Britain before they could reach Ireland. This perhaps explains why Ireland has no species of quadrupeds which are not also found in Britain.

If we look at the seas around Ireland we find that at first glance the likeliest location for some sort of 'land-bridge' is the raised shelf stretching from Scotland, through the Isle of Islay to County Derry. As the Ice Age ended much of the earth's waters were still locked up in glaciers. If the sea level was fifty-five metres lower than it is today, then the passage between Scotland and Derry would be open. The isthmus between south-east Britain and the continent is only thirty-seven metres below the current sea level. So as more and more ice turned to water and the seas gradually rose, Ireland would have been cut off from Britain, long before Britain was finally severed from Europe. This would have allowed species to continue their advance into Britain even though Ireland had become unattainable.

The species that made it to Ireland would have been the pioneers, the hardier animals that first began the new trek north. This may explain why Ireland has so few reptiles and amphibians. Although many of the British species that are not found in Ireland, like the common toad (*Bufo bufo*), the viper (*Vipera berus*) the grass snake (*Natrix natrix*) and the crested newt (*Triturus cristatus*) have pushed on as far as northern Scandinavia, being cold blooded they would not have moved up north until summer temperatures at least approached an optimum. Even the frog (*Rana temporaria*) seems to have been an introduction – probably for food in the late Middle Ages. Only the common newt (*Triturus vulgaris*) and the lizard (*lacerta vivipara*) actually reached Ireland in the earlier post-glacial period. The lizard's survival in cold conditions may have been helped by the fact that it produces live young, not eggs. Its early arrival may also be indicated by the fact that it is the only reptile or amphibian found on Cape Clear and other offshore islands.

Unfortunately, the 'land-bridge' theory is fraught with controversy. The sea–bed has changed since early post-glacial times. It must have been greatly depressed by the weight of ice, and it may be unwise to draw conclusions from its contemporary profile. The notion of animals trooping cheerfully backwards and forwards in single file over dry land is no longer favoured. If a connection did exist – and it seems that some of these animals did reach Ireland before man – then it is the pigmy shrew that could hold the key to what it looked like. Pigmy shrews are found in Ireland; common shrews are not, even though the latter is much the more numerous species in Britain. Pigmy shrews have a catholic diet and survive well on boggy ground. Common shrews like earthworms best of all and require dry land. If our land–bridge was an extended marshy

water-land, dissected by innumerable streams and rivulets, it might have excluded the common shrew and let the pigmy through.

This suggestion, which has been put recently by several scientists, assumes that the ecology of these animals has remained unchanged over the last 10,000 years. It also assumes that the third British shrew, the rarer water shrew (*Neomys fodiens*) would not have arrived in Britain in time to avail itself of this gradually submerging isthmus, or that its burrowing tendencies, like those of the common shrew and the mole (*Talpa europaea*) would have excluded it.

Perhaps, after all, the connection was not a land-bridge, but an ice-bridge.

To pursue the question any further would take us too deep into the realms of zoological and archaeological debate. Suffice it to say that some sort of connection between Ireland and Britain probably existed for a while after the Ice Age; that ever since the ice melted numerous organisms have been attempting to establish themselves in Ireland but that, among the mammals, only a handful of species have succeeded without the intervention of man.

Where Ireland's Species Come From; The Lusitanians

The movement of species from other land masses across Ireland continues today. The air carries the seeds of flowers. Insects travel hundreds, sometimes thousands of miles. The painted lady butterfly (*Cynthia cardui*) for instance, works its way up through Europe to our shores every year all the way from Africa. And, of course, there are the migrations of birds. Each winter our estuaries and wetlands throng with waders, geese and wild swans down from the Arctic, our fields are visited by lapwings (*Vanellus vanellus*) from northern Britain, and our hedgerows by thrushes from all over the north of Europe. In summer the swallows and swifts, the cuckoos (*Cuculus canorus*) and warblers return from the far south to breed.

One of the finest places in Ireland to witness these migrations is Cape Clear. Ornithologists have long been attracted there in spring and autumn, not only by the regular passage of birds but by their irregular and unpredictable movements as well. A sharp-eyed birdwatcher might astonish himself by spotting a 'vagrant', perhaps a little yellow-browed warbler (*Phylloscopus inornatus*) from far away Asia, a golden oriole (*Oriolus oriolus*) up from the Mediterranean, or even something like a white-rumped sandpiper (*Calidris fuscicollis*) blown in from America.

Such observations are the life-blood of the collector, but more usefully they remind us of the wide variety of species that continually drop in on Ireland. This, if you like, is the visiting process through which successful colonizers will be selected. The vast majority of the established species of plant, bird and animal found in Ireland belong to the broad family of central-western and north European organisms, with a preponderance of oceanic species as the climate would dictate. But the story of the colonization of Ireland is by no means complete, as the history of a bird like the fulmar, and the more recent arrival and spread of the collared dove (*Streptopelia decaocto*) from Turkey would indicate.

Furthermore, there are some Irish species which lie outside the main grouping. There are species of plant, for example, that have North American affinities, in particular the blue-eyed grass (*Sisyrinchium bermudiana*) and the rush (*Juncus tenuis*). As we shall see when we examine the Burren in chapter six there are also a few plants with distinctly Mediterranean or high Arctic origins.

There is one much larger family of 'exceptions' in Ireland, however. These are the so-called 'Lusitanians' and they deserve particular attention here. They include numerous plants, some invertebrates and even one amphibian, and they are all organisms whose main centre of distribution lies down in the warmer lands of northern Spain and the Pyrenees (the area the Romans called Lusitania). Several of Ireland's Lusitanians, like St Patrick's cabbage (*Saxifraga spathularis*), Mackays heath (*Erica Mackaiana*), the beautiful Kerry lily (*Simethis planifolia*), and large flowered butterwort (*Pinguicula grandiflora*), are not native to Britain, while most others—Irish spurge (*Euphorbia hyberna*) or pale butterwort (*Pinguicula lusitanica*)—have very limited distributions there.

Ireland's most notable Lusitanian invertebrate (although it may not be genetically identical to the European species) is the Kerry slug (*Geomalacus maculosus*), which is found round Killarney and also, incidentally, on Cape Clear. If I can persuade anyone to think of any slug as beautiful then this is the one to do it. The Kerry slug is slender, not a gross sort of slug at all. It

is a rich black colour painted most attractively with neat cream spots and it has the charming habit of rolling up like a hedgehog when disturbed.

Finally we come to the natterjack toad (*Bufo calamita*), an attractive, warty little animal with a yellow stripe down its back. It is rare in Britain, and in Ireland it only occurs on a handful of sand dune systems in north-west Kerry.

Most of Ireland's Lusitanian species are found mainly, if not exclusively, in the mild south-west. Aware that this area might have remained free of ice during the Ice Age, Ireland's great natural historian, Robert Lloyd Praeger, author of the first modern *Natural History of Ireland*, believed that the Lusitanians were survivors from a previous era in which dry land between southern Europe and Ireland and the distribution of the Lusitanians upon it, had been more continuous. After all, he scoffed, the alternative was to picture something like a load of toads being shipwrecked off the Kerry coast!

From what we suspect now, however, about the behaviour of the ice and the fierceness of the permafrost even on unglaciated land, the likelihood of a permanent, cosy refuge for Lusitanian species in Kerry becomes remote. Other naturalists have suggested the existence of islands a bit further south where our Lusitanians sat out the Ice Age, but as the contemporary mammalogist James Fairley has observed in his *An Irish Beast Book*, these 'lands' have now conveniently disappeared.

The only convincing explanation for the presence of Ireland's Lusitanians is that they are the result of a limited post-glacial colonization, that a chance element has contributed to the arrival of the toads (perhaps they came in sand used as ballast in ships) and that, taken together, they are proof of the general rule that every type of climate and topography eventually attracts appropriate tenants.

Whatever way they have arrived in Ireland, an assortment of appropriate tenants have indeed taken up residency in all Ireland's habitats, in its sand dunes and heaths, on its mountain-tops and in its peat bogs, in its woodlands and hedgerows, its grasslands, rivers and lakes. But before we look at these ecosystems in detail, there are a couple of points still to be made about the effect of isolation on Irish nature.

Isolation and Endemism

There is another handsome slug on Cape Clear—one common all over Ireland—called *Limax marginatus*. When it comes out during the rain and stretches itself along the stone walls you can see that it measures two to three inches in length and along its buff-coloured flanks it usually has two dark stripes. I say 'usually' because sometimes the stripes turn out to be a line of black spots. Regular variations in colour like this can be thought of as a sign that the species' genes are 'experimenting' with new designs. Now it so happens that naturalists visiting Cape Clear have noticed a curious thing.

The island is shaped like a figure eight, joined at the 'waist' by a strip of land only a quarter of a mile wide. It seems that the stripey form of *Limax marginatus* is found mainly on the eastern side of the waist, while the spotty ones nearly all live out on the western bulge.

This may be the result of pure chance, but let us suppose, for fun, that there were only spotted rocks in the west of Cape Clear and striped rocks in the east, and that, furthermore, there was nothing to eat but turnips in the west, while only potatoes grew on the eastern bulge. Given time and isolation and the fact that the two bulges would probably become separated by the sea, we could imagine the evolution of two brand new and unique species of *Limax* slug. One would be a strictly turnip-eating spotted slug and the other would be a stripey potato freak, and the only place they would be found on earth would be on their respective islands of Cape Clear west and Cape Clear east.

On truly isolated oceanic islands this process has actually occurred. It is called endemism. When Darwin arrived at the Galapagos Islands with the crew of *The Beagle* he found a whole group of finch-like birds (*Geospizinae*), all broadly similar, but with very different beaks. Some had finch beaks, others had parrot beaks, woodpecker beaks, flycatcher beaks or warbler beaks. They were all 'endemics', found nowhere else, having evolved only on the Galapagos Archipelago. Darwin deduced that a single ancestral species had undergone what we now call 'adaptive radiation'. It had evolved new shapes and types of behaviour in order to fill a whole variety of roles, or 'ecological niches', that were available since no other small birds had managed to reach the islands. We now know that the same phenomenon had occurred 3,500 miles to the north-west, on the Hawaiian Islands. There, just one species of honeycreeper (*Drepanididae*) had 'radiated' into no less than twenty-three unique and different species of bird, and an additional twenty-four subspecies.

We have no cases of adaptive radiation in Ireland and no endemic species, but we do have several endemic subspecies. A subspecies is a recognisable distinct local race within a species, separated from other races more by geography than genetics. An Irish coal tit, therefore, could breed successfully with a French coal tit if the two were to meet. By contrast, two different species—a coal tit and a great tit, say, cannot breed together. Occasionally 'hybrids' are produced between species but they are infertile.

The most obvious Irish endemic subspecies are the Irish hare (*Lepus timidus hibernicus*), the Irish stoat (*Mustela erminea hibernica*), the Irish jay (*Garrulus glandarius hibernicus*), the Irish coal tit (*Parus ater hibernicus*) and the Irish dipper (*Cinclus cinclus hibernicus*). Each of these has some distinguishing feature in its colouration. The Irish stoat, for instance—which incidentally, has also colonized the Isle of Man—has no white rims to its ears and is smaller than the British stoat. Ireland's hare has a much browner coat in summer and does not turn white in winter as other races of the arctic hare do. The Irish

jay has more of a blue tinge on the back of its head, the coal tit is cream or buff on the parts where European coal tits show white, and Ireland's dipper lacks the rich chestnut belly of 'normal' dippers. All these endemics are, also, noticeably darker than their British or European counterparts as are many specimens of the Irish otter (*Lutra lutra roensis*). This so-called 'melanistic' tendency, which is also exhibited by several Irish invertebrates, including ladybirds and moths like the yellow shell (*Camptogramma bilineata hibernica*), is sometimes explained as the response to a cold wet climate, since dark colours absorb warmth. Among fish there are Irish races of charr (*Salvelinus spp*) and pollan, (*Coregonus spp*) locked away in Ireland's isolated lakes, and some of the most varied species of plant, particularly the hawkweeds (*Hieracium spp*) and the brambles (*Rubus spp*) include Irish endemics.

Isolation and Extinction

Finally we come to the last aspect of Ireland's isolation, the business of extinction. One of the most charming birds to be seen on Cape Clear is the chough (*Pyrrhocorax pyrrhocorax*). It is a neat, glossy, purple-hued crow with red feet and a slim, red, down-curved beak which it uses to dig insects out of the turf-lined soils of the clifftops. Chough fly in pairs or, when their two

or three young are on the wing, in small family groups, calling sharp, double cries which sound like ricochets over the rocks.

In Ireland they are sedentary birds, rarely travelling more than twenty miles from their birthplace at any season. So the chough on Cape Clear are probably an old, local family, perhaps a little inbred. Inbreeding is a hazard for isolated populations of any organism. It reduces the genetic vigour of the group and it is just possible that Cape Clear's chough might one day die out. In that case they might not be replaced by birds from the mainland. Isolation also leaves a species more vulnerable to disasters. As it happens, chough have already become extinct around the coast of Cornwall in

England, and they have declined over most of western Europe. Although Ireland, with between 600 and 700 pairs, remains a major stronghold for the species, the source of possible reinforcements is getting further and further away, so a catastrophe now—an unforeseen pollution problem, for example —could remove chough from Ireland forever.

Extinction is often the result of a failure to adapt. The dinosaurs or the giant deer, for example, failed to cope with climatic change and diminished food supplies. Loss of habitat may also be the deciding factor. The wild boar could not survive in Ireland once it was denied the cover of the forests, and much more recently the exploitation of part of the Bog of Allen has wiped out the pretty little Rannoch rush (*Scheuchzeria palustris*) in Ireland.

Some extinctions have been the result of deliberate campaigns of persecution. So, intensive agriculture and the use of herbicides have weeded out the ancient alien corn cockle (*Agrostemma githago*) from the Irish flora, just as relentless harrying had earlier removed the wolf.

Extinction, too, can involve mysterious biological functions. For example, the passenger pigeon of North America (*Ectopistes migratorius*) was not wiped out (the last one died in a cage in 1914) because trappers caught every last one. The problem appears to have been that in order to breed they had to be in clumsy, inefficient but vast colonies (rather like guillemots). What the trappers may have done was to reduce the population to below the level at which vast colonies could exist, and so the surviving birds simply stopped breeding. Perhaps the corncrake (*Crex crex*) which is now becoming so rare in Ireland (see chapter four), is also suffering from an unidentified biological syndrome.

We do not know the full extent to which extinction—rather than the failure to colonize—has been a contributory cause of Ireland's comparatively limited fauna and flora. But one thing is certain: when a species becomes extinct on an island like ours, the clock is set back on thousands of years of colonizing effort, and now man is here, such an organism is unlikely to make its way back again.

For this reason alone—apart from the beauty and wonder of their existence —it is well to study the animals and plants that we still have, and to understand the contexts, the habitats, in which they are most likely to flourish.

3
The Green Sandcastle:
The Dunes Of Murlough

Every sixty seconds the fog-horn booms out a warning across Dundrum Bay at Murlough in County Down. The black bulk of Slieve Donard, the mountains, and all the folds of Northern Ireland have disappeared and only a thin strip of shore is visible through the mist. Out at sea there's been a storm. The pounding waves have pulverised the rocks further down the coast and the churning waters have scooped up the sediment in the sea bottom. Now a gentler current, its power ebbing, slides across the shallow shelves of the bay. It empties its burden of storm-ground sand, pushing it up ripple by ripple onto dry land as the water laps the foreshore. The last tail of the wind dries the sand and whips it in snakes and gusts over the surface until something, a piece of driftwood, jetsam, or a plant, catches and holds it. Then the sand piles up in mounds, like newly delivered building material waiting for someone to come and restore the lost land.

This is the first beginning of a sand dune system. Looking at it, we can witness the birth of a wildlife habitat from scratch. Few of the children who crowd the beach, after the winds and the spring storms fade into summer, have any inkling of the wonderful story of this birth. They probably never notice how nature smooths away the battlements of their abandoned sandcastles and begins to fashion a more permanent edifice. And few of the families trudging back across the dunes on summer evenings will observe how they grow old beneath their feet. Crossing a dune system is like being in a time-machine. All the ages of a habitat, from youth to maturity, are laid out and easy to perceive as you travel inland. Hundreds of years of growth and colonization can be examined in a few minutes' walk.

Out of the sand a complete ecosystem will grow, colonized first by plants, then by insects, then by birds and mammals. Its members will sort themselves into a coherent 'sand dune' community, dependent on each other and specifically adapted to the prevailing conditions—to salt, for instance, to

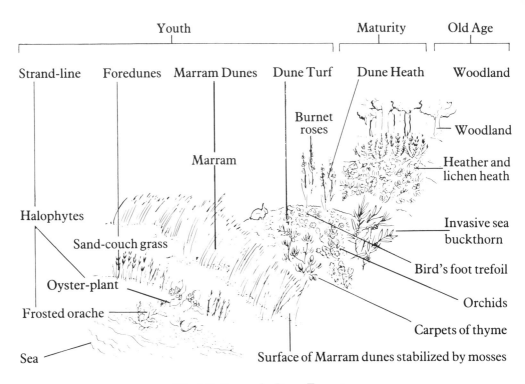

Youth   Maturity   Old Age

Strand-line   Foredunes   Marram Dunes   Dune Turf   Dune Heath   Woodland

Burnet roses

Marram

Woodland

Heather and lichen heath

Halophytes

Sand-couch grass

Invasive sea buckthorn

Bird's foot trefoil

Oyster-plant

Orchids

Frosted orache

Carpets of thyme

Sea

Surface of Marram dunes stabilized by mosses

The Life Story of a Dune Ecosystem

drought and to an immature soil. In the life cycle of a sand dune childhood is bare sand turning to light, grass-covered dunes; youth is a rich turf, full of violets, clover and orchids; maturity means robust, stable hills, dotted with blackthorn, carpeted with grey lichens and old age is the gradual merging of heather-clad dunes into farmland and woods, the beginnings of the rest of the countryside.

Ireland has many beautiful dune systems. There's hardly a twenty-mile stretch of coast without some sort of beach and sandhill. There are the playgrounds of Brittas Bay in County Wicklow, worn thin by generations of holiday-makers. There are the dunes of Rush, north of Dublin, trimmed and penned into golf courses, but still fringed with flowers of the rare green-winged orchid (*Orchis morio*). There's Bull Island, sitting right in Dublin Bay, where every dog-loving north-side Dubliner walks his pet on a Sunday, and where delicacies like autumn lady's tresses (*Spiranthes spiralis*) grow. And, of course, there are the remoter sand dunes, the wild, windy west coast systems like those in north-west Kerry, the only area in Ireland where the natterjack toad can still be found.

The dunes of Murlough, in Northern Ireland, however, are a particularly good example of how a habitat develops. All those stages of a dune's life are represented. The whole system has been preserved—protected from agricultural and recreational development—first by the Downshire family who owned it from 1800 onwards, then by the British National Trust who took it over in 1950. But before looking at the plants and animals of the dunes, it is worth examining the sand itself, seeing, in a little more detail, what it is made of and how it is delivered to the shore.

Sand comes from three main sources: it consists of fragments of rock worn from the coastline cliffs; it includes particles of stone carried from the land to the sea by rivers, and it also contains the shattered shells of crustacea and the powdered bones of innumerable marine creatures. Shells and bones are rich in calcium so fresh sand will always have a calcareous or limey quality, and this, as we shall see, is significant for dune flowers.

The proportions of shell and rock can vary enormously. At one extreme, for example, we have the beaches of western Donegal whose sands are made of quartzites and granites. These beaches occur at the mouths of Donegal rivers whose waters are heavy with glacial material endlessly washed from the granite outcrops inland.

At the other extreme are the beaches of Connemara, further south on the west coast, where tiny seashells have, over thousands of years, formed vast deposits offshore, and the sands are mostly 'organic'. In one or two famous spots near the townland of Roundstone, the sand looks like coral and consists almost entirely of the crushed hardened remains of a *Lithothamnion* seaweed. The Connemara sands have actually blown inland in places, creating a limestone habitat on top of acid soils. The Murlough sands are something in between, an average mixture of seashells, and granite brought down by the Carrigs River from the northern foothills of the Mournes.

The way the sand is delivered to the shore is influenced by the lie of the land beneath the water and, of course, by the direction of the current. 'Normal' beaches are formed by a current travelling parallel with the shore. Sand spits grow where the land suddenly cuts away from the current leaving shallows, giving the sand a base to build on. Rarer features, called tombolos, develop when sand builds up between an island and the mainland. Again, the fractured coastlines and sediment-laden waters of south-west Connemara are disposed to meet in this way. But however much sand is carried by the sea and however much the offshore gradients are able to trap the sand, dunes cannot form where the coast is unprotected from the waves. The power of a winter storm will quickly carve away an exposed beach. And indeed this is the normal cycle of life for most beaches, of growth tide by tide in the summer and sudden collapse in the winter.

So why are there dunes at Murlough? Clues have been found by geologists examining the shingle bars that are exposed by the wind from time to time. The shingle contains pieces of rock from far away formations, from the counties of Tyrone to the north-east, from northern Antrim, and from the Scottish Firth of Clyde. It seems that vast glacial deposits, channelled by the profile of the surrounding hills, ended up in Dundrum Bay. The modest flow of the Carrigs River pushed the deposits aside to form the arms of the bay and the sea's current fashioned them into a sort of anchor for the sand to cling to and build upon, thereby rising above the water.

The oldest dunes at Murlough, now a mile inland, grew up thousands of years ago. Under their low hills archaeologists have excavated artifacts 5,000 years old, and used by Neolithic man. Closer to the sea, forming a sort of spine down the centre of the system, younger sands have been piled on top, sometimes in hills of thirty metres and more in height—evidence, it is said, of great storms that struck the coasts of Europe in the thirteenth and fourteenth centuries. Over these ridges and stretching back towards the sea's edge lie the new dunes and the fresh sand. These are the accumulations of the last 500 years, where the life of the dunes begins.

Life On The Bare Sand

On an early morning at the end of summer, if you are very lucky, you can creep down onto the Murlough sands and find them occupied by seals. Common seals breed up on the northern sands of Dundrum Bay, and away round the corner on the islands of Strangford Lough. The fluffy grey pups are born on the sand or even in the water in late June. They can swim and dive right away, suckling their mothers under water, and are weaned within three weeks. By August they are off on hunting trips to Murlough with their parents. Hunting trips are not too arduous. There's plenty of time allowed for lying out on the sandflats, bodies curved like bows, a head and a flipper raised here and there into the sunlight.

When the tide is out at Murlough, sands half a mile wide appear, and the seals are safe, far away at the water's edge. The tide rises, and dinner arrives: molluscs and crustacea, and best of all, the flat fish, the flounders (*Platichthys flesus*), that are so common here. The seals slip into the water and begin to feed.

In these damp inter-tidal expanses, half sand, half sea, lives another easy prey for seals, the slender nine-inch sand eel (*Ammodytes tobianus*) which lives with the tides. As the water level goes down, the eels squirm and wriggle their way deep into the sand. When the sea returns they emerge again to swallow the plankton and crustacea that wash past their burrows. In August and September, the female sand eels lay piles of tiny oval eggs—often as many as 20,000—further out, where the sand slopes away into deeper water.

The provision of a nursery for sand eels is one of the most important contributions that the dune's inter-tidal zone can make towards the productivity of the sea. For almost everything eats sand eels: not just seals, but

4 *Top Left* Gannets.   5 *Top Right* Puffins.   6 *Bottom* Trawkieran Harbour, Cape Clear.

7 *Top* Razorbills and guillemots returning to Cape Clear's coastline.   8 *Bottom* Cliff colonies of kittiwakes, guillemots and razorbills on Great Saltee.

9 *Top Left* Marsh fritillary on devil's-bit scabious.   10 *Top Right* Bee orchid.
11 *Bottom* The Murlough dunes with Marram and sea buckthorn.

salmon (*Salmo salar*) and mackerel (*Scomber scombrus*), cod (*Gadus morrhua*) and turbot (*Scophthalmus maximus*), and most of the cliff-nesting seabirds, like puffins and guillemots, that breed around the sea coasts of Europe.

Apart from its role as a park bench for seals and a home for a whole range of specialized sand and mudflat dwellers (see chapter seven), the sandflats are essential as a protective girdle for the dunes. They dissipate the waves, smoothing them into gentle ripples which push the surface sand in lines slowly up the shore.

This freshly delivered dry sand offers the harshest of environments to any would-be colonizers. It is always on the move and it is quickly subjected to extremes of temperature. Even the inter-tidal sands, for all their moisture, can turn into death traps on very hot days. Occasionally, in summer, the sun is so strong during the day-time low tide that the sand bakes, the oxygen is boiled away and hundreds of sand eels spurt out from their holes, gasping and asphyxiated, before the sea can return to save them. How much more hostile is the dry surface sand up on the shore.

But the biggest hindrance to plants that want to grow on the strandline is salt. So close to the sea, the sand is continually drenched in fine, salt sea spray. Salt is toxic to most plants. It 'burns' their protoplasm, their living cells. It also stops them from taking up moisture through their roots because salt can absorb the available water more quickly than the plants.

One group of plants, however, can cope with the salt. They are called *halophytes*—salt plants. Not only are they not damaged by salt, but most of them can actually absorb it and use it as a sort of water-absorbing tool within their own cells. Halophytes include the seaweeds, that spend most of their lives immersed in salt water, and the plants of salt marshes. At Murlough, salt marshes develop where the sand and mud line turns inland to meet the estuary of the Carrigs River. Their damp, often flooded, salty ground holds typical halophytes like glasswort (*Salicornia europaea*)—which looks a bit like a long thin robot with lots of bumpy green segments—the dark, waving, branch-leaved seablite (*Suaeda maritima*) and sea plantain (*Plantago maritima*), which resembles an ordinary plantain except for its narrow spiky leaves.

There are also a few halophytes that manage to grow along the strandline, on the bare sand just above the high tide mark. The most specialized of these is probably the frosted orache (*Atriplex laciniata*), a silver-green spinachy sort of plant with roughly diamond-shaped leaves. It is an annual, growing from seed each year and so not expecting to survive in one place for very long. And it has a system of glands which can exclude salt when the plant has acquired sufficient moisture.

Above the orache grow slightly less salt-resistant halophytes—like the fleshy-stemmed sea sandwort (*Honkenya peploides*) with its bright little yellow star-shaped flowers, and sea campion (*Silene maritima*). Where veins of shingle are exposed, the blue-flowered oyster plant (*Mertensia maritima*) sometimes

12 *Top* Hen harrier chicks in the mountain heather.
13 *Bottom Left* Bog asphodel, a common plant of blanket bogs.
14 *Bottom Right* Young peregrines nesting in the Mournes.

finds a footing. It comes and goes at Murlough, depending in part on how much shingle the winds uncover, and how much it gets trodden on by visitors. It disappeared completely between the 1950s and 1977. (The leaves of oyster plants are supposed to taste like oysters—in other words slightly salty and like nothing very much, without the lemon.) The shingle also supports opportunist plants common both to the seashore and to waste-ground, like curled dock and common cleaver (*Galium aparine*).

At this stage, then, the plant life of the new, dry sand consists of a scattering of halophytes and just plain chancers.

The Building of the Dunes

Those first pioneering plants on the dry sand are stragglers. They grow in ones and twos, rarely enough to form colonies, and they have only a minimal influence on the sand itself. At most they provide the occasional obstacle for blown sand to pile up against, the first excuse for a dune to form.

The greening of the dunes, the real spread of vegetation, is begun by highly specialized grasses. The first to arrive is usually sand couch (*Agropyron junceiforme*). Sand couch is closely related to scutch grass (*Agropyron repens*) whose ability to choke a flower bed between one weekend and the next drives gardeners to despair. Sand couch grows fast, first by seed and then by underground stems called rhizomes. These fan out quickly under the sand sending out new colonizing shoots at intervals. If a storm scatters the new dune and fractures the young grass, every fragment of rhizome can form its own shoots and develop into a separate plant.

Sand couch is not a true halophyte, but it is more tolerant than most plants of salt on its foliage or round its roots. It can even survive the occasional flooding by an extra-high winter tide. This it must be able to do, because it is a perennial, a longer lived plant that does not die away in winter. Being a perennial makes it an effective trap for sand. Its leaves are there all year round, catching the particles, and they also act as a miniature wind break, reducing the shifting of the sand and increasing the rate at which the first line of dunes grows. These, the foredunes, are very important. They form a barrier to the wind-blown spread of salt spray and they stop the tide licking its way inland. They are the essential outer ramparts of the ecosystem that is about to develop.

The other plant that helps to create the foredunes is lyme grass (*Elymus arenarius*). An attractive, blue-grey grass, it is rare in Ireland perhaps because it suffers from its own special parasite, a type of fungus which spreads up the stem and seals the flowering spikes. It grows on dunes in north Donegal and along the shore of County Dublin, but is absent from almost the whole of the south and west Irish coast. When it does take root, lyme grass has the same robust ability as sand couch to spread rapidly through the sand. At

Murlough, the first patches of lyme grass were found in 1969 and within ten years it had crept along one and a half kilometres of shoreline—not very vigorously, but the plant was established.

In any case, on most Irish beaches, the thin wispy grass you find closest to the sea will be sand couch. But it has only a limited role to play in the life of the dunes and although it will begin to erect a second, inner line of hillocks, it cannot tolerate trampling, it is often heavily grazed by rabbits and once the dune sand begins to mass on top of it, the plant weakens and dies. However, just as the sand couch begins to fade, another grass takes over the job of building the dunes. This is marram grass (*Ammophila arenaria*). Marram is not so keen on salt as sand couch, and it needs the protection of the foredunes before it grows. But whereas sand couch cannot survive under more than about thirty-five centimetres of sand, marram positively thrives on being covered over.

Marram has a most tenacious root system. It fans out its stringy root tentacles just beneath the surface of the sand. When the wind blows and the plant is covered by a new layer of sand, the marram stem just grows up through it. It splits and branches out a second root system, above the original roots and again just beneath the new surface. As the dune keeps piling up, the marram stem keeps dividing and developing fresh roots. Each tussock of marram that you see is supported by an infinitely intricate network of fibres down in the sand. They act like a pattern of girders, endlessly reinforcing the structure of the dune as it grows.

How Marram Builds a Dune

The Marram stem produces new root systems just beneath the surface of new sand as it piles on top of the plant.

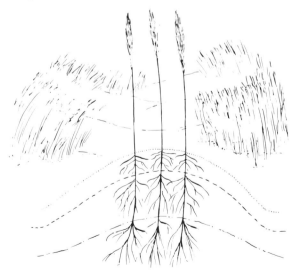

A single marram plant can provide the skeleton for a dune twenty-five metres high. What it cannot do, however, is stop the sand from blowing about on the surface. This job is accomplished by the next regiment of dune colonizers. After rain, enough moisture remains in the sheltered nooks and crannies between the marram stems for the wind-blown spores of various mosses to germinate. Soon the little star-shaped whorls of *Tortula* and the fingers of *Bryum* appear. These are the commonest mosses on the marram dunes, and they are accompanied by a new type of grass. Sometimes called sand cat's-tail (*Phleum arenarium*), this binds the horizontal surface of the dune in much the same way that the marram has consolidated its vertical profile. The cat's-tail sends its roots out sideways, pushing up a fresh shoot every couple of inches. Soon the sand is punctured with tiny grass stems, all standing up in straight lines like little soldiers, and the patches of bare sand get smaller and smaller once the mosses, the cat's-tail and other grasses and lichens become established.

When the sand no longer moves, the dune stops growing. At that point the marram loses its vigour. It seems that its roots require the challenge of accumulating sand to stimulate strong growth. The physical infrastructure of the dune ecosystem has now been built and the marram's work is complete. It stops advancing, and a more varied plant community begins to appear.

Coping with Aridity

The problem of salt has now receded. The sandhills are stable and their surfaces are no longer blown away by every breeze. But there are still several obstacles which stop just any old plant from setting up shop on the dunes. The most significant is drought.

It may be hard to conceive of a desert in Ireland, but this is what the dunes are in their early stages of development. Plants have to depend for their moisture on dew and rainfall. The sand is still too loose to hold water between its particles, so a week of summer sunshine can result in a serious shortage.

All the pioneering dune plants have evolved ways of dealing with the lack of water. Some of those that grow closest to the sea, like the tall, lilac-flowered sea rocket (*Cakile maritima*) have thick, succulent leaves. Sea rocket leaves look like green rubbery fingers. To some extent their succulence may be induced by the presence of salt—or its chlorine constituent—in the cells, but in any case it enables the plant to store water and use it when the going gets tough.

Marram grass also has a special trick of its own. During dry spells and in the heat of the day, it rolls its leaves in on themselves, turning them into long tubes. This halves the area of leaf that is exposed to the breeze. Breezes stimulate plants to give off water through the normal process of transpiration

—the vegetable equivalent of sweating—so, conversely, being able to hide from the wind is a useful precaution if you want to hold on to your moisture. Sand couch and lyme grass can roll their leaves as well.

Next there are mosses. Mosses usually grow in the dampest locations and they build up their own humus which often stores enough water for their purposes. The typical sand dune moss (*Tortula ruraliformis*), however, has amazing powers of survival in dry weather, hanging on even when it seems totally desiccated. An interesting experiment can be carried out by finding a patch of *Tortula* on a sand dune and visiting it with a bottle of water on a hot day. The moss will look dead, dried up and frizzled into stubby twigs. But as soon as you pour a little water onto it, the moisture seeps through the whole plant and it comes back to life, slowly opening its star-shaped fronds, one by one, like little eyes. So during the heat, tortula can reduce its metabolic demands to almost nothing by letting its green parts shrivel, and yet it is ready to respond and awaken immediately to the first drops of rain or dew.

Another tactic is to evade the drought altogether. In late February and early March the Murlough dunes are sprinkled with the tufts and threads of minute white crucifers (four-petalled flowers). These are the flowers of whitlow grass (*Erophila verna*), whose leaves form a rosette, and sea mouse-eared-chickweed (*Cerastium diffusum*)—quite similar but its leaves run up its thin stems. They are not just annuals, they are 'ephemerals'. They get the whole business of life—germination, growth, flowering and seeding—over and done with in a few short weeks in early spring, before the summer's warmth begins. In this way they can live the rest of their year as dry seeds —the most drought-resistant stage of a plant. (So drought-resistant, in fact, that seeds of one common dune-land plant, the kidney vetch have been known to germinate after ninety years—presumably a record for an Irish species.)

Although these ephemerals are well adapted for life on the bare dunes, that's not the only place they will grow. One of the commonest of them at Murlough, the hairy bittercress (*Cardamine hirsuta*), is found elsewhere on all sorts of bare, open ground, even in town. Bittercress has an amusing method of setting its seed. When its pods are ripe they wait for a passing animal, a waving grass stem or even a breeze. At the slightest touch their lids peel back like springs, firing a shower of seeds in all directions, and another bit of dune is colonized.

One other group of plants can cope with the arid dune conditions: the vulgar composites like dandelions and ragwort have very deep roots able to delve down through the sand, sometimes to firmer ground that holds water. They quickly establish themselves in places where other plants with shallower roots cannot make it. But by now there is enough vegetation on the dunes to support colonies of invertebrates. Most of them are mobile and avoid

getting dried up, but not the snails. A snail risks his all when
he sets off in search of a juicy leaf on a hot day. Normally
snails keep cool in their shells by squeezing under stones
or by piling deep into the foliage of larger plants. But
the dunes don't provide this sort of cover so dune snails
have to adapt like the pioneer plants. They have learned
to aestivate. Aestivation is like hibernation but it is
done in the summer. The snail slithers off and sticks
himself halfway up a stem of marram or sea rocket
where he can be wafted by the cooling breezes. He seals
the mouth of his shell, shuts down all systems and
simply waits until the heat is off.

The Growth of the Dune Turf

Ecologists will tell you that there are three factors controlling the development of plant life in any habitat. These are the climate—warmth, moisture
and light (the climatic factor)—the state of the soil (the edaphic factor) and
the effect of other organisms—competition or interaction with other plants,
predation by insects, birds, mammals, disturbance by man (the biotic factor).

We have now moved away from the sea, over the first waves of dunes.
We have crossed the hills covered with marram and sealed with mosses and
pioneering grasses, and arrived at the line of gently sloping hollows. Here,
lack of moisture is not a critical issue any more. There is enough vegetation
for water to be held for a while in the ground. In fact, in many dune systems
in Ireland the deeper hollows are damp enough for wetland sedges and rushes
and even willows and alders to grow. These are called dune slacks. There
are none at Murlough, only an occasional moist patch beside which the odd
pair of ringed plovers, a common shoreline wading bird, sometimes nests.
But, at any rate, desert conditions no longer rule.

The climate of the hollows becomes increasingly stable. There are no
extremes of temperature. There is plenty of light and no larger plants to
monopolize it. Furthermore, the rain—which in the long run will change
the chemical composition of the soil—is at this stage merely useful in keeping
the moisture level topped up.

Biotic factors have not yet become significant, though they soon will. The
plant community is still too young to support very sophisticated societies of
other wild creatures. So, at the moment, by far the most important influence
is the edaphic factor, the soil.

How does sand become soil? Though salt and drought have ceased to be
a problem, one hurdle remains for dune plants to conquer: the lack of certain
nutrients. Sand, unlike a mature soil, contains little or no nitrogen of its own
and no humus—no dead organic matter for essential bacteria to work on.

Plants require a whole range of elements in order to survive. They need phosphorus to help them store and convert energy, potassium to control the flow of water through their cells, sulphur for the creation of proteins, magnesium to make chlorophyll so they can 'feed', lime for their cell walls and tiny amounts of zinc, iron, boron, copper, chlorine and molybdenum. Sand probably contains enough of all these—and a surfeit of some, like lime —derived from the original rocks, seashells and seaweeds that sand is made out of. But more than any of them, plants need nitrogen—a major constituent of proteins and genes.

There is nitrogen in water, in dead and living plants and animals and in humus. But sand is a 'soil' without a history, so it depends on the greatest store, the air itself, which is 80 per cent nitrogen. Only a few plants, however, can tap this source directly. They are the nitrogen 'fixers', the plants that can breathe in nitrogen from the atmosphere, use it and then deposit it in the soil. Algae are nitrogen fixers—they grow amongst the mosses as part of the structure of the lichens—and so, to some extent, is marram. Although mosses in particular provide the first layers of humus, changing the texture of the sand to soil, neither they nor the lichens process much extra nitrogen for other plants to share. This is done by the fixers of 'fixers', the legumes —clovers, trefoils and members of the pea family.

If you look at the roots of legumes you might find tiny lumps, like miniature galls. These are called nodules and in each one lives the bacterium rhizobium. Rhizobium can only survive in the safety of a nodule, but it pays a sort of rent for the protection. As the atmosphere percolates into the sandy soil, the rhizobium absorbs nitrogen and mixes it with oxygen to produce a nitrate. This is passed first to its host and from there into the soil.

The most conspicuous and productive nitrogen fixer at Murlough is birdsfoot trefoil (*Lotus corniculatus*). This is a small, bright yellow pea flower, very common on sandy and grassy areas all over Ireland. It gets its name from its seed pods, which are long and pointed, and grow in clumps, three forwards and one back, strikingly like the claws of a bird. In some of the hollows nearest the sea, birdsfoot trefoil encounters so little competition that it gathers in uniform golden swathes covering hundreds of square metres.

From now on, with humus and nitrogen building up, the development of a dune turf is rapid. All sorts of beautiful flowers appear. There are always tufts of purple thyme (*Thymus drucei*), filigrees of scarlet pimpernel, the dancing heads of mauve or yellow pansies (*Viola tricolor*), and the stalked pink cups of common centaury (*Centaurium erythraea*). The powdered remnants of seashells in the sand give the turf a calcium, or lime-rich quality which always makes these dune hollows a rewarding place to search for rarer flowers. Every dune system has its specialities. At Murlough they include the spikey, yellow-brown discs of the carline thistle (*Carlina vulgaris*) and the tall blue trumpet-flowers of viper's buglos (*Echium vulgare*), that throb with visiting bees in midsummer. There are also the tightly wrapped pink triangles of the pyramidal orchids and, perhaps the most extraordinary of all the Murlough flowers, the bee orchid (*Ophrys apifera*).

The Bee Orchid

One of the most exciting experiences you can have at Murlough is to find the flowering spikes of bee orchids. There are not many of them and you have to be lucky, as you pick your way carefully over the colourful dune turf on a warm June morning. But it's worth hours of effort, for the flower of the bee orchid is an astonishing creation and the life-cycle of the plant tells us a lot about the interdependence of life forms in a habitat.

The flower is brown and rounded and engraved with gold markings. It is held to the stem by the wings of three sugar-pink sepals and it looks, not like the lip of a petal, but like a solid object, for all the world, in fact, like the body of a visiting bee.

This is no accident. The bee orchid belongs to a large family of orchids, most of them growing in southern countries and warmer climates, whose flowers have evolved an amazing technique for pollination. They 'deliberately' imitate the shape and colour of female wasps or bees; most of them adopt the identity of one particular species and time their flowering with critical precision. Because the male insects hatch out before the females, the flowers pop up offering, not nectar, but their bodies as substitute mates. The excitable male, programmed for speedy reproduction, flies down and 'copulates' with the flower, collecting pollen on its head, with which it will fertilize the next plant it assaults. Mind you, once the genuine females have appeared, with all moving parts in order, the flowers quickly lose their appeal.

Those 'insect' orchids whose ranges extend up into the unromantic north, however, come to rely less on their relationship with bees or wasps and resort instead to self-pollination. Insect behaviour, like the weather, becomes less predictable. So, despite their exotic looks, the bee orchids at Murlough are probably never visited by bees. After waiting in vain for a few days, their pollinia, the little stems inside the flower that are loaded with millions of pollen grains, simply shrink and bend forwards until they touch and adhere to the female stigma. It is a little disappointing that our bee orchids don't employ their so carefully developed powers of attraction, but at least they retain their exotic appearance as a symbol of the complicated pathways that evolution has taken.

One other relative of the bee orchid grows in Ireland though, and it is still pollinated by insects. The fly orchid (*Ophrys insectifera*) has a smallish brown flower with a metallic-looking blue patch which glints like the closed wings of a wasp catching the sunlight. It even has dark 'antennae'. The pollinating job is done by a little burrowing wasp (*Gorytes mystaceus*), which like the flower, is found as far north as Scandinavia. The fly orchid doesn't grow on sand dunes but prefers more sheltered locations, like woodland edges, where it may be that insects are more trustworthy. Just in case, it too is capable of self-pollination, which is convenient but, of course, it increases the risk of 'inbreeding': individual peculiarities are locked into the offspring—as they are in incestuous human relationships—and in the long-run genetic variety and vigour may diminish.

Bee orchids, like all the Irish and British orchids, have an extraordinary life-cycle. It cannot begin until the dune turf contains enough humus to support the growth of fungi. Fungi, in fact a particular type called the mycorhizal fungi, are intimately involved with the development of orchid seedlings.

Most plant seeds contain enough stored food to germinate and feed new shoots until they reach the surface. This usually only takes a few days or weeks. In orchids, however, several years elapse before the germinated seed grows its first leaves. Since the seeds themselves are tiny and quite incapable of hording sufficient nutrients the only way the orchid seedling can survive is to 'catch' an infection of mycorhizal fungus. The fungus uses its enzymes to ferment dead matter in the humus and turn it into food which it spoons into the orchid. But the relationship is not entirely friendly. It is more like a battle, with the fungus thriving in winter, and the orchid pulling ahead in summer. The fungus hangs on long after the orchid's dependence has subsided.

Bee orchids take from five to eight years to build up the energy to flower —a risky strategy since a seedling is likely to be destroyed before it can reproduce. Presumably, it is to compensate for this risk that they, like all the orchids, produce millions of powdery seeds. Having flowered, the bee orchid dies and disintegrates. So when you find a flower you really are witnessing a unique event.

Their appearance from year to year is unpredictable. Botanists still record the season in 1924 when thousands of bee orchids were found together at Magheramorne in County Antrim. The next year observers returned to the spot and found only nine flowers. When we finally spotted them at Murlough we decided to film them immediately. The following morning we returned, drawn by their special bumble-bee appeal to take some more shots. Every single flower had been eaten by slugs.

Insects on the Dunes

Slugs and snails are not the only invertebrates on the dunes for a populous and ordered society is developing. Under the grassy turf the new soil is beginning to team with 'earth processors', microscopic mites (*Acarina*) and springtails (*Collembola*), while nitrate levels are being enriched by the efforts of industrious characters like *Typhaeus typhoeus*. *Typhaeus* is a burly, scarab-type beetle. It is large, horny, roundish and black and it feeds on rabbits' droppings. When the male is not eating the dung, he rolls it around the dunes in search of his mate who will be busy digging a hole. The male doesn't dig because his showy armour-plating inhibits his movements. The female pushes the dung down her hole, lays her eggs over it and seals the future generation underground with its larder. Since the beetles bury much more dung than they actually use, the excess is efficiently distributed through the soil as fertilizer.

Above ground, small grey-brown weevils like *Sitona griseus* are nosing about with their long snouts between the marram stems, feeding on leaves and occasionally stumbling into the camp-sites of wolf-spiders (*Pisaura mirabilis*). The wolf-spider is like a desert bedouin. It spins a sort of tent in the marram grass which doubles as a nursery for the hundreds of baby wolf-spiders born inside and as a trap for unwary bugs caught and fed to them during their first days of life.

Among the flowers, a hundred species of flies are flitting about helping with the work of pollination. And every patch of flowers conceals a predator. Crab spiders (*Thomisa Spp*), for example, adopt the colouring of the plant they hide in. On the sand dunes they are often tiny and yellow, sitting motionless on the petals of the birdsfoot trefoil. They don't spin webs but rely on their crab-like mobility, pouncing sideways, backwards or forwards, whenever a fly alights on their flower.

But the spiders don't live their lives in tranquillity either. Most dunes have solitary wasps that live on the sand. At Murlough one of the most interesting is the rare *Arachnospila anceps*, which is a specialist at killing spiders. When the adult wasps emerge from their lonely underground pupae in midsummer they rush to mate. The male wasp is an effete chap who spends the rest of his time swanning about the dunes visiting flowers and sipping nectar. The female, however, is a lethal hunter. As soon as she has mated she scours the dune turf for spiders, scaring them out of their flowers or rousting them from their webs and burrows. With her long, slender legs she is an agile sprinter and she has little trouble in running down her prey, seizing it from behind and paralysing it with a terrible sting to the abdomen. Indeed, most spiders are so terrorized that they don't even resist. With her mandible and legs the mother wasp then excavates a nest chamber, drags the spider inside and deposits a single egg on top of it. Finally she flicks over a few grains of sand to close up the nursery-tomb before flying off to make provision for her next egg.

Many duneland insects are particular about what they eat. Another of Murlough's rare solitary digger wasps, one called *Crabro peltarius*, stocks its

burrows with just one species of fly, a long-bodied, hairy fly known as *Thereva annulata* whose larvae live in the dune soil.

Moths and butterflies also have specialized diets. One of the first moths to colonize the dunes is the coast dart (*Euxoa cursoria*). It is a dull, fluffy, buff-coloured moth, common at Murlough, and its caterpillars feed close to the sea on sand couch and sea sandwort. Next comes the shore wainscot (*Leucania litoralis*), with wings the shade of coffee and cream. It feeds entirely on marram—the adults come to the flowering grass heads and the larvae eat the leaves.

As you walk on the dunes, however, on a June afternoon, the moth you are bound to notice fluttering over the marram is the six-spot burnet (*Zygaena filipendulae*). Its front wings are grey-black decorated with six bright red spots and its back wings are a pale red edged with black. This arresting pattern is supposed to warn hungry birds that the moth is not very tasty. It is its only defence since, unlike most moths, the burnet flies and feeds by day. The cocoons from which the adults emerge are fastened halfway up the marram stems where they resemble closed buds. There are often hundreds of them and the fresh young moths, with wings hardly dry, will be mating right beside their newly vacated cases.

Before climbing the marram to spin the cocoons, though, the black-and-yellow striped burnet caterpillars gorge themselves for over a year exclusively on birdsfoot trefoil. Trefoil is also the gourmet choice of several butterfly caterpillars, like those of the dark green fritillary (*Argynnis aglaia*), a splendid, orange-brown, restless butterfly, and the azure common blue (*Polyommatus icarus*). But this adherence to one food plant reaches a spectacular climax with the marsh fritillary.

Marsh fritillaries (*Eurodryas aurinia*) are extremely beautiful. Their brown wings, orange below, are segmented with black lines, like stained-glass windows, and every segment has strips of colour, of black, of orange, of cream, of pearl white, sometimes of red. The caterpillars feed only on the tongue-like leaves of devil's-bit scabious (*Succisa pratensis*). There are only a few patches of this at Murlough and when the fritillaries hatch out all together in the first few days of June and sit quite still, every handful of leaves seems to have flowered into a butterfly.

Weevils, beetles, the larvae of flies, indeed lots of insects, show these specific preferences for particular plants. This has an interesting effect on the distribution of flowers in the dune garden. As the soil improves there are more and more plants wanting to move in and the uniform marram and trefoil blankets give way to variety. To avoid excessive predation by their particular insect pests each species of plant spaces itself out on the turf so that caterpillars, for instance, cannot easily crawl from one individual to the next and wipe out the colony. The gaps between the individual flowers of one species are filled by other plants. Consequently a mosaic develops, and its diversity is partly the result of the activities of insects.

Rabbits and the Dune Garden

The brilliant floral mosaic of the dune turf—its orchids and bedstraws, its thyme, pimpernels, storksbills and violets—is what attracts botanists to places like Murlough. But it is only one stage in the development of the dune system and it cannot last forever. As the colourful turf spreads inland and the soil improves, it comes under constant siege from invading shrubs. Once these taller plants establish themselves they will monopolize the light and the ground-hugging flowers beneath will wither away.

As in any garden, however, invaders can be kept at bay by constant vigilance. The guardian of the dune flowers is the rabbit. Their digging disturbs the ground, ploughing little furrows where small annual flowers can take root for a season. But, much more significantly, rabbits are mammalian mowers. They trim everything, giving the turf its close-cropped, well tended look. A shrub that can grow three metres tall or a pansy that flutters a couple of centimetres from the ground, will both end up the same height while rabbits are around.

The small flowers thrive until the soil becomes sufficiently rich in humus for shrubs and tall grasses to produce more young shoots than the rabbits can deal with. Under normal conditions this only happens on the older dunes, well inland.

There are some four million rabbits in Ireland. Each one is capable of eating a third of its own weight, or about one pound of grass or young shrubs, at a sitting. But there are two particular aspects of the rabbit's biology which make it such an effective dune gardener. The first is its digestion. Like most animals that eat grass and greenery, because plants contain cellulose which is hard to digest, rabbits need a specialized way of feeding. At the end of a meal they find a safe hiding place and excrete soft pellets of half-digested material. They then settle down to eat these all over again. Passing their food in this way twice through their very long digestive tracts helps them get the maximum amount of nutrition from it.

The rabbit's second distinction is its notorious reproductive ability. A four-month-old female can start breeding even though she is only half grown. Each pregnancy lasts just four weeks and most females are pregnant again within two days! The mother buries her young in a small hole like a play-pen so she can get on with the business of eating and mating, only visiting them once a day to suckle them. After three weeks she leaves the door open to encourage them to fend for themselves and she starts on her

next brood. She frequently produces six litters and a total of thirty young in a single breeding season. Still more extraordinary, in an area where there are too many rabbits or there is not enough food, the mother can reabsorb the foetus into her uterus and not waste her energies producing babies that would be bound to die.

Rabbits, of course, are not native to Ireland. They were shipped here from Europe, probably by the Normans, and for hundreds of years they were 'farmed' for their meat and fur. The earliest known map of Murlough, dating from 1702, identifies the sand dunes as an official rabbit warren. Murlough was part of the Dundrum Estate, owned by the successors of Sir Francis Blundell who bought it in 1636. According to the estate's financial accounts, the warren was treated as a valuable asset. Between January 10th and April 1st 1755, for instance, 3,614 rabbits were trapped there. They fetched a penny halfpenny a pair. The meat was disposed of locally and the skins were taken to the fur market in Dublin.

Ireland's native grazing animals, the red deer and the Irish hare, must once have played part of the rabbit's role in dune systems, and hares are still an important influence on grasslands like the Burren. So the cropping of the young dune turf is not an unnatural process.

Nevertheless, deer declined many centuries ago, and rabbits gradually replaced hares in most lowland areas of Ireland. Up until the 1950s there were between five and ten times the rabbit-numbers we have today. In Britain, for example, around sixty million were culled every year before the Second World War.

So many rabbits eating so much vegetation were bound to have a significant effect on any habitat. Conversely, if you had killed 99.9 per cent of them, you would have expected some fairly major changes to occur. This is precisely what happened when myxomatosis arrived.

Myxomatosis is a natural disease spread by fleas. It affects various species of rabbit in South America and California. But because they have been in contact with the virus for thousands of years, in them it causes only a mild affliction leaving its victims with slight bumps on the head. Its catastrophic effect on the European rabbit was discovered by accident. Laboratory animals in Brazil, bred from European stock, caught the disease and died, having first developed the now gruesomely familiar symptoms of pus-filled eyes and swollen, seeping glands. From there, the virus was deliberately introduced to France and Australia and in 1953 it 'escaped' from a laboratory in Kent, in the south of England. By 1954 it had spread to Ireland.

At Murlough, the disappearance of the rabbit was the signal for shrubs to conquer the dune turf. Aggressive sea buckthorn (*Hippophae rhamnoides*) spread in dense thickets over acres of dunes, reaching almost to the sea. And the blue buglos, the rare carline thistle, the pale spotted orchids and one small species of heather, cross-leaved heath (*Erica tetralix*), almost vanished.

But it is not in the interests of a virus to destroy its host. After those first lethal years the vehemence of the myxoma virus—in terms of the time it took to kill any individual rabbit—declined greatly. Since then, scientists in Britain have tracked the ebb and flow of the disease's intensity. They have shown how it evolves new strains and keeps in step with the development of resistance in the rabbit. This relationship between disease and host will probably continue forever, with rabbit populations slowly increasing as the virus selects its own weaker strains in order to preserve the maximum number of hosts.

Taking Britain and Ireland together, rabbits are now back to around 20 per cent of their pre-myxomatosis numbers. In Britain, in 1986, they were blamed for causing £120 million worth of damage. In Ireland, too, their return will be costly to farmers, but for the fragile flora of the Murlough dunes it will be like the arrival of the cavalry.

The Growing Community

Sea buckthorn, Murlough's most invasive shrub, grows naturally along the sandy coasts of southern and eastern Britain. It is not a native Irish plant but was introduced to Ireland because of its ability to stabilize coastal sands. Like sand couch and marram its roots and shoots spread quickly and, like trefoil, it has root nodules infected with nitrogen-fixing bacteria. It was first brought to Murlough in the 1880s and it has come to play an interesting role as a sort of halfway stage between the young dune community and the more mature scrub and heath which inevitably develops as the dunes grow older.

As long as the rabbits can keep it at bay, buckthorn makes several valuable contributions to life on the dunes. Its little creamy-white blossoms, appearing in March and April, are wind pollinated and probably offer little nourishment to early insects. But the large orange berries, strung over the hills like fairy lights in autumn, attract busy flocks of thrushes and chattering fieldfares from the far north. The trunks and branches of the shrubs also offer a habitat for lichens—around thirty species have been recorded so far, which is three times the number found on the dune floor.

The leaves of the buckthorn, however, are its greatest treasure. In May, they are eaten by millions of winter moth (*Operophtera brumata*) caterpillars. These are voracious little eating machines, found more commonly in woodland (see chapter five). They are quite aggressive, and will frequently swivel to nip each other when they are jostling for space on the same twig. Within a few weeks the caterpillars have stripped many of the shrubs to skeletons. At this point the green, fleshy moth larvae are very easy for birds to see.

The chaffinch is the ultimate buckthorn inhabitant. Without the shrubs and their caterpillars, chaffinches (*Fringilla coelebs*) would hardly be found at all on the dunes. This sprightly woodland finch—the male, with his white wing bars, blue face and orange breast is one of Ireland's prettiest birds—builds its nest in a fork in the buckthorn's trunk and lines the inside with lichen from the branches. Though adult chaffinches normally eat seeds, they feed their young on insects, which are easier to find in spring. The only problem in having dinner on the premises like this, is that the chaffinches' own home bushes sometimes get defoliated by the indiscriminate caterpillars, leaving their nests exposed to predators.

Meadow pipits (*Anthus pratensis*) do not run this risk. They benefit even more from the surfeit of caterpillars supplied by the buckthorn. Their young are just fledging when the caterpillars come on the market and it would hardly be surprising if they turned into winter moths themselves, since that's all they get to eat for ten days or so! Meadow pipits are extremely common. After skylarks they are the second most numerous bird on the dunes. They are small and brownish with creamy underparts streaked with short black lines. Males and females are alike, but if you watch a pair carefully you will notice that the male's breast streaks are darker and more distinct.

There are nearly fifty meadow pipits' nests per square kilometre at Murlough and they conform to a regular design pattern. They are always very well hidden, concealed on the ground at the end of a short passage in the grass stems. They tend to be on the inside slope of a dune crater, so the immediate vicinity of the nest is protected from general view, and there is usually a look-out post, a small thorn bush or the like, nearby. From this station the parents can survey the distant dunes for predators, cheeping nervously through beakfuls of caterpillars. When they finally decide it is safe to approach the nest they never fly direct to the lip, but creep with exacting caution through the grass.

What they are trying to evade is the unwanted attention of cuckoos. The female cuckoo's antisocial habit of laying her eggs in the nests of other birds and leaving her young to be reared by these unwitting babyminders is notorious. But some aspects of cuckoo behaviour are not quite so well known. In Ireland the cuckoo's most frequent victim is the meadow pipit. Contrary to popular belief, the cuckoo's egg is not usually a perfect match with those of its host. For instance, it is almost half as big again as a meadow pipit's egg and must feel very different to sit on. Although Irish cuckoos can sometimes produce fair imitations of the eggs of robins, chaffinches, sedge warblers (*Acrocephalus schoenobaenus*), dunnocks and wheatears (*Oenanthe oenanthe*), as well as meadow pipits, and each cuckoo concentrates on one preferred host, they don't always get the right pattern of egg into the right nest. A motley meadow pipit type often turns up among plain blue dunnock's eggs, for instance.

In other ways, however, cuckoos are cleverly adapted to their piratical lifestyle. They have short legs so the female can easily straddle the nests of

smaller birds, and her eggs have reinforced shells that can survive an unexpected drop. The eggs also appear to be incubated for several days inside the mother's oviduct before they are laid. This gives them a head start in the race to hatch out first among the stranger host's own eggs. Getting a lead is useful, since the newly hatched cuckoo will have to clear the nest of other eggs or chicks. Nevertheless, it only takes him three minutes to manoeuvre a rival egg backwards up the nest cup and over the rim, and a two-day-old cuckoo can eject a seven-day-old baby meadow pipit.

Finally, the cuckoo's long tail and rounded wings make her look like a sparrowhawk as she skims over the dunes. Her disguise helps her to find nests by testing the reaction of the meadow pipits to a 'predator'. The closer she is to the nest-site, the more anxious they become. In the end, however, she has to resort to rooting on the ground, and it may easily take her seven hours to locate the nest itself.

With such a high density of meadow pipit hotels on offer, Murlough becomes a veritable cuckoo metropolis in May and June, and an excellent place to study the bird's vocabulary. Cuckoos don't only say 'cuckoo'—which is anyway the male's prerogative—but they employ a complex language of coughs and gurgles. When the male chases a female he often hisses at her and when he catches up and displays to her he utters a number of gentle 'oohs'. The female, in her turn, will sit mewing thoughtfully when she is watching a potential victim, and she often lets out a significant long 'chuckle', particularly after she has laid an egg.

The poor old meadow pipits have to watch out for other predators as well. There really are sparrowhawks (*Accipiter nisus*) sometimes, cruising over the dunes from the woods further inland, and hooded crows (*Corvus corone cornix*) are a continuous menace to all small birds. These heavy, hungry crows, with their black faces and wings and their pinkish-grey shoulders and underparts, nest in solitary trees out on the older dunes. But, although they are always on the look-out for juicy chicks and can rip a pipit's nest to tatters in a few seconds, at Murlough they have taken with equal enthusiasm, to seafaring. The mussel beds in Dundrum Bay, exposed at low tide, offer easy pickings to parent-crows with two or three insatiable youngsters in tow. So, indirectly, the proximity of the sea provides a little respite for Murlough's pipits.

Maturity: From Heath to Woodland

All through the summer days skylarks hang over the dunes, climbing higher and higher as if worked by invisible strings, reeling out their long trilling songs without breath or pause. When they come down to earth they fall like parachutes, their feathers splayed and the white edges of their tails catching the sunlight. In countless cups of grass, nestfuls of tubby skylark chicks— all tufts of down and gaping pink mouths—are waiting to be fed, while the females, too busy for music, stalk among the flowers in search of grasshoppers or dig for grubs in the turf.

Beneath them, in the soil, a change is occurring. Decades of rain, pattering the surface and draining down deep through the turf, have dissolved the lime out of the earth. Without lime, that ancient legacy of seashells and fish bones in the sand, the maturing humus of the ageing dunes becomes increasingly acidic. At this stage one of two things will happen. Either the dunes will develop into heathland or, more rarely, they will suffer a blow-out.

Blow-outs occur when the high winds which can arise at any season rip the heart out of a dune, exposing the sandy soil so the whole process of stabilization and the growth of a turf has to begin all over again. In this case, when the turf flora is restored it will contain some newcomers, plants that are more attuned to the acid conditions. At Murlough these include a rarity like shepherd's cress (*Teesdalia nudicaulis*). It has a short leafless stem, topped with a puff of tiny white flowers, growing from a green rosette and is only found in one other place in the whole of Ireland.

After a few years, the turf on these disturbed, mildly acid dunes, is full of plants common to older grasslands and woodland, like primroses and tall two-leafed orchids called twayblades (*Listera ovata*). In the late summer they will be shaded, too, by dense stands of bracken.

The contribution of bracken to the dune habitat differs significantly from that of buckthorn in that its foliage is not eaten at the beginning of summer but at the end. The fresh leaves of bracken contain a form of cyanide which keeps them safe from insects. As the weeks progress, however, the poison disappears and various moth caterpillars and the larvae of sawflies and other insects begin to feed among the fronds. One group of small muscid flies of the *Chirosia* family make a habit of mining the bracken leaves and you can see the effects of their work where the ends of the fronds curl up and wither.

This 'late-opening' insect larder is very useful for birds like the willow warbler (*Phylloscopus trochilus*) that breed later in the season, especially as their young have to fatten themselves up for a long migration down to North Africa. Willow warblers rear their offspring in grassy balls at the foot of the bracken stems. If you are patient they will usually tell you where their nest is. They give a short 'hooweet, hooweet' call when they are anxious and sooner or later they cannot resist flying over their patch and dipping, ever so slightly, to make a passing check on their chicks.

Whether the sand is affected by blow-outs or not, it must eventually go the way of all dunes and turn into heathland. At first, a solid grey matting of large-leaved lichens forms, giving the surface of the dunes a middle-aged look. On Murlough the lichen-heaths are dominated by two species of *Cladonia*. They are *Cladonia arbuscula* with its yellowish-grey, branched, hollow-stemmed tentacles and an intriguing lichen called *Cladonia floerkeana*. This species produces small, grey-blue, individual fingers, capped with bright red spore 'factories' which look almost like wax matchsticks stuck in the ground. The lichens often stretch for hundreds of yards, across the wide hollows between the old dune ranges. This is a sign that rabbits were long ago at work, pruning the shrubs and leaving the less palatable *Cladonia* behind. But the shrubs grow back and the final stage of the dune system is marked by broad stands of heather (*Ericaceae*). Rings of gorse (*Ulex*), or whin, as it is called here, surround the feet of the hills with sharp prickles and yellow flowers. The white smudges of burnet rose (*Rosa pimpinellifolia*) bushes litter the rolling heathland, blackthorns (*Prunus spinosa*) and hawthorns stand out against the sky and lonely sycamores, carved by the wind into submissive triangles, huddle in the folds.

Gone now is all memory of the sandy marram dunes or the lime-rich turf with its orchids and thyme. The sea is just a distant whisper, rarely glimpsed beyond the massed lines of younger hills. Here, instead of easy sand to walk on, you struggle against the wiry grip of waist-high ling (*Calluna vulgaris*). This is the nesting ground of the heathland birds, of the reed bunting (*Emberiza schoeniclus*) and the chattering whitethroat (*Sylvia communis*), and, all around, you can hear the metronome clicks of stonechats (*Saxicola torquata*).

The dunes have grown up and the ecosystem is complete. A fox picks its way daintily through the lichen, following a favourite path. Badgers have set up ancestral homes in the old hills. The badgers' estates at Murlough are obvious because bluebells (*Endymion non-scriptus*), split by their digging, proliferate all over the entrance halls of their burrows.

Away inland, the dune heath smooths into farmland and a line of woods. There among the birches and pines a creature of the trees, a long-eared owl (*Asio otus*), waits for nightfall. The glow of the evening sun catches the edge of its ear tufts as it turns to look back over the dunes where it will begin the night's hunting. So a grain of sand has turned into a forest.

4
The High Road: Colonizing The Mountains Of Mourne

The Mountains of Mourne are not the highest mountains in Ireland. That honour belongs to the Macgillycuddy's Reeks and the 1,041 metres summit of Carrauntoohil in County Kerry. Their flora is considerably less interesting than that of Ben Bulben in Sligo, the Wicklow Mountains south of Dublin probably have a greater diversity of mammals and birds, while for sheer remoteness I would choose the lonely hills of Donegal, looking out as they do on the empty ocean of the North Atlantic. And yet . . .

And yet the Mournes are unusually beautiful. They rise from the plains of County Down in the south-east corner of Ulster, a cluster of tall, deeply carved peaks—all of them around 600 metres or more—with sharp profiles, steep ravines and romantic names. There is Slieve Lamagan, the clinging-mountain, Bearnagh, mountain of gaps, Binnian, of the little horns, and Muck, of the pigs. And tallest of all, is the great blue pinnacle of Slieve Donard, 850 metres high, which dominates the coast, hangs over the sands of Murlough and is named after St Domhangart, a local chieftain, first a doubter, then a disciple of St Patrick, who is supposed to have fashioned himself a stone cell on the summit.

The Mournes are built from pillars and pyramids of granite, the summits bare and exposed and the shoulders and slopes clothed with grasslands, heather and bogs. Granite is an 'igneous' rock made from magma, molten material which welled up from a hot spot under the earth's crust and then cooled. Molten rock contains the element silicon in large quantities. It also contains oxygen and a varied assortment of metals and other elements. The nature of the dry rock which it produces depends on how quickly it cools. When thrown clear of the crust during, say, volcanic action it cools quickly to form smooth, fine-grained materials like basalt. When it cools in a vast block under the surface the process is slow and gives rise to the formation of large, hard crystals. This is the case with granite. The silicon combines with oxygen to form a quartz, with potassium and sodium to form feldspar, and with iron and magnesium to form mica. Quartz, feldspar and mica, then, are the main constituents of granite, which is an exceedingly hard rock.

The reason the Mournes magma was able to cool so slowly is that, at the time, some sixty million years ago, the whole region was roofed with a thick cap of much older sedimentary shale from the Silurian period of 440 million years ago. Somehow the granite was able to intrude into this like the filling in a sandwich, and cool off in isolation. Geologists have devised a theory, the 'cauldron subsidence' theory, to account for the intrusion. A vast chunk of Silurian rock fell from the bottom of the roof into the pan of molten rock beneath. Some of the magma was consequently pushed up to fill the gap and there it remained, gradually surrendering its heat between the fallen slab of rock under it and the intact cap above.

Over the next millions of years most of the Silurian cap eroded away, particularly in the high Mournes, leaving the new granite exposed. The hot climate which lasted until the Neogene era, twenty-five million years ago, probably 'rotted' the stone in parts. So when, in the late Ice Age, the Mournes summits were avoided by the glaciers sliding down from the north-west, their bare protruding faces were split and shattered by the frost, creating the spectacular peaks and tors that are so attractive now to mountaineers.

This little bit of geological history is important to the naturalist. The shape of the mountains has a bearing on their wildlife. The piles of splintered scree, for example, that lie beneath the summits, produce a constant ebb and flow of pioneering plants and insects. The profusion of crags and ledges on wild inaccessible rock faces ensures ample nesting-sites for peregrine falcons (*Falco peregrinus*), so the Mournes probably have a denser population of these rare birds than anywhere in Ireland.

More significant, however, is the influence on plants and animals of the granite itself. For granite, as we shall see, increases the inevitable 'acidity' of the mountain soil, making life more difficult for upland species. In this context, too, it is valuable for a botanist, especially, to know where relics of the original Silurian rock cap still exist. Silurian rocks are softer than granite and release their minerals more generously into the soil creating a more nutritious environment for plants. On the eastern crown of Slieve Muck, for example, a slender Silurian ridge is marked conspicuously by the sudden appearance of rare alpine plants like the yellow-flowered rose-root (*Sedum rosea*) whose presence would otherwise be unthinkable on a granite range.

The patchy survival of the Silurian cap has, likewise, influenced agriculture and the extent of human invasion of the Mournes. The western foothills form a crescent-shaped terrace 1000 feet and more below the High Mournes. There the granite is mainly covered with shales and agriculture is profitable. On the next terrace up, the shales extend to just one plateau, called Deer's Meadow, below the western ridge of Slieve Muck. The area was flooded for a reservoir in 1959 after the building of the Spelga dam—dam of 'the splintery rock'. Previously, however, its grasses were so much richer than the surrounding pastures that it was one of the last places where 'booleying' was still practised—the farmers of mid-Down used to herd their cattle up here from the lowlands for the summer grazing.

The Belfast water authorities have left their mark in other ways than the Spelga dam. There is an earlier reservoir in the deep gorge of the Silent Valley and, most remarkable monument of all, there is the 'Mournes wall'. Built between 1904 and 1922 to keep trespassers out of the watersheds, two-and-a-half metres high and just over a metre deep, it toils for twenty miles across the ridges and valleys of the entire mountain range.

It was with Mournes granite that the docks of Belfast and Liverpool were built, and large blocks were used for the Albert Memorial in London. Until the Second World War the granite was split with hammer and chisel—the 'plug and feathers' method. Now there are large commercial quarries using dynamite. The stone-boats that carried the granite to England returned with sturdy roofing slates from Wales. This is how the whitewashed cottages of County Down came to be among the first in Ireland to exchange their thatch for 'Bangor blues'. Some of them, my wife's family's included, still boast their original slates.

High on the Mournes hilltops, however, there is little rumour of this. In places the peat layers have been cut long ago, leaving criss-cross ridges and raised peat hags, but otherwise the impact of man is minimal. All day long you hear the wind and the magical solitary croaking of the ravens.

For many naturalists the raven (*Corvus corax*) epitomises the spirit of the

mountains. This great black crow, as big as a buzzard, with its distinctive diamond-shaped tail and its hollow call, always seems to be away, high in the air, shy and far from humanity. It is a rugged bird, one of the first in Ireland to breed each year, feeding its young on the carcasses of animals that have died in winter and on the afterbirth from the earliest lambs. For nesting sites ravens even outdo the peregrine falcon in their choice of impossible cliff-side overhangs. And when you watch them tumbling and rolling in the vast sky for sheer pleasure, the exhilaration of the upland is communicated far more movingly than by words.

In this chapter we will follow an imaginary path—'the High Road'—across these dizzy, 'raven-tongued' heights. We will examine how plants and animals respond to altitude and how their communities develop from the bare mossy heaths of the summits, through high montane grasslands and cold stands of dwarf shrubs, down through the peat bogs and the heather moors to the lower sheep pastures and finally out to the richer farmlands in the valleys below.

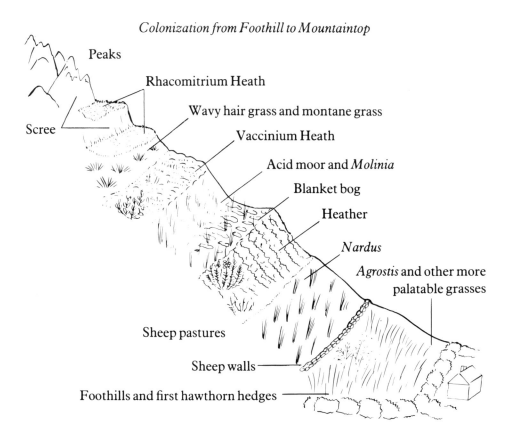

Colonization from Foothill to Mountaintop

Peaks

Rhacomitrium Heath

Wavy hair grass and montane grass

Scree

Vaccinium Heath

Acid moor and *Molinia*

Blanket bog

Heather

Nardus

Agrostis and other more palatable grasses

Sheep pastures

Sheep walls

Foothills and first hawthorn hedges

The humpbacked tops and stony peaks of the Mournes may not be high, but they can be treacherous. I remember one vivid morning setting off up Slieve Donard to film the rare nest of a ring ouzel (*Turdus torquatus*), the mountain thrush which lives on the high shoulders of the hills. It was a brilliant dawn, an unmarked blue sky with fresh rays of sun catching the beaded spiders' webs in the heather. Above us, the summits shone benignly, like touched-up photographs as we climbed towards them. Yet no sooner had we stopped, pitched our hide and angled our camera towards the birds than the mists fell on us. Everything was drenched with cold and dissolved into nothingness—the sky, the hills, the rocks, the grasses and ferns—all disappeared as if they'd been cancelled. Just ten yards away our precious ring ouzels came and went like ghosts, rarely visible, passing to and fro through solid walls of cloud.

We huddled there in blindness for three hours, hearing only the occasional cries and whistles of the shepherds piercing up from the clear foothills almost 300 metres below. Then a sudden wind ripped away the mist. It tore the hide from its moorings and hurled the camera on top of me, while the shrieking peaks swirled back with a changed aspect, grim and bitter. So began a succession of summer gales and storms that lasted a week or more.

It is important, in understanding how colonization begins on the mountain-tops, to see the peaks at their fiercest, for that is their usual mood. So many factors up there militate against the establishment of life. There are the extra-long upland winters, the splintering frosts and the all too brief growing periods of summer. There are the ceaseless skyline winds, the soils, thin to vanishing point, and the unkind nature of the rock itself. For granite is not a nourishing sort of stone. It contains few of the mineral nutrients that plants can use and its weathered fragments increase the unwholesome acidity of the soil. It is a hard rock, slow to erode, slow to crack and unwilling to offer the clefts and toeholes essential to plants in such an exposed environment.

But there is life at the top and, in the Mournes as on most Irish mountains, it follows a predictable pattern. First to colonize the bare rock are the alpine lichens. They require no soil and no crevices. All they need is clean air, plenty of light and a stable surface. (It is this last requirement, by the way, which stops them from being the first pioneers on sand dunes.) Lichens reproduce through spores which are scattered by the wind. Wherever they settle, even on the smoothest rock face, provided it is sheltered from the most vehement of prevailing gales, they can set up their miniature nitrogen factories.

The most obvious lichen up on the high Mournes is one called *Rhizocarpon geographicum*. It grows in large, emerald green patches, and from a distance it gives the impression that some colourful hillwalker has been clambering around splashing the rocks with green paint.

Lichens create the earliest vestiges of soil by weathering the rock and adding to the minute granite particles that they unpick from the surface the relics of their own dead growth. This provides just enough encouragement for the most pioneering of all mosses, *Rhacomitrium lanuginosum*. Sometimes called woolly hair moss, *Rhacomitrium* is amazingly resistant to cold and wind and will grow anywhere on the mountaintops, where the relief flattens out sufficiently. Indeed up on the stony detritus of the summits, where the rock fragments are ever on the move, *Rhacomitrium* will even precede the lichens.

It is a fluffy, greyish moss with stems that branch into numerous tufts and every narrow leaf is finely pointed with long 'hairs'. It often seems to be the only plant growing over dozens of acres and because it forms such extensive mats this type of vegetation has acquired its own ecological tag. It is known as rhacomitrium heath.

Once the heath is established, the brittle fingers of the grey-white *Cladonia* lichens spread into the gaps, and then the first mountain grasses appear. Wavy hair-grass (*Deschampsia flexuosa*) is a beautifully shaped grass. It produces a loose scattering of flowerheads attached to the main stem in groups of three by the slenderest of threads. The other common upland grass is sheep's fescue (*Festuca ovina*) whose flowers hug the stem rather like the ears of the wheat plant. Neither of these is restricted to the mountains by any specialized adaptation—indeed they can be found on poor ground all over Ireland. But they are hardy grasses able to root themselves in the shallowest of peaty soils and to feed on the meagrest of nutrients. Up in the rhacomitrium heath they crop up in stunted, isolated clumps. Their seedlings germinate in the humus created by the moss. They are nourished by the nitrogen supplied by the lichens and protected, as they grow, by the dense moss bedded around them. Once in place they spread freely down the high mountain slopes, thriving in the absence of lusher species whose demands could never be met on the top of the Mournes.

But life is still precarious. Those sudden winds can scalp the heath top, shifting the bared stones and forcing the lichens and woolly hair moss to begin their work all over again. This cycle of colonization and obliteration can continue for years. Indeed on some north-westerly exposures, facing the dominant gales, vegetation never really does get going.

One of the best places to examine the pioneering process at work is on the scree slopes. There among the frost-bitten piles of rock you will find stones covered with lichen, others packed together and grown over with woolly hair moss and, near the foot of the scree, carpets of grass beginning to form. Each winter these plant assemblages will be shuffled around as new frosts and winds get to work among the stones. Eventually, however, the mountain grassland becomes a permanent mantle. The first pioneering task is complete and new plants arrive. Dwarf shrubs, ferns, other grasses and rushes, even flowers, form the next community and their survival depends, most of all, on how they cope with cold and wind.

The Effects of Cold

The Irish mountains in winter are never quite as bleak as the Highlands of Scotland. Nevertheless, incorrigibles who have chosen to walk off their New Year's celebrations by clambering over the Mournes will know that the hills are pretty chilly at that time of year. On average, you can reckon that for every 100 metres you ascend, the temperature drops by 1 degree Fahrenheit.

This means that in the mountain regions of the Mournes, those areas above 600 metres, the air temperature hovers continuously around freezing point from the middle of December through to February. The fierce night-time frosts assault the plants' food reserves and their early buds. They also split the soil, extracting the stones like loose teeth. This may help to aerate the compacted earth, but it also adds to the instability of a plant's environment.

Almost more severe, however, is the effect of the cool summers on the hills. Although the potential growing season may last for four months, the heavy cloud cover obscures the sunshine. Even in July, average temperatures rarely climb much above 50 degrees Fahrenheit, so just when plants might expect a bit of warm encouragement their growth is suppressed. The most conspicuous result of the cold is the concept of the 'treeline', the height above which trees simply cannot exist. In Ireland the technical treeline is around 600 metres, though in practice you will rarely find trees above 300 metres and in the Mournes there are hardly any trees at all.

Cold inhibits all growth, not just that of trees, and this decides what sort of plants *will* survive in the uplands. Slow growth means that a normal life-cycle cannot be completed in a single season. This is why annuals—the quick-in-and-out plants, producing seed from seed in under a year—rarely make it up on the Mournes. Instead, nearly all the mountain plants have to be perennials, longer living plants which use food reserves collected in previous years to get them growing and flowering each spring as soon as they get the chance.

Botanists define four types of non-aquatic perennials and they give them magnificent names which describe their winter strategies. Two of the types are successful in mountains and two are not. *Hemicryptophytes* prepare their buds in the autumn and keep them protected, at or just below the surface of the soil, by a fringe of the previous year's leaf remains. Typical examples are the rosette-forming plants like starry saxifrage (*Saxifraga stellaris*), which is common in the Mournes, and tussocky herbs—the grasses, sedges and rushes. *Chamaephytes* include the dwarf mountain shrubs like blaeberry (bilberry) (*Vaccinium myrtillus*). They also have overwintering buds which are attached to their permanent woody stems and held fractionally above ground level.

The advantage of both these strategies lies in the fact that the impact of cold is minimised at the soil surface, so buds retained there are unlikely to be damaged or retarded by the frost. Indeed the inevitable layer of snow will actually insulate them, which is why mountain plants often flower so promptly when the snow around them melts.

The two 'lowland' types of perennials cannot survive heavy frosts nearly so efficiently. The *Phanerophytes* are the larger shrubs and trees and their buds sit at least a foot up in the air where they would be exposed to mountain winds. *Geophytes*, whose buds are buried underground near their food storing bulbs or rhizomes, risk being locked in the earth by a deep-biting upland frost long after the surface has warmed up.

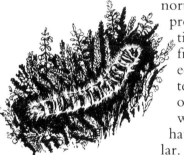

The inhibiting effects of low temperatures are not only felt by plants. The northern eggar moth (*Lasiocampa quercus callunae*) produces a magnificent brown caterpillar, sometimes nearly two inches long. Its thick fur coat, fringed with whiskery hairs, separates into dark-edged segments like a swiss roll divided ready for tea. The northern eggar is an upland race of the oak eggar, which breeds in Irish hedgerows and woods. The oak eggar flies in July and August, having spent a single winter and spring as a caterpillar. But the slower growth rate enforced by mountain conditions means that the northern eggar has had to extend and adapt this one year life-cycle. Instead, it passes one winter as a small caterpillar, uses a complete summer to go on growing to its full size and then 'hibernates' as a pupa in the second winter. It can then take advantage of the full upland summer by emerging as an adult in the May of its second year of life.

It also appears that the cold temperatures of the uplands can disrupt close associations between plants and insects. The moor-rush (*Juncus squarrosus*) for example, is common all over the Mournes. The cold at higher altitudes does not restrict the size of the plant itself, but it retards its production of flowers and seeds. Moorgrass frequently hosts a tiny buff-coloured micro-moth called *Coleophora caespititiella* whose larvae feed on the seeds of the rush. The moths hatch out in late June and spread up the hillsides in search of *Juncus* flowerheads in which to lay their eggs. The larvae and the seeds then develop together. But at heights above about 550 metres, the rushes will not have flowered by the time the adult moths are on the wing so the moths are unable to colonize the higher hills.

Cold, however, is not merely measured in degrees Fahrenheit and Centigrade. Wind makes the cold colder. The mountain gales that whirl around the ridges of the Mournes and hurtle down the hillsides have also had to be catered for in the evolution of life in the uplands.

Coping with Wind

At 600 metres the speed of the wind is likely to be double what it is at sea level. Gales are so frequent that, except in the most sheltered positions, tall plants would be snapped off or uprooted in no time. Consequently, nothing pushes its head up more than a few inches above the ground. As you walk down through the high grasslands of the Mournes in summer and pick your way among the pink bellflowers or the purple-black berries of the little blaeberry plants, it is hard to believe that you are actually crossing a vast shrubbery. That, however, is the case, for at these altitudes only the dwarf forms of woody plants can survive.

The alpine shrubbery of the Mournes develops once the grasses have firmly stabilized the soil, and it extends down the hillsides until heather takes over or until blanket bogs begin to form. Sometimes called vaccinium heath, it contains four common species of miniature bush. As well as blaeberry which has palish green, slightly toothed leaves, and is the only deciduous member of the mountain 'berry' bushes, you will usually find cowberry (*Vaccinium vitis-idaea*). It has smooth, dark evergreen leaves, its flowers are more pointed than bell-like and its berries are red. Then there is crowberry (*Empetrum nigrum*), with its pointed leaves and black berries, and occasionally the creeping dwarf willow (*Salix herbacea*) which produces little yellow catkins just like its large relatives, the 'real' willow trees.

Vaccinium heath grows on all Irish mountains and in the north-west, from Donegal down to the hills of Connemara and the Burren, the community is also joined by a rare little shrub, the bearberry (*Arctostaphylos uva-ursi*). It has bell flowers like a blaeberry and red berries like a crowberry.

Wind, like the cold, does not only control the size of upland plants, it influences their shapes—rosettes and cushion formations are effective wind defences commonly employed—and it also affects where they will grow. Even in very exposed locations, the sheltered side of a boulder may be quite richly vegetated. Lichens, mosses, shrubs and ferns will nestle into the protective shape of the stone while on the windy side only grass may be growing. Sometimes, the maturer vaccinium shrubs can themselves provide this sort of shelter. The gales prune them into elongated triangles, leaning away from the wind, and in their lee mosses and younger shrubs get the chance to develop. The result is a sort of wave-like vegetation with larger and smaller plants alternating in a regular pattern over the hillsides.

It is on methods of reproduction, however, that the wind has its most profound effect. There are not many insects up on the high ridges. The average fly might be blown from one summit to the next in the time it took

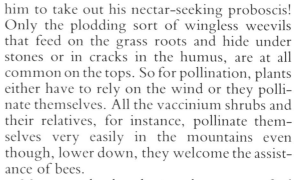

him to take out his nectar-seeking proboscis! Only the plodding sort of wingless weevils that feed on the grass roots and hide under stones or in cracks in the humus, are at all common on the tops. So for pollination, plants either have to rely on the wind or they pollinate themselves. All the vaccinium shrubs and their relatives, for instance, pollinate themselves very easily in the mountains even though, lower down, they welcome the assistance of bees.

Many upland plants, however, find specially adapted short-cuts to the business of propagation, doing away with pollination all together. Lichens, mosses and ferns, as we know, breed from wind blown spores. But in the barren mountain landscape, spores are often cast fruitlessly against hard rock and lost, so one common species of fern, the hard fern (*Blechnum spicant*) has a back-up system. It produces two completely different types of frond. One is a fertile, spore-bearing frond which stands up from the main growth of the plant, is tall and slender-leafed and dies away in winter. The other is infertile and evergreen, has harder, thicker-fingered leaves and grows in the form of a rosette which can spread vegetatively along the ground.

Much rarer in Ireland is the beautiful little parsley fern (*Cryptogramma crispa*). It is a speciality of the Mournes since, although it is not uncommon in northern Britain, it is found almost nowhere else in Ireland. Parsley fern is even more of an upland specialist than hard fern and it too develops fertile and infertile fronds. The edges of the narrow fertile fronds curl underneath to protect the spores from wind until they have grown, while the smaller infertile fronds have a broad, feathery appearance very like parsley—hence the name.

Another very interesting 'short-cut' is taken by a common mountain grass called viviparous fescue (*Festuca vivipara*)—a very close relative of the sheep's fescue. Instead of dropping seeds and leaving them to the mercy of the wind, it develops complete miniature plants on its stems. When these fall to the ground they are ready to root themselves immediately without waiting, as a seed would have to for germination. This form of reproduction can only occur in areas like the Mournes, where there are very high levels of humidity.

Finally, there are the clubmosses. Clubmosses are one of the oldest forms of life on earth. 400 million years ago they grew all over the world as huge, tree-sized plants. Now, however, they have shrunk into tiny finger-like growths, restricted to the hill-tops where they do not have to compete with the more efficient vascular plants and where their peculiar system of reproduction is still a useful means of survival. There are five species of clubmoss in Ireland, and two of them are common in the High Mournes, often growing where the rhacomitrium heath is developing into grassland. Fir clubmoss (*Huperzia selago*) grows in groups of upright fingers that look like pigmy conifer forests. Alpine clubmoss (*Diphasiastrum alpinum*) branches out like little flat hands along an often lengthy prostrate stem. Both can spread vegetatively, the alpine clubmoss being particularly adept at creeping over the surface of the moss, taking root at intervals. Both can also reproduce through spores, which are fertilized safely underground, and fir clubmoss, at least, has even a third wind-proof method of propagating itself. It produces bulbils. A bulbil is a robust type of clone, more than a seed, less than an independent plant, which drops off and develops into a replica of the parent clubmoss.

Acid Moor

Most Irish mountain soils are acidic, and in the Mournes they are particularly so. But what exactly is meant by an acid soil? We know that acid means sour to the taste, but in chemical terms it means the concentration of hydrogen ions present in any mixture.

Chemists long ago devised a simple formula for expressing hydrogen concentrations which we still use as the 'pH' system. It looks blindingly mathematical but it is actually quite straightforward. For instance one hundredth of a gram of hydrogen ions per litre of soil would be written by a mathematician as $1/10^2$ gm/L and by the chemist as pH2. Similarly one thousandth of a gram of hydrogen is written as $1/10^3$ gm/L or pH3, one ten thousandth is $1/10^4$ gm/L or pH4, and so on. The pH scale extends from 1 to 14 (from acid to alkali). Pure water (not rainwater) has a level of pH7, and what ecologists call a lime-rich soil will be pH 6.5 or above. So, by these measurements, distinctly acid soils are equivalent to pH 4.0 or below.

The acidity of upland soils is mainly caused by leaching, the process by which rainwater washes the mineral nutrients, derived from the rock, out of the soil. Rainwater consists mainly of hydrogen and oxygen. When the rain soaks into the ground, its oxygen content mixes chemically with the minerals to form various salts. These run away downhill, leaving the hydrogen behind.

In the lowlands the effects of leaching are countered, particularly during the summer, by evaporation which draws up water and, with it, fresh supplies of minerals from underground. The roots of the rich plant life help to do the same thing and the lowlands also receive some of the minerals washed down from the hills.

In the mountains, however, the vegetation is sparse and rainfall far outpaces evaporation. Even in mountains made of mineral-rich rock leaching is inevitable. Most hill ranges, however, are not particularly well endowed in the first place. The Mournes granite is mainly mica and quartz. With so little mineral variety, granite soils become acidic as soon as they are stabilized.

An acid soil means a poor soil. This is because acidity discourages the microscopic bacteria and fungi that would normally make nutrients available to plants (see chapter five). The typical leached acid soil is known as 'mor'. It will not support the most effective nitrogen-fixing plants like clovers and is peaty and infertile, containing comparatively few invertebrates. Ants, earthworms, millipedes and snails, for example, will be absent. In this respect, 'mor' contrasts with what is called 'mull', the fertile leaf moulds, full of insects, which are found in lowland forests.

The poverty of the high Mourne soil affects everything. Apart from the ubiquitous mites and springtails present in almost all humus, the only common invertebrates in the upland soils are leatherjackets, the larvae of the hardier species of daddy-longlegs (*Tipulidae*). Like the hilltop weevils, they feed mainly on grass roots.

Such a limited insect fauna explains why you see so few small birds up near the summits. In fact, there are only three regular species. The most striking is the wheatear. The male has a smooth grey head and back, with a black ear and an orange-brown breast, while his mate is a neat, sandy-coloured bird. Wheatears sit on the bare rocks, flicking their tails and 'chatting' at you and when they fly away what you are most likely to notice is the con- trast between their white rumps and black tails. Wheat- ears come in sum- mer and are very dextrous at re- moving leather- jackets from the ground. But there is not much else for them to eat and, since they and their young

15 *Top Left* Common sundew.   16 *Top Right* Peat turf, cut and stacked to dry on a bog in the Wicklow Mountains,   17 *Bottom* Sheep country in the Mournes.

18 *Top Left* The skill of scything the hay.   19 *Top Right* False oxlip.   20 *Bottom* Ox-eye daisie

21 *Top Left* Bird's nest orchid.   22 *Top Right* The flowers and fruit of Arbutus.   23 *Bottom* Oakwoods in Killarney.

have to fly back to the Sahara in autumn, they need to range over a whole mountainside to find enough food for such a journey. Indeed, on the average upland stroll you rarely meet more than one pair of wheatears.

The other birds of the mountain grasslands are the meadow pipits, which at these altitudes rely on things like rush moth caterpillars, and the wren which hunts up the weevils. The wren is a tiny bird with a giant heart. It has a big voice—a continuous sharp, piercing, trill and whistle—that can fill a valley and it is the only Irish bird that seems equally at home in the depths of a wood or on the top of a mountain. Actually wrens suffer terrible mortalities during harsh winters, but survivors fight back the next spring by laying up to a dozen eggs in a clutch and rearing several broods, so the hills are rarely without their songs.

Poor acid soils can only support plants that make low nutritional demands. In other words, 'poor' plants that don't eat much. Since plants rarely contain more nutrients than the soil on which they grow, this controls the population of grazing animals that can survive on the hills. The only native vegetarian up in the Mournes is the Irish hare and in order to stay healthy it has to make very selective use of the mountain menu.

Leaving out the mosses and lichens, there are four main communities of upland plant that the hare can choose from. On the high ridges, as we have seen, there is the fescue grassland, and the vaccinium heath. Lower down, there are the damp moors and bogs surrounded by purple moorgrass (*Molinia caerulaea*) and heather, and containing sedges like bog-cotton (*Eriophorum vaginatum*). Finally, there are the dense tangled masses of another grass species, called matgrass (*Nardus stricta*).

On average, none of these offers as much nutrition as a decent lowland pasture. If we take three criteria, nitrogen–protein, phosphorus and lime, the lowland field will have 50 per cent more protein, 25 per cent more phosphorus and two-and-a-half times as much lime as the fescue grassland. Matgrass has even less nutritional value—half the protein, a third of the phosphorus and quarter of the lime. No wonder that wherever a foothill pasture is reclaimed and fertilized in the Mournes, groups of half a dozen hares and more slip down of an evening to get in a good feed.

But supposing our hare stays up near the hilltops where he is safe from disturbance, what should he eat? If he sticks to matgrass he'll starve. If he eats *Molinia*, he'll get plenty of protein but only one seventh of the lime available in blaeberry. Heather will also give him sufficient lime, but contains only a third as much phosphorous as bog-cotton, which in its turn has almost no lime at all. But the Irish hare is no fool. He eats a bit of everything, building up a healthy diet from a cross-section of plants, none of which is particularly nutritious on its own. But this means he has to travel over a wide acreage so hares, like the wheatears and other small birds, are rarely very numerous in the mountains.

24 *Top Left* Wild garlic.
25 *Top Right* Male bullfinch.
26 *Bottom* The fox, Ireland's commonest predator.

The Formation of Bogs

As you come down off the high steep grasslands and vaccinium heaths, the shoulders of the mountains smooth into less precipitous inclines. There are scoops and hollows and wide plateaus, sodden with water and treacherous underfoot. These are the beginnings of the great peat bogs that spread across all the damp hillsides of Ireland. In late July their perimeters and expanses are flagged for the unwary walker by the white, loose-spun seed heads of the bog-cotton, dabbed like candy floss sometimes as far as the eye can see.

Bogs tend to form wherever drainage is poor, where, for instance, the rain falls at a faster rate onto the soil than it can seep out of it. The Mournes, as we know, are made of granite. Granite is impermeable so rainwater cannot soak through. It can only flow away where the slopes are steep enough to allow it to run downhill. As soon as the relief flattens out for a while, the ground becomes waterlogged.

The Mournes are wet. They receive about 1,500mm of rain each year. But many Irish mountain ranges are even wetter. Parts of Donegal get 2,000mm a year. In Kerry the figure can be 2,400mm a year and the Connemara hills practically dissolve under 2,800mm. So much rain means that, even on rocks that are not impermeable, waterlogging will occur through the simple process of leaching. On the steeper slopes leaching washes the soil's minerals away downhill, but in the upland hollows it carries them deep into the ground. There they eventually concentrate into a hard 'metallic' layer or 'pan' which won't let the water through. From then on the nutrient-empty soil or 'podsol' above becomes increasingly sodden.

The standing pools of stagnant water gain a film of algae and upon this the first layers of bog mosses, or sphagnum, develop. The sphagnum mosses are extraordinary plants. They feed on nutritive salts in the water, but because bog water actually contains so little nourishment, each sphagnum plant must be able to pass vast quantities through its system to collect the little bit of food it needs to survive.

To achieve this requires a very special structure. The outside of the plant is lined with a mat of capillary 'hairs' which suck in the water. Inside, the leaf consists of two types of cell. There are large empty dead cells, used as water storage tanks, and very long narrow cells where the business of photosynthesis and growth is carried on. The cell walls contain remarkable compounds to which biochemists have given the unfortunate name of *unesterified polyuronic acids*. These speed up the sphagnum's feeding process by swapping hydrogen ions, which the plant itself produces, for scarce but essential minerals in the water. In this way the sphagnum gets the goodies while the water around it becomes increasingly acidic and hostile to other forms of life.

There are at least fourteen species of sphagnum commonly found on Irish bogs. Each one has a slightly different role to play in the growth of the bog. The bright yellow starry *Sphagnum cuspidatum*, for example, is one of the earliest arrivals, and is found in the wettest areas. It is quickly followed by the larger-leaved, green-brown *Sphagnum papillosum* which is probably the most common of all, while on the raised hummocks of the well-established bog the fetching red stems of *Sphagnum magellanicum* take over.

They are all soft and bulging and full of water like sponges, and as a group, they are the most important plants in the evolution of peat. Peat, or 'turf' as it is called in Ireland, is a sort of half-way stage between wood and soil. It consists of half-decayed plants—leaves and flowers, roots and stems—that have lain in waterlogged conditions and have therefore never been able to decompose properly. It has developed, over thousands of years, from the sodden and compressed remains of flooded forests, of shrubs and of reed beds. But most often it is made from layer upon layer of dead sphagnum, the commonest plant on drenched landscapes.

Peat, then, is a product of arrested decomposition. But why does this occur? The answer lies in the supply of oxygen in the bog. As the sphagnum grows over the surface of the still bog pools, it shuts off light and air to the water beneath it. Without oxygen most of the common 'aerobic' bacteria that help to break down dead matter cannot survive.

A few types of bacteria, however, do not require so-called 'free' oxygen, that which is available in air and in aerated soils and water. Instead they use 'engaged' oxygen, unlocking it for instance, from sulphuric acid, which exists in very dilute forms in bogs. In a sense, these 'anaerobic' bacteria feed chemically rather than biologically. Sulphuric acid consists of hydrogen, sulphur and oxygen (H_2SO_4). When bacteria use up the oxygen (O_4), they leave behind hydrogen sulphide (H_2S) and this is what gives some bogs their terrible smell of bad eggs. No oxygen is left over to help with the process of decomposition which is therefore very slow.

There are two types of bog in Ireland, the blanket bogs that spread over poorly drained land mainly in the uplands, and raised bogs. Raised bogs are a more complicated phenomenon, occurring in the lowlands, in the depressed basin of central and eastern Ireland. They are usually part of the life-cycle of a fen (see chapter seven), developing on mineral-rich waters. Dead vegetation gradually seals the fenland nutrients beneath it. Bog mosses growing on top are consequently irrigated solely by rainwater, which is mildly acidic, acid conditions take over on the surface and a 'raised' dome of peat forms over the old fen.

Raised bogs are potentially fertile. Many have been drained for agriculture, while the turf of both raised and blanket bogs has always been a valuable commodity. For hundreds of years turf has warmed the hearths of Irish households and now it fuels eleven large power stations whirring out electricity twenty-four hours a day.

Bogs, for so long taken for granted, exploited and despised, have become a seriously threatened habitat. This is very sad because the peculiar conditions prevailing in bogs—high acidity and the scarcity of oxygen and nutrients—have helped to evolve a specialized wildlife community. It is a community of intrepid plants and insects that are now growing rarer each year.

Surviving in the Bog

The surface of the mountain blanket bog does not consist of a uniform film of sphagnum. The moss is only visible here and there, rooted in the most recent layer of its dead ancestors. The sphagnum carpet supports a diverse society of acid-tolerant flowering plants which grow up through it: small flowers like golden tormentil (*Potentilla erecta*), low shrubs like cross-leaved heath and sedges like deer sedge (*Trichophorum cespitosum*) and white beak-sedge (*Rhynchospora alba*).

In the Mournes, the first sign that a bog is developing occurs when the dry montane fescues give way to the red wiry stems of purple moorgrass or *Molinia*. *Molinia* grows in clumps across the drier areas of the bog. Damper patches are filled with swathes of the conspicuous cotton sedge, and ringed with the yellow flowers of bog asphodel (*Narthecium ossifragum*). Open pools of water, evidence of the latest rainfall, may contain the broad leaves of bogbean (*Menyanthes trifoliata*) and are fringed with black bog rush (*Schoenus nigricans*).

Throughout this community food is in short supply, but the bog plants have evolved a number of diverting strategies for coping with this problem. The most devilish device is the one employed by the sundews. There are three species of sundew in Ireland. The commonest, and the one that occurs all over the boglands of the Mournes, is the round-leaved sundew (*Drosera rotundiflora*). The oblong-leaved sundew (*Drosera intermedia*) and the larger great sundew (*Drosera anglica*) have narrower, more oval-shaped leaves, and are more numerous in the vast blanket bogs of the wet west of Ireland. Sundews eat insects. They are all small plants growing on the wet surface of the peat or on the sphagnum itself. Their broad, green, fleshy leaves are about an inch long and covered with shiny red spines. Each spine is dabbed with a dew-bright blob of sticky liquid which is irresistible to insects. Small midges, froghoppers, hunting flies, even dragonflies, land on the spines hoping to feed on the juice. But they get stuck in it and as they struggle they pull the leaf slowly closed around them like a jaw. The spines become the bars of a fatal trap where the insect's proteins are broken down by an enzyme secreted from the centre of the leaf and gradually absorbed into the plant.

In late summer sundews send up a fragile flowerhead that bends at the top very like a minute shepherd's crook. The flower itself is a little white star which only opens briefly in the brightest sunlight, has no attraction whatsoever for insects and has to be self-pollinating.

Then there are butterworts. The long leaves of the butterworts are pressed flat against the bog's surface, like vegetable starfish. They are bright yellow and shiny, as if smeared with a coating of butter, and are sticky and deadly as sundews, catching and digesting insects in a similar manner. Again there are three species in Ireland, each distinguished by its flowers. The common butterwort (*Pinguicula vulgaris*) produces a most beautiful deep blue flower, like a slightly trumpet-shaped violet with a white, feathery heart. It is the only butterwort found in the Mournes and is common in bogs right across Ireland except in the south-west where its larger, altogether more dazzling blue relative, the larger-flowered butterwort is found. The third species, the pale butterwort, is a white shade of pink, small and unassuming, and grows in lowland bogs.

There are five other species of 'carnivorous' plants in the bogs and acid waters of Ireland. These include the bladderworts (*Utricularia*), whose leaves swallow their prey in open water and the pitcher-plant (*Sarracenia purpurea*) which was introduced to the Irish midlands from North America in 1906. It has leaves like cups, half-filled with liquid, into which insects are supposed to tumble.

The bog plants that don't supplement their diet with insects have to be punctilious about recycling their nutrients. At the end of the summer the minerals that have been drawn into the sharp leaves of the bog asphodel and the slender foliage of the bog-cotton to make them grow, must all be returned safely to the plants' rhyzomes under the sphagnum. There they will be lodged until required again in the spring.

It is a delicate balance that has to be maintained. This becomes obvious when sheep-farmers try to exploit a bog. If sheep are grazed on it, their droppings, the occasional carcass, even their wool, help keep the nutrients in play. But if the shepherd cuts the bog plants to carry them off as fodder the minerals are lost for ever and the plants cannot grow back again.

Methods of reproduction, too, are carefully fashioned to suit life in the bog. The seeds of bogbean, for instance, are buoyed up with air sacks so they can float and disperse on the water, while bog asphodel can actually be pollinated by rain. Its golden flowers are fluffy and raindrops are captured on the long hairs on the stamen. There the water forms a sort of bridge over which pollen can float between anther and stigma.

The surface of the bog, of course, is in contact with the air and during the summer parts of it will dry out, ensuring that the top few inches remain reasonably well aerated. This is where most of the bog plants root themselves, and where most of its invertebrates are found.

The dark anaerobic zone beneath, however, is hostile to nearly all forms of life. Nevertheless, one or two insects have found ways of surviving even there. The larvae of chironomid midges which hatch out deep down in the bog water contain haemoglobin enabling them to hang on to any oxygen they manage to absorb. But the cleverest aqualung system has been devised for its young by the handsome metallic-coloured bog-cotton beetle (*Plateumaris discolor*). Its larvae have two hollow spines on their bottoms which they plug into the air spaces in the roots of the bog-cotton. This allows them to breathe while they construct a cocoon around themselves. As they change into pupae they give up their spines and rely on the communicating air passage between the cocoon and the adjacent root. The adult beetle matures in September, but this is a rotten time to emerge in an upland bog so it passes the winter quite happily where it is, munching the sedge's roots and using the plant as a breathing tube.

The Heather Moors

No one who walks in the Mournes in July and August can ignore the mauves and purples of the heather, drawn like a broad belt round the midriff of the mountains. Heather marks a sort of boundary between the uplands and the lowlands. Above it are the peaks, the mountain heaths and alpine grasslands. Around it, and sometimes beneath its roots are the bogs, while below it stretch more ordered pastures and the world of men.

Without men the wide expanses of the heather moors would not exist as they do today. At the moderate altitudes where heather now grows most luxuriously, it is not a 'climax' plant. In the natural course of colonization it would merely indicate a halfway stage in the development of upland woodland. But the pines, the birches and, lower down, the sessile oaks, have been felled far back in history. Grazing and burning have kept them at bay and so heather has become the most important plant in the mountain 'tree zone'.

I say 'heather', and many people would probably think of it as one plant, but there are, of course, lots of species of heather. If you travel west to Connemara, you might find the separate pink bells of St Dabeoc's Heath (*Daboecia cantabrica*) or the densely clustered flowers of Irish heath (*Erica erigena*). Both are plants more common in south-west Europe, and neither grows in Britain. While you're there you might also visit the single colony a few miles west of Galway, of Dorset Heath (*Erica ciliaris*), a species otherwise found only on the heaths of Dorset, Devon and Cornwall in England. Or you could turn up the rare bogland heather known as Mackay's Heath.

In the Mournes as on most Irish hillsides, only the three commonest heathers are found and they each occupy slightly different locations. Bell heather (*Erica cinerea*) is a compact shrub whose flowers are of the deepest red-purple and are kept half closed like globes. It only thrives on the driest soils usually on the steeper slopes and the sides of the valleys, where drainage

is most efficient. Cross-leaved heath, on the other hand, likes the wet edges
of the bogs. It is the 'vulgar model' of the Mackay's Heath. Its flowers are
pink and grow in a sort of fist of eight or nine bells on the end of a short
stem. The leaves form distinct and separated crosses climbing up the stem
from the ground. Finally there is ling, the most numerous heather of all. Its
requirements are intermediate in nature. It will grow on the drier parts of
the bogs or on the damper slopes. Its only overriding need, like all of the
heathers, is for a suitably acidic, peaty soil. The flowers of the ling are the
least conspicuous, but if you stop to examine them carefully, they are
the most beautiful. Their buds are like threads of pale beads stitched across
the moors. When they open they reveal almost star-shaped flowers, mauve
on the outside and creamy within and with long, delicate red-tipped styles
reaching out from the centre.

The flowering season for heathers lasts from July through September. The
first to emerge is usually cross-leaved heath, followed by bell heather, with
ling opening some weeks later. This staggered and extended blooming time
is very important for insects. Their life-cycles, as we have seen, are frequently
delayed by the altitude, so hungry, flower-sipping adult flies, bees and moths
tend to be more numerous in the hills near the tail-end of summer. In fact,
throughout much of the year the heather moors are a giant cafeteria to which
most upland invertebrates have free entry. Heather provides not only its rich
crop of flowers, but acres of leaves, miles of underground roots and, in
spring, tender nourishing shoots. The larvae and adults of beetles, weevils,
flies and thrips (*Thysanoptera*) feed on it, attracting, in their turn, the carnivorous invertebrates. Hunting through the heathery undergrowth, striped marsh
spiders (*Dolomedes spp*) haul their egg sacks, round and white like little golf
balls, clamped to their bellies. Voracious killer flies like *Empis tessellata* sit on
the leaves waiting for their prey. You can often find them squatting in
tandem: a large black female with her proboscis sunk into the flesh of a
hapless dung fly, sucking out its life juices while her mate clings to her back
fertilizing her.

Heather is a chief food and hiding place of the magnificent emperor moth
(*Pavonia pavonia*). It has a four centimetre wing-span with four startling circles
like eyes on its wings, and its furry body is as bulky as a bumble bee's.

There are several more specialized heather-munchers. Cross-leaved heath,
for instance, suffers the particular attentions of a scale-bug of the *Eriococcus*
family which causes galls that twist the stems into spirals. The most notorious
non-paying guest on heather, however, is the heather-beetle (*Lochmaea
suturalis*). Half a centimetre long and dark brown in colour, this little beast
can do a lot of damage. It strips the young heather of leaf and bark leaving
it a rusty red colour. Its eggs require a humidity of 70 per cent and more to
survive, so they are usually laid conveniently in neighbouring sphagnum
bogs. Sometimes they hatch out in plague numbers and, in the grouse-

shooting moors of Britain this phenomenon has become synonymous with commercial disaster.

In the Mournes, the heather moors help to feed the Irish hares and support a fair population of birds. The highest reaches straggling up the mountain ravines, and surrounded by cliffs, will hold the occasional ring ouzel's nest. Lower down in the foothill heathers you will find the heathland birds that we met on the old acidified dunes at Murlough: skylarks, whitethroats, reed buntings and stonechats. If you're lucky in late July you may also see a family of plump little orange whinchats (*Saxicola rubetra*), waiting in line on a barbed wire fence to be stuffed with daddy-longlegs by their parents. Uncommon relatives of the stonechat, whinchats breed on the moors and heaths in central and northern Ireland. Like the wheatears and ring ouzels, they are only here for the brief upland summer.

The bird most closely associated with heather, of course, is the red grouse (*Lagopus lagopus*). When a pack of them explode into flight at your feet you don't forget it in a hurry. But large populations of grouse require deliberate management. The heather must be burnt to maintain a constant supply of new shoots which the birds feed on. But too much burning removes essential nesting cover. Sphagnum must be drained to discourage the heather-beetle from breeding, but too much drainage causes erosion. Although the speckly dark brown plumage and the red eye-patch of a grouse can meet you on most Irish mountains they are nowhere very common. In all the weeks we were filming in the Mournes we only saw seven birds.

The other three species of British grouse, incidentally, are not found in Ireland. The giant capercaillie (*Tetrao urogallus*) became extinct here around 1790 through upland forest clearance, while black grouse (*Lyrurus tetrix*) and ptarmigan are simply not on the record books.

The Mountain Raptors

The kingdom of Mourne is one of the ancient realms of the north and although its boundaries have long since been erased and forgotten, it still has a king. For today the undisputed ruler of the summits is the peregrine falcon. The peregrine swoops on its prey at terrifying speed. With wings closed and body angled like a fighter-plane, it can clock 120 mph or more, striking its victim a thundering blow with one clenched talon on the back of the head. From a vantage point high on a cliff top or circling up and up above the mountain bogs and grasslands, the peregrine sees every movement on the hillsides. Nothing that flies is safe. Peregrines kill birds, and the combination of their awful velocity and perfect timing means that even geese and herons, birds many times their size, can fall beneath them.

Ornithologists in Ireland and Britain have recorded an astonishing number of birds in the peregrine's diet—117 different species so far. In the Mournes, snipe (*Gallinago gallinago*), meadow pipits, wheatears, skylarks, the occasional grouse, starlings, and passing mallards are all likely prey. Best of all, however, peregrines like doves—feral doves (*Columba livia*), wood pigeons (*Columba palumbus*) and homing pigeons.

You might suppose that such lethal hunters would make rather prickly companions. In fact, you would probably be right. Although peregrines usually mate for life, members of a pair pass the winters in comparative solitude. Each year, in early spring, they come together to celebrate a complicated routine of spectacular courtship displays. They circle and roll and dive, in unison and alone, calling their high-pitched wild, 'whickering' cry. They touch beaks in mid-air caresses, and practise talon to talon manoeuvres which, later on, they will employ in earnest when the male takes on the job of delivering food to the brooding female. Such demonstrations of intimacy are essential. They serve to remind two very dangerous birds not to hurt each other. They also cement a relationship in which, over the long months of rearing the young, mutual reliability must be absolute.

Males and females look alike. Both are slate-grey above and white or pale buff below. Their throats are streaked, their breasts and stomachs barred with dark grey and their cheeks are marked with conspicuous dark 'moustaches'. But if you are privileged to watch a pair together you will notice immediately that the female is the larger bird. She, after all, must be able to hunt even while she carries her developing eggs inside her. On average she is 15 per cent bigger, but a really hefty female can be double the weight of a modest male.

All the more reason for the male, who actually holds the territory, to be polite to her. Even before she has begun laying—around mid-April on the Mournes—he brings delicacies to her at the chosen nest-site, usually a narrow ledge on a steep, inaccessible rock face. The selection of the site is not difficult, for each territory will only contain a couple of alternatives, and generations of peregrines use the same eyries. Indeed some nests occupied today were recorded in falconers' notes way back in the Middle Ages.

The male helps a little with the incubation of the eggs—normally a clutch of three—and, until the chicks fledge, two and a half months after the first egg is laid, he does most of the hunting. In the Mournes both parents will still be guiding and feeding their full-grown young in the early autumn.

The female is a surprisingly tender mother. She stays beside her chicks almost constantly for the first weeks of their lives, offering them morsels of meat delicately poised at the tip of her beak. The nest itself looks a casual affair—just a pile of twigs or a shallow scrape. But on one occasion we filmed a mother returning from a brief exercise flight to find one of her fluffy, white, three-day-old chicks had strayed right to the cliff-edge. She carried it gently to the back of the nest and spent the next hour excavating a safety barrier of earth with her beak.

During the 1950s and 1960s the peregrine came perilously close to extinction. In Ireland numbers fell from about 190 known pairs in 1950 to only nineteen successful nests in 1968. In Britain the decline was identical, from 700 pairs to just sixty-eight, and the story—a well documented one—was the same throughout Europe. The cause of the catastrophe, as many people now realise, was the widespread spraying of corn with organochloride insecticides particularly Dieldrin and DDT. These pesticides are 'persistent'. They remain in the environment for years and once ingested they cannot easily be excreted from the body tissues. Because peregrines stood at the top of the 'food chain', feeding on birds like pigeons that had eaten infected corn, they absorbed many 'pigeon-fulls' of poison.

One result, of course, was death, but another was more common and more insidious. Female peregrines—and many other raptors were affected, particularly sparrowhawks—could rid themselves of at least half the toxin by including it in their eggs. Eggs became infertile, or their shells so thin that they fractured during incubation, so even birds that survived could not breed.

After severe restrictions on the use of pesticides were introduced in the mid 1960s, it took a further ten years for peregrines to show definite signs of recovery. In Ireland and north-west Britain, Dieldrin and DDT were less intensively employed and, with increased protection from other threats like shooting and egg collecting, the Irish peregrine population has now soared encouragingly to 350 pairs. In other parts of the western world, however, it has not been so lucky. In Finland numbers have fallen from 1000 pairs to twenty and the bird has died out completely in eastern North America. The story serves as a warning that even in the mountains, with their clean air and undisturbed landscapes, the long reach of pollution cannot be evaded.

Nevertheless the uplands provide the main breeding grounds for Ireland's other raptors. Golden eagles (*Aquila chrysaetos*) became extinct in Ireland in 1912, but an odd pair cropped up in Antrim to breed between 1953 and 1960. A few pairs of the smaller 'common' buzzard (*Buteo buteo*) also hang on in the Antrim Glens, in the Sperrins and in Donegal and, like the rangy hen harrier (*Circus cyaneus*), they are occasionally seen hunting over the Mournes in winter. Hen harriers nest in the heather or young forest plantations on many of the hills and moors of Ireland except those of County Down (including the Mournes) and Connemara. They are long-winged, long-tailed birds, the male a beautiful silvery-grey, whose buoyant, see-saw hunting flight is very distinctive.

Buzzards prefer rabbits, and hen harriers catch mice and numerous small birds. Merlins, however, eat meadow pipits. The merlin (*Falco columbarius*) is Ireland's other montane bird of prey. It is a small brownish falcon—the male has blue-grey wings—not much bigger than a blackbird. It chases its prey in dashing flights just above the level of the heather. Since meadow pipits supply half its diet and since they are so very numerous, it is odd that merlins are growing increasingly rare in Northern Ireland. They still breed close to the Mournes, but their stronghold is away west in areas like Connemara. Even there they seem to be declining. A study there in 1985 found that successful nests tended to be on inaccessible lake islands out in the bogs. So for merlins, as for most birds of prey, the key to survival is an undisturbed environment.

Sheep and Shepherds

We now move downhill, below the bogs and the heather moors, to the lower foothills. Here, sheep and shepherding begin to influence the landscape, often profoundly. Most picturesque are the dry-stone sheep walls threading their jig-saw patterns across the harsh pastures. The traditional Mournes design is like a honeycomb. Piled slabs of granite are interspersed with holes as if someone had removed stones at regular intervals (a handy saving on materials). They are much more solid than they look but the sheep distrust

them and won't risk clambering over. Stoats, however, have no such
scruples. They can weave in and out of the walls, ambushing rabbits on
either side at will.

Probably the real champion of the sheep walks, though, is the little sheep
tick (*Ixodes ricinus*). The tick larva emerges in the summer, hatching from
one of the 2,000-odd eggs its mother has laid. It then climbs to the tip of a
grass blade where it waits for a sheep, hare or you or me, to come past. As
soon as its station is disturbed it gets excited, sitting up on its hind legs ready
to make a grab at dinner with its front pincers. If it is out of luck it can sit
on for several days but then it has to crawl back down the grass stem to soak
up some moisture. The matting of grass near the soil, even if it is only a foot
lower down, is out of the breeze and therefore at least two and a half times
more humid than the grass tip. Without this damp resort the larva would
die.

The larva lives its life going up and down its bit of grass as if it were on
an elevator, and it can last out like this without feeding for two years. Success
means four days of drinking someone else's blood, even a bird's will do.
Then it drops back down into the matting and turns into a nymph. (An
immature insect is called a 'nymph' if it resembles an adult without wings,
and a 'larva' if, as in the case of caterpillars and butterflies, it looks totally
different.) The process must be repeated before it can become an adult, and
again before it can breed. At this final stage only the female feeds. She must
fill herself with mammalian blood in order to trigger ovulation. The male,
meanwhile, empty and minute, creeps around the twitching skin of the host
until he finds an engorged female. And a new throng of ticks will be on its
way.

The bleating of the sheep—whether or not they are troubled by ticks—
adds greatly to the atmosphere of the summer hillsides. But, under certain
conditions, their grazing can significantly alter the vegetation. Sheep don't
eat everything on the lower grasslands. One plant they do not like is matgrass,
or *Nardus*. *Nardus* is easy to recognise. It is a buff-coloured grass and its seed
capsules grow in a line together on just one side of the stem. If you pick
some and try eating it you will find out why the sheep are not so keen on
it. *Nardus* is full of fibre, its stiff husks stick in the throat and even for a
sheep, it is extremely difficult to digest.

If too many sheep are put out on a hill, they will graze down all the more
palatable grasses, the *Agrostis* and *Festuca* species. *Nardus*, left untouched,
will take advantage of the extra light and space available and will spread.
The same thing happens if heather is burnt indiscriminately and excessive
numbers of sheep allowed to graze all the new shoots that result. The heather
won't grow and *Nardus* will invade.

As we have already seen, *Nardus* is one of the poorest of grasses in terms
of its nutrient content. It hosts few insects and is avoided by hares and rabbits

so where it takes over it reduces the overall productivity of the uplands for wildlife as well as man. It is not so often in our temperate lands that man actually makes the environment less hospitable for himself and his crops and animals. In the fertile lowlands, after all, we have forced the soil to produce more and more through imaginative technological advances. But the mountains are less forgiving, and the balance of nature there is altogether more fragile. A few sheep can make all the difference.

From here on down into the valleys the hillsides are no longer under the sovereignty of nature. Climate, altitude and the state of the soil, which held such sway over the wildlife communities near the summits, now give way to the workings of man. Commercial considerations—EEC grants favouring beef over dairy herds, the preference for oil seed rape rather than corn or silage over hay—these are the criteria that govern the look of the lowland landscape. The simpler rules controlling the processes of natural colonization become obsolete.

If you stand at the Spelga dam, with the ridge of Slieve Muck behind you, you look down across the vale of the River Bann where the limited nutrients of the Mournes have been carried by thousands of years of rainfall. It is a gleaming plain of pleasant farmland stretching away to the town of Banbridge and beyond. Before leaving this, the last skirt or flounce of the mountain range, it is worth giving some brief consideration to the role of the farmer down there. For, in a sense, his activities can be compared to any large organism—a rabbit on the dunes or a deer in the forests—that modifies its environment.

Farm and Farmer

Since the Land Acts of a century ago, the typical Irish farmer has been an independent small-holder. Until the last ten years his methods have been 'traditional', implying a relatively unchanging agricultural regime, and he has had two overriding influences on the landscape: he has planted hedgerows and cut the grass.

Hedges were first laid out round the large estates on the rich farmland of Dublin and Cork. That was 300 years ago and their use spread all over Ireland, except to the rocky lands where the stone wall—or ditch as it is often called—is still the field boundary. A good hedge is a multi-purpose plantation. Its staple trees are hawthorn and blackthorn, to keep livestock in or out. In the past, ash or sycamore might have been added for firewood, hazel and willow for wattles and baskets, crab and apple (*Malus spp*) for fruit. Fuchsia, which adorns so many Irish hedgerows and cottage gates with the red ballet-dancers of its flowers, was introduced from South America. Hedgerows have provided shelter for generations of cattle and have shielded fields against erosion by wind and rain.

To wildlife they offer some of the facilities of woodland. Ecologically they are similar: they have the same three-tier-structure—flowers in the hedge bottom, shrubs in the middle and mature trees protruding at intervals to form a loose canopy at the top. They follow the same cycle of leaf fall, decay and nourishment of a rich soil fauna, and they share with woodland an intricate animal community based on the individual tree (see chapter five).

In fact, hedgerows are like a thin ribbon of forest looped back and forth across the landscape as a modest compensation for the loss of Ireland's primeval woods. They provide a continuous line of wilderness along which creatures can move in secrecy and safety. Mammals, apart from hares, avoid open terrain. Rabbits, for example, rarely stray into the centre of a field—on average they feed within fifty yards of their burrows, which are frequently in hedges. If you watch a hunting fox you will notice that he, too, usually keeps to the field boundaries.

Hedges also act as an extensive frontier between 'woodland' and grassland where species from both habitats can meet, sometimes with interesting results. For example, the primrose (*Primula vulgaris*) is a typical wood and shade plant while its relative the cowslip (*Primula veris*) is a flower of the open fields. Hedges bring them into close, though 'unnatural', proximity with each other and when this happens they can produce a hybrid—the false oxlip which is tall like a cowslip but has the large open flowers of the primrose. The 'frontier effect' also ensures that hedges and their grassy fringes provide a haven for field plants and animals displaced by intensive agriculture.

All in all, then, hedges shelter a diverse fauna and flora—nearly a third of Ireland's common breeding bird species and more than a third of its flowering plants. But life on the Irish farm has changed. Farms are getting larger. In 1940, 57 per cent of farms in Ireland were smaller than thirty acres. In 1980, the proportion had dropped to 45 per cent. The number of farms over fifty acres, on the other hand, has increased from 41 per cent to 52 per cent. Farms have also become much more mechanized. In 1939 there were only 2,100 farm tractors in the Irish Republic. By 1960 43,000 Irish farmers were tractorized and by 1980 the figure was 145,000.

Large farms require fewer boundaries. Mechanization requires larger fields. Both mean the destruction of hedgerows. Since 1936 14 per cent of Irish hedges have been grubbed up. This is a serious loss, even though, for comparison, the figure in Britain is 25 per cent.

And so we come to the business of cutting the grass—the area where the greatest agricultural impact has been felt. The traditional Irish meadow was grown with a dozen grasses, full of plantains and knapweeds, and, in its damper patches, held dense stands of white meadowsweet (*Filipendula ulmaria*) and the pink flags of ragged robin (*Lychnis flos-cuculi*). It was ablaze with flowers and humming with insects. It was cut for hay once a year, cut by hand and piled cock by patient cock, with all the townland sharing the labour and the cutting helped to restrain the most invasive plants and retain the floral diversity.

But now the meadows are cleared and drained and planted up with rye grass. They are a dark green monoculture, forced and fertilized and machine-mown for silage twice or thrice in a season. All this makes economic sense. Farmers can feed more cattle without the desperate anxiety over the weather and rain-spoiled hay. But the beauty and the wealth of wildlife are diminished. Ireland's lowland pastures have changed from a habitat into a factory floor.

Probably no species has suffered more than the corncrake. It used to be one of the 'characters' of the old countryside. There isn't a country person in Ireland who doesn't remember the 'scrape, scrape' call of the male out in the rough fields on summer evenings. It was always a hard bird to see—like a thin golden partridge with black flecks on its back and a greyish throat—preferring to skulk in the grass rather than fly. But occasionally a male,

keen to advertise his territory to best advantage, would choose an unusual prominence from which to deliver his message. There is an amusing record of one that habitually used the bumper of a parked car. One day, the owner kept awake by the incessant craking, hid the car round the back of his house. But the corncrake found it and the following night he was back on the bumper again.

Now, however, in most of Ireland corncrakes are neither seen nor heard. A nationwide survey in 1978 found them to have disappeared from most areas east and south of a line from Belfast to Kerry. Only in Donegal, Mayo and Galway was the population still relatively healthy and more recent studies show further weakening there too. Many Irish naturalists believe the corncrake is now heading for extinction in the country, just as it disappeared, thirty years ago, from much of England.

The explanation for this decline involves several factors. Despite their apparent unwillingness to get up on their wings, corncrakes actually migrate to central and eastern Africa in the autumn—and droughts in their wintering grounds may have put severe pressure on them. But their collapse in Ireland coincides with the intensification of agriculture, just as the areas in which they are still found are the areas where farms are still small, chemical dressings less used and the grass-cutting regime less demanding on the land. It has often been assumed that corncrakes have been killed at the nest by mowing machines. This may be true, but ample safe sites still exist all over Ireland, on the edges of lowland bogs, near hedgerows, in bracken and on all sorts of rough ground. The real problem is likely to be food. Corncrakes eat everything the meadows have to offer—crickets, spiders, beetles, caterpillars, flies, worms and seeds. The new farming systems reduce the variety of most of these. Corncrakes are not strong flyers. They must use a huge amount of energy on their African journey. If they, and especially the inexperienced young birds, set out on empty stomachs they will never get there.

Whatever the case, the old order is changing in the lowland farmscape and the loss of the corncrake is a symptom of this change. Compared with the barren summits and cold heaths of the Mournes, the lowlands are highly fertile. But their fertility is increasingly conscripted into our service, not into the nourishment of wildlife. As the potential productivity of the land increases, quite obviously so does the influence of man. Which is why if you want to see the fabric of nature and the patterns of colonization intact, you should study the hilltops.

5
Woodland Layers: The Killarney Oakwoods

If you stand, one October day, on a mountain shoulder of the Macgillcuddy's Reeks, you see below you to the east the long lakes of Killarney. Round their shores, folding over the low foothills and stretching woody tentacles up the vertical seams of the slopes, lie the last great Irish forests.

All around on the moors the red deer stags are groaning out the challenges of the rut. Streams are full and bounding down the hills into the woods. Leaves are on the turn, red squirrels are brandished by gusty winds like little mops in the tree tops, and whistling gangs of thrushes—redwings (*Turdus iliacus*) down from freezing Scandinavia, blackbirds, mistle thrushes and song thrushes from Britain, Germany and the Balkans—are stripping the berries from the yew trees.

This is the season, too, for admiring the arbutus (*Arbutus unedo*), the strawberry tree. In sheltered coves on the rocky lake shore, the last of the bees cluster on its small sticky white bellflowers, and its straight red fruits sparkle like incongruous Christmas decorations.

Arbutus is a plant of oceanic lands far to the south, lands like north-west Spain. That it is also native to this part of Kerry is a symptom of Killarney's warm, dripping wet climate, a climate, perhaps, that favours trees rather than men.

For the remoter Killarney woods are probably the nearest thing that Ireland has to ancient 'natural' woodlands: the only stretches of land in the country that have been covered with trees continuously since the end of the last Ice Age. These forests include stands of birch and alder, ash, hazel and yew, but they are dominated by sessile oaks (*Quercus petraea*)—the ultimate trees of steep 'Atlantic' valleys. They have survived intact though not unchanged—they have been felled and replanted but never cleared away—while the rest of Ireland has been all but stripped of its trees.

Woodland in Ireland has experienced a cataclysmic history, one of evolution through climatic change, followed by wholesale destruction (see

Chapter Two). It marks the climax of nature's colonization of the land. Nothing larger than a tree can grow and nature produces nothing more fruitful and intricate than the plant and animal communities that the tree supports.

Different types of woodland develop under different conditions. All that is left in Ireland of this climax mosaic are a few pockets of native trees: alders along the sodden shores of lakes and rivers, hazel on rocky limestone in the Burren, pedunculate oaks (*Quercus robor*) on the central lowlands near Abbeyleix and Charleville in County Offaly, and sessile oaks on the acid soils that are most common in Ireland. The finest of the semi-natural sessile oak forests grow in the valleys of Glengarriff in West Cork, near Glendalough in County Wicklow, in Glenveagh in northern Donegal, on the coastal slopes above Rostrevor in County Down, in the Glens of Antrim and best of all in Killarney.

The sessile oak is distinguished by its acorns which do not hang from stalks, like those of the lowland 'pedunculate' oak, but sit tight to the twig. Both species are native and in Britain they have hybridised, sometimes becoming hard to distinguish. There are probably not enough of them growing side by side in Ireland for hybridisation to be so common—and in Killarney the sessile stands are remarkably pure. Sessile oaks tend to support less life than pedunculate oaks. Nevertheless, in Killarney they host many hundreds of species of invertebrate, twenty or thirty species of bird and several types of mammal.

The dominant trees in the forest have a profound influence over other woodland organisms. Their leaves, flowers and fruits provide food, their canopies, branches and trunks give shelter. Their roots control the supply of water and nutrients in the soil, and their cycles of death, decay and leaf fall determine the rate at which used nutrients are returned to the earth.

And there are more subtle influences. Tree trunks, for instance, are invertebrate highways. During the day the traffic is motionless and, apart from the activities of birds and larger animals—and in Killarney the incessant attacks of invisible and voracious midges—the forest can seem quite still. But at night everything is on the move. Up and down the trees slugs and ants, spiders, beetles, weevils, and caterpillars travel to and fro to feed. So the location and density of the trees provide a sort of road map, dictating the main routes that insects follow throughout the woods.

The life strategy of the trees is important too. Trees can, of course, be either deciduous or evergreen. By dropping their leaves in autumn, deciduous trees like the oaks are hibernating. They do not waste energy maintaining their leaves and trying to make food when light is in short supply. This is a good way of life in a region where winters are dull and long but not too cold. Trees may adopt the evergreen technique for two contrasting reasons: in warm lands, like the Mediterranean, broadleaf trees can keep their leaves and go on 'feeding' in the normal way throughout the year. The strawberry tree is a 'broadleaf evergreen', living near the northern edge of its range in Killarney; conifers, on the other hand, produce needle-like leaves, that are resistant to cold because they provide a small surface area to the winter winds. What the conifer loses by keeping its leaves throughout the winter it more than compensates for by being ready to start work as soon as the first glimmers of the short northern summer appear.

So the deciduous cycle of the oaks affects the character of all life in the Killarney woods. The autumn fall of leaves sparks off feverish activity among the invertebrates of the leaf litter. The long season of leaflessness ensures a supply of uninterrupted light to plants on the ground, influencing the way some of them behave. The profound renewal of spring concentrates the breeding efforts of almost every woodland organism. These are patterns we take for granted, but they might be different if the trees were different—if nature had devised other ways for its most glorious creations to respond to climate.

Life in the forest co-exists in three distinct layers: in the canopy of leaves formed by the crown of the dominant trees; in the branches of the low shrubs beneath; and on the woodland floor. In Killarney the canopy and the floor are the most significant habitats and I will describe them later in greater detail.

The shrub layer is like a junior canopy and offers less food and shelter to other organisms than the true oak canopy and is less varied in its make-up than the ground layer. It consists of that handful of species of trees and shrubs that can reach maturity under the shade of the oaks.

Every tree in the Killarney forests has its place. Birch for instance can sometimes be found growing under oaks, but it is not a true member of the shrub layer. It is a colonizer, one of the first trees to move into clearings or to spread up hillsides on the edge of the forest. It prepares the ground for the oaks, but does not survive to maturity once they arrive. Arbutus, too, is clearly a shrub, but again it is not a member of the shrub layer. It only survives in Killarney on open ground that is not shaded by full-grown oaks. It is a relic from an earlier stage of colonization, before the climax vegetation had evolved, when areas that are now forest were still heathland. Yew, on the other hand, is a climax tree in its own right. In Killarney it forms the canopy on twenty-five hectares of bare limestone where the soil is too shallow and limey for oak. This is the only natural yew wood in the whole of Ireland.

Apart from brambles, the main natural plant in the Killarney shrub layer is holly. (In the last hundred years rhododendron (*Rhododendron ponticum*) has flourished as well, but it was introduced by men and is not part of the natural structure of the forest.) Being evergreen, holly benefits from the extra supply of light in autumn and early spring when the canopy is bare. It likes dampish acid soils and the combination of sessile oak and holly is such a regular feature in the west of Ireland that ecologists describe it as an 'association'—a predictable community. On the more neutral soils in eastern Ireland, holly is replaced under the oaks by ash and introduced hornbeam (*Carpinus betulus*). These distinct associations are found elsewhere in central Europe, western France and the Mediterranean.

In Killarney the chief role of the shrub layer is to provide deeper shade for certain ground plants, hiding places for mammals and nesting-sites for birds. Chaffinches, for example, the commonest birds in Killarney, build their comfortable, feather-lined nesting-cups almost exclusively in the shrubs. It is on the woodland floor and high up in the canopy, however, that most of the forest life occurs.

The Leaf Canopy

The forest canopy is like a vast power station. Its millions of fluttering leaves absorb energy from the sun and convert it into forms which are not only useful to each individual tree but which help to nourish countless other woodland creatures as well.

To give an idea of the sheer size of this energy generator, you can estimate that every mature oak tree in Killarney has about 150,000 leaves. Spread out side by side on the ground they would cover about seventy square metres. So, all the leaves on the trees in the Killarney oakwoods combine to form a solar cell with an area of 200 square kilometres.

The essential unit of power is the leaf. The leaf is the only piece of equipment on earth which can regularly make food out of sunlight, water and air. If there were no plants and no leaves, the rest of the earth's living organisms would not be able to use the sun's energies, other than to keep warm. We would only be able to sunbathe and starve!

What makes the leaf so special of course is that it contains chlorophyll. Chlorophyll is a green pigment which absorbs the red, orange and blue rays of sunlight and is contained in special cells called chloroplasts. These are microscopic discs, stacked into conducting rods that work rather like tiny eyes. But instead of transmitting light in the form of images they transmute light into chemical energy. The chlorophyll uses this immediate energy to mix water, sent up from the roots and transported along the leaf's veins, with carbon dioxide absorbed from the air. The result is sugar in the form of glucose. This process of manufacturing glucose is what biologists mean by photosynthesis (literally, manufacturing with the aid of light). Like any chemical process it is a sort of recipe: take six parts, or molecules of water; add to six parts of carbon dioxide, in the presence of sunlight and, if you are a leaf, you get one part of glucose and six parts of unwanted oxygen which you exhale.

Glucose is energy in a suitcase. It can be 'opened up' and used even when the original energy source, the sun, is not around. Thus, at night, the tree stops 'breathing in' carbon dioxide and breathes in oxygen instead. Respiration with oxygen can occur, though more slowly, during the day as well. Oxygen is used to burn the glucose and this helps to fuel the tree's metabolism. It gives it the energy to draw up minerals needed for growth from the ground, to make protein and fats, to build its trunk, extend its branches and develop more leaf factories.

For long-term storage, surplus glucose is converted into more complex carbohydrates, like starch. But it is not only the tree that will use these stores. Almost as soon as a fresh leaf has unfurled in early summer its food shelves, its glucose and starch, are pilfered by invertebrates. In this way, the sun's energy, so cleverly parcelled up by the leaf, will be distributed beyond the confines of the tree, throughout the forest ecosystem.

The Robbers of the Leaf's Stores

The greediest, and the most conspicuous, robbers of the leaf's stores are moth caterpillars. At least fifty species feed on the oak leaves of Killarney.

These include caterpillars of the pale brown mottled umber (*Eranis defoliaria*), whose female looks like a beetle, has no wings and sits around on the tree trunk at night awaiting fluttering masculine visitations. There are also the disguise specialists, the peppared moth (*Biston betularia*), the oak beauty (*Biston strataria*) and the august thorn (*Ennomos quercinaria*) whose caterpillars look like twigs. Most common of all, however, are the caterpillar gangs of the ubiquitous winter moths and of the green oak moth (*Tortrix viridana*), a tiny creature with bright green forewings whose larvae feed only on oak. Millions of these hatch out, particularly in May and June, and devour the leaves voraciously. In a good caterpillar year they can all but strip some trees of their leaves, and the pattering of caterpillar faeces falling on the ground fifteen metres below can sound almost like rain.

The leaves, however, are not as vulnerable as they look. Like most tree leaves, the oak leaf has a waxy, shiny surface. Clinging to feed on such a slippery foothold, while it shakes and spins high above the earth, requires specialist skills. Caterpillars, with their suction-powered legs, get along pretty well. Anchored by their back feet they wave and reach until they find a suitable leafy rim to munch on. But even then they frequently get blown off their footholds. This risk is avoided by a clever adaptation developed by some of the mini-moths (Micro-lepidoptera). The larvae of *Eriocrania subpurpurella*—fifteen adults would fit into the space taken up here by its name—excavate a labyrinth of little feeding passages safe inside the leaf. From outside these show up as distorted blotches often covering half the leaf area. It is not so surprising, however, that of the rest of the many thousands of invertebrate species in Ireland, only a relatively small proportion have learnt to tackle oak leaves.

In any case, the great moth caterpillar armies, that attack the leaves in spring, are only given a few weeks to enjoy their feast. For by midsummer the oak leaves have built up high levels of tannin in their cells, making them much less palatable. The increase of tannin helps to maintain a balance between leaf and caterpillar. It also explains why you find such a concentration of moth caterpillars in the trees during the first half of summer. This, as we shall see, has a significant influence on bird-life in the canopy.

In late July, the oaks need to replace their ragged and wind damaged spring 'power units', whose efficiency has been reduced by wear and tear and daylight robbery. So they produce a second crop of leaves to enable them to go on manufacturing and storing carbohydrates into the autumn.

By now most of the caterpillar hordes have either turned into moths or been eaten themselves. The new leaf crop is a handy insurance against excessive defoliation but it too has its plunderers. There are the bugs—various aphids and shield bugs (*Pentatomidae*) —that spend most of their lives in the leaves. There are late broods of sawfly larvae and regular second broods of another tiny leaf moth (*Phyllonorycter quercifolia*) which lasts well into November. There are cunning giants like the fluffy pale tussock moth (*Calliteara pudibunda*). Its four-centimetre-long pinkish or yellowish hairy caterpillars only appear in autumn. They concentrate on the late leaf crop, when there is less competition, and take their chance with encroaching bad weather.

Finally there are the gall wasps (*Cynipidae*). The little spangle gall wasps of the *Neuroterus* family, for instance, have a fascinating life style. They inject their eggs inside the oak leaf in late July, and the leaf responds by producing a cancerous tissue—a round, pink space module—in which the wasp caterpillar can safely grow. In autumn the little flying saucer separates from the leaf and floats down to the ground. There, under the leaf litter, its passenger pupates. But when the wasp emerges as an adult in April it, and all its siblings, are female. For them, spring is not a joyous mating season since there are no male wasps around. Yet they manage to lay eggs, usually producing red, current-shaped galls in the male catkins of the oak. These eggs are never fertilized, but they still produce the mixed male and female gall wasps whose offspring grow in the spangle galls. This mystery of virgin-birth is actually quite common among insects. Entymologists call it parthenogenesis (from the Greek *parthenos*, virgin and *genesis*, origin). It is a way of increasing the productivity of the species and, in some gall wasps and sawflies, males have become almost totally obsolete.

Canopy Birds

Leaves are the intermediary between the sun and the forest ecosystem. They alone can 'digest' the sun's energy. Caterpillars cannot digest sunlight but they can eat the leaves. Blue tits cannot digest leaves but they can eat the caterpillars. Sparrowhawks, the only common birds of prey in Killarney, cannot eat caterpillars but . . .

The blue tit is probably the most significant bird in the Killarney oak canopy. This perky, energetic little forager, with its sky-blue cap, only weighs about eleven grams. Nevertheless, it runs on 150 caterpillars a day during the summer. Now caterpillars are not always easy to see. Most of those that are found on oak leaves are pale green like the leaf. All can freeze into total immobility and some, like the peppared moth and the mottled umber, are brown and nobbly and straighten up like twigs. Most of the time the blue tit has to flutter all day from branch to branch, hanging upside down among the leaves, searching endlessly to fill his recipe.

So how does he cope in the breeding season when he and his mate have nine or ten hungry fledglings calling for service in a hole in an oak trunk? At the beginning of June, when the chicks are getting ready to fly, the parents have to deliver a caterpillar to the nest every minute. They have to be able to find them almost without looking. Consequently blue tits have to time their breeding and particularly the fledging of the young to coincide precisely with the spring climax of the caterpillar 'bloom'. This means that the blue tits as well as the caterpillars are controlled by the level of tannin in the oak leaves. If the blue tits time their breeding incorrectly, if there is a climatic hiccup or a poor caterpillar season, the numbers of young blue tits will be greatly reduced. The neighbourhood sparrowhawk, in his turn, will have to look further afield for its food.

Once the young blue tits have left their nest and can feed themselves the situation is less critical. Although the family continues to eat the same large quantity of insects, they don't have to find them all within a few yards of the nest. As the weeks progress and the chicks spread out, a less concentrated invertebrate population will suffice.

Other birds apart from blue tits feed on the woodland caterpillars. Magpies and jays pick them up off the ground when they fall, and the robins that live in the shrub layer under the trees pluck them from the lowest branches. Round the margins of the lowland woods jackdaws stop their usual ground-feeding in the fields and head for the trees during the busiest caterpillar weeks —and there are other canopy birds as well.

The common canopy dwellers in Killarney, after the blue tits, are great tits, coal tits, goldcrests (*Regulus regulus*), willow warblers, chiffchaffs (*Phylloscopus collybita*) and blackcaps. All have rather different habits. The great tit is like a large blue tit with a black head. It is a 300 caterpillar-a-day man but it also tends to go for larger prey, like tree beetles, lower down the trunk. The small, black, grey and white coal tit prefers conifers and is more common in the yew woods of Killarney, where it supplements its insect diet with conifer seeds. The goldcrest is tiny, Europe's smallest bird. It lives in the very top of the canopy, feeding on the minutest aphids and weaving its little basket-like nest, ten or twelve metres up, from the threads of the lichens which grow in the tree tops.

The three warblers, willow warblers, chiffchaffs and blackcaps, are all summer visitors. They winkle out the larger summer aphids, and are most conspicuous for their voices. Willow warblers and chiffchaffs, small yellowish birds, would be almost identical if it weren't for their songs. All through late May and June, the chiffchaff makes an endless repetition of its two little high-pitched notes. The willow warbler, on the other hand, whistles five or six notes on a descending scale. This might just be confused with the much fuller, chirping, descending scale of the chaffinch, which rings out right across Ireland from March to May.

The blackcap, a larger grey-brown warbler—the male has a black crown, the female and immature a brown one—has an excitable, tuneful song. In autumn blackcaps turn from insects to feed on fruit and berries. In recent years they have become more common all over Ireland and have taken to overwintering occasionally in the comparatively warm Killarney woods. Their flexible diet may well have helped them to adapt to Irish Decembers.

Certainly the so-called 'resident' canopy birds, that stay in the woods in the winter as well, have to look for other food once the leaves are down. Blue tits, for instance, will squeeze the oil from the spores of winter mosses and great tits make a speciality of hazel nuts and the seeds of wood-sorrel (*Oxalis acetosella*), one of the commonest woodland flowers. Really cold spells are rare in Killarney, but when they occur the canopy birds gang together. In mixed groups of forty or more they twitter along the forest floor, turning over leaves, and rooting through the litter so that they can all benefit when someone turns up a scarce cache of hibernating invertebrates, of moth eggs, of fallen oak galls or weevils.

Indeed, a bird like the blue tit is the ultimate woodland inhabitant. Though it may specialize in canopy living, during the changing course of the seasons it will rummage through every layer of the forest, from leaf gall and fruit, lichen and moss on the branches, to fungi on the trunk, and dead wood and leaf litter on the ground. And every nook and cranny that it rifles is provided, directly or indirectly, by the oak tree.

The Waste-Disposal Team

The death of an oak tree is a great event in the forest. Locked up in the trunk and branches is a huge legacy of nutrients. There are stores of proteins and fats that the tree had been making before it fell, and there are numerous minerals that it had drawn up from the soil. All these assets have to be reorganized into usable commodities and shared out among the plant and animal beneficiaries in the wood. There's a lot of work to be done, employing an enormous team of undertakers.

Let's just take the proteins as an example. When the tree ceases to live, its proteins turn to ammonia. Ammonia itself is useless to green plants, but it can be reprocessed by bacteria. A primary group of bacteria turn the ammonia into insoluble nitrites. A second group get to work on these and produce nitrates, the nitrogen-bearing salts which are soluble in water and can therefore be taken up by plants through their roots.

Alternatively the ammonia can be absorbed and fed upon directly by fungi. Fungi contain no chlorophyll so they cannot make their own food. Instead they 'drink' decaying proteins, mainly from dead plants. They produce a feeding web, called the mycelium, which grows deep into, say, the trunk of the dead tree and sucks up its ammonia through tubular filaments, or hyphae. The part of a fungus that you see growing outside the tree trunk, the toadstool or mushroom, has nothing to do with this feeding process. It is a 'fruiting body', solely responsible for making spores which will float away on the wind and germinate into new hyphae elsewhere. The fungal powers of reproduction are prodigious. The average common mushroom, for example, can generate 16,000 million spores. There's little unemployment among those that survive the vagaries of the wind, so vital is their role in recycling the nutritional elements of the forest.

To complete their job, of course, the mushroom and toadstool bodies themselves have to be eaten and there is an extraordinarily complex division of the spoils between at least four different groups of invertebrate. Some adult flies, for example, feed mainly on the spores before the wind takes them. The larvae of a different class of flies and of small moths develop inside the living tissues of the fruiting body. When the fungus dies miniature beetles tend to take over, including species of staphylinid beetles that will only be found on that particular type of fungus. Finally, the fungus-corpse, mined by caterpillars, holed by slugs and sodden by rain, begins to rot. It then attracts the common invertebrates that feed on carrion and dung. Scientists in Britain have found at least 220 species of invertebrates breeding inside fungi.

Returning to our fallen oak tree, the dead wood of branch and trunk is eaten by bark-beetles, by thrips, by sixty-odd species of mites, by woodlice and by slugs. Digesting the wood and passing it out as microscopic faeces, the hungry invertebrates act like millions upon millions of mincing machines.

But reducing the tree to powder and merging it into the soil is a long process. Many generations of mincers are needed for the job and they support a hierarchy of specialized predators. The reddish centipedes of the family *Geophilidae*, for example, eat mites and woodlice, hunting them deep inside the dead wood. Centipedes can curl and slide their sinuous bodies into the most confined spaces, disabling their prey with their poisonous front pincers. In the meantime, the passages leading into the dead trunk will be invaded and excavated by ants who, though they forage out across the leaf litter, often choose to lay their eggs in the safe galleries of a fallen tree. When winter arrives, wood wasps, bees and larger beetles will cluster in to hibernate. All in all a single dead oak can easily house 200 species of invertebrate.

Oaks, however, are long-lived trees so deaths in the forest do not occur very frequently. But of course a bit of regular dying, enough to keep the undertakers busy, occurs every autumn when the leaves tumble. Oak leaves are toughened with tannin and take several seasons to break down, but there are other leaves to be worked on as well, those of the plants of the forest floor.

Death, as always, is a leveller. Plants that formed exclusive habitats for particular invertebrate species when alive become general 'dead plant matter' to the workers in the leaf litter. So nettles support their very own nettle-weevil (*Cidnorhinus quadrimaculatus*) which you would never find on an adjacent piece of dog's mercury (*Mercurialis perennis*)—one of the commonest Killarney plants. Nor, for that matter, would you find the dog's mercury beetle (*Hermaeophaga mercurialis*) on a nettle. But when they die, both plants will be eaten by the same pill millipede (*Glomeris marginata*).

To put it another way, only about thirty species of invertebrate have been found feeding or breeding on bracken, whereas some 230 species are specifically associated with oaks. But when they die they are both equally attractive to the disposal team waiting on the woodland floor. The disposal team—bacteria, fungi, beetles and slugs—have three related roles to play in the forest. They clean up the corpses of tree, leaf and animal. They ensure that nutrients return to the soil where they can be used again by a new generation of plants. Finally, the invertebrates, in particular, help to feed a range of woodland birds and mammals.

Birds and Mammals of Dead Wood and Leaf Litter

Dead wood alone supports about a fifth of the woodland's insect fauna. Yet in Killarney, with all those trees, only one species of bird is anything like a dead wood specialist. Certainly the tits will prise beetle larvae out of crevices in dead branches during their ceaseless tours of all the tree's resources. Only the tree creeper (*Certhia familiaris*), however, lives and feeds regularly in the standing carcasses of trees.

Climbing jerkily up a tree trunk, the tree creeper looks like a little brown mouse. But it's a cleverly designed little bird. Its back is mottled and flecked most beautifully, with amber and grey and brown of many colours, just like a piece of variegated bark. It has long claws and toes for defying gravity and slipping happily along the undersides of high branches. And it has a long, down-curved beak for winkling wood weevils and bark beetles out of their holes.

Tree creepers nest in hollow stumps or behind the flaps made where folds of dead bark start peeling away from dying tree trunks. They have a curious history: on the continent they are a bird of upland pine forests and their place is taken in deciduous lowlands by another, very similar species, the short-toed tree creeper (*Certhia brachydactyla*). But in Ireland and Britain, native pines disappeared 1,500 years ago, and because the short-toed tree creeper never reached these islands our tree creeper was able to switch its preference to deciduous trees. Perhaps its flexibility and its subtle camouflage have enabled the tree creeper to survive almost total deforestation in Ireland. For although there are so few woods left, there are tree creepers all over the country, often simply living in hedgerows. The other, brightly coloured woodpeckers, the green (*Picus viridis*), great and lesser spotted (*Dendrocopos minor*) woodpeckers, and the little blue nuthatch (*Sitta europaea*), that would accompany the tree creeper in an English oakwood, are not found in Ireland.

Two other small brown birds, that specialize in sifting the leaf litter for insects, will also search dead wood once it has fallen. They are the dunnock —it has a slate grey chest which in the breeding season can look astonishingly blue—and the minute wren. Both are skulkers—hard to see under the shade of the bushes. Much more conspicuous are the birds that don't make their entire living on the ground, like blackbirds, who crash around in the undergrowth, jerking piles of leaves over with their beaks to get at worms and larvae. Robins do much the same but more daintily; magpies too feed part of the time on the ground though mainly in glades and clearings, while, as we have seen, the canopy birds concentrate on the leaf litter in hard weather.

Among the mammals, a significant hunter in the leaf litter is the pigmy shrew, significant not because it is especially common, but because it eats so much. The pigmy shrew is Ireland's smallest mammal. It is less than four centimetres long, weighs about four grams, and has to eat all the time to survive. It gets through twice its own weight of woodlice, beetles, mites and spiders, flies and bugs, every single day. Its favourite of all favourite dinners is the little woodlouse *Trichoniscus pusillus*, which is one of the commonest invertebrates in the Killarney leaf litter.

More common, particularly in the drier leaf-litter, is the beautiful chestnut-brown wood mouse, with its long tail, pale underparts and large, startled eyes, whose diet has been thoroughly investigated in Killarney. In autumn and winter they feed on the profusion of fruits—acorns, holly berries and yew berries—that fall from the trees above. Only in late winter, spring and summer do they concentrate more on invertebrates.

Since 1964, the bank vole has also been found in Killarney. Previously unknown in Ireland this dumpy, short-tailed little rodent seems to have spread through most of Kerry and on into Clare and West Cork. Presumably imported accidentally into Ireland, the bank vole is common in Killarney where it prefers dense cover. It eats green plants and fungi as well as fruits, but leaf-litter invertebrates still make up about a third of its diet.

Slugs are considered a great delicacy by hedgehogs, as are millipedes, snails, caterpillars and almost anything else small and squashy that lives on the ground. Even a large mammal like the fox is not above rooting through the leaves for beetles and worms. And then there is the badger.

The badger is a sort of mammalian blue tit. He'll eat almost everything the woodland has on offer. He'll raid the nests of wasps and bees, dig up the roots and storage tubers of bluebells, nip off new shoots of dog's mercury,

and crack open acorns and hazel nuts. He can also save himself time and trouble by catching a hedgehog—which he scoops out from under its prickles as if he were swallowing an oyster—or by carving up a nest of young rabbits. But no badger's meal is complete unless it is garnished with a generous mouthful of beetles. Slugs, snails, caterpillars and worms are delicious, but beetles are best of all.

The Field Layer

Over the seasons, the massive fallen tree trunk softens and sinks. Its shell has been processed into a mildly acid humus which quickly grows a soft skin of mosses and decorative trailing spleenworts (*Asplenium spp*). Slowly it is folded into the green contours of the woodland floor. The leaves and branches that fell with it have long since been absorbed, with their nutrients, into the soil. They help to nourish the growth and flowering of a multitude of plants that cover the forest understorey.

This often colourful carpet is called the field layer. Its patterns of flowers are not woven together haphazardly. They consist, instead, of distinct groupings or associations of plants whose composition is determined by three major factors: whether the soil is wet or dry, whether it is acid or lime, and how much light is allowed to reach the ground through the canopy of the trees above.

On most days in Killarney it either rains or it rains harder. So the soil nearly everywhere in the woods is moist. There are extremes, of course. Round the shores of the lower lakes there are flooded inlets half way between land and water. This is where the alder swamp-woods have developed, the alder trees sometimes standing on tiptoe, using their roots like stilts to keep above water. Beneath them there can only be a matting of sedges and reeds. Or there are the bare limestone outcrops, where rain drains freely away and spinneys of arbutus and yew have grown gnarled and dry on almost no soil at all.

Most of the rest of the Killarney soils, however, are either wet and acid or wet and slightly limey. Why the difference? Well, Killarney actually straddles two of the most important and opposite Irish rock forms. On the eastern side of the great lowland lakes the carboniferous limestone of inland Ireland is just petering out. On the western shores rises the old red sandstone which climbs up the valleys towards the massive Macgillycuddy's Reeks, and away to frame Ireland's south-western coast.

Modestly endowed with nutrients and poorly drained, the sandstone gives rise to an acid soil. The limestone produces a base soil, but it is not pure like the Burren limestone, so its other minerals contribute to the formation of peat—hence only slightly limey, or neutral conditions.

In late May, in the lowland woods, it is obvious at a glance what sort of soil you are standing on. Battalions of bluebells indicate mild damp acid. The many base soils, however, can be covered with an even more dazzling display. Sheets and sheets of wild garlic (*Allium ursinum*) spread their dense green leaves, and their flowers like bulbous white stars, over acres of woodland, filling the air with the delicious aroma of French cooking. When we were filming the insect life of the garlic we could not avoid crushing leaves underfoot and the smells left us feeling permanently hungry.

Flowers, their nectar and their leaves, are important feeding stations for invertebrates. A cluster of flowers in the middle of the wood can be an oasis to a passing butterfly, while flower sheets like the garlic become a sort of metropolis. Gangs of speckled woods (*Pararge aegeria*), the commonest butterfly of the woodland shade, hover over the garlic flowers, slender leaf slugs slide down the folded cups of the leaves and craneflies, hatched from their 'leather-jacketed' larvae in the damp earth, dance in the light or mate, cemented together on the flower stems.

Coal tits, nesting in the yew woods on the drier limestone nearby, make regular shuttles to snatch the craneflies and many a coal tit nestling is raised on garlic-flavoured insects.

But even more than soil and moisture, light or the lack of it is the controlling influence on flowers in the forest. Oak trees in summer only allow 20 per cent of sunlight to reach the floor below. Beech trees—not native to Ireland but growing freely in many areas, including the Killarney lime soils—absorb all but 5 per cent of the light.

There are three ways in which flowers can cope with woodland shade. Firstly flowering can be completed in early spring. Since leaf production in the forest is generally staggered—field layer in February, shrubs in March, canopy trees in late May—this gives the maximum amount of light. Wood anemones (*Anemone nemorosa*) and, a few weeks later, bluebells and wild garlic, grow copious leaves which work overtime, storing extra food underground in the bulbs. As soon as they flower their leaves die, and the plants feed on their reserves for the rest of the year. Alternatively, growing in glades and clearings or on the edges of paths allows the advantages of flowering in full summer when insects are busy. Typical woodland clearing plants in Killarney are foxgloves (*Digitalis purpurea*), the blue-flowered, leafy bugle (*Ajuga reptans*) and the red campion (*Silene dioica*). All are pollinated by summer bees, and large flies. Indeed red campion hides its nectar in a tube behind the flower so that only flies that are big enough to pollinate it can reach the proffered reward.

Thirdly, some forest flowers are able to evolve the ability to survive at a slower rate of photosynthesis. This is very effective in enabling them to grow in the woodland shade, but is a disadvantage in more open ground where plants with faster metabolisms will elbow the slower ones out. Yellow pimpernel (*Lysimachia nemorum*), early purple orchid (*Orchis mascula*), wood avens, dog's mercury, wood sanicle (*Sanicula europaea*) and wood sorrel are the common plants of the shadier Killarney field layer. The last two have an extra trick: they are 'wintergreens'. They grow their new leaves in the autumn, not the spring, and they keep active for most of the year.

In the heart of the forest, however, as the trees get older and the canopy more lowering, flowers gradually drop out of the field layer. Other methods have to be devised to cope with the deepest shade.

Plants of the Deep Shade

One way of surviving in deep shade is to give up your reliance on light altogether. This is what the bird's nest orchid (*Neottia nidus-avis*) does. It has no leaves and no chlorophyll, only pale ghostlike flowers on a wan-looking stalk. It does not make food by photosynthesis, instead it lives on 'carrion', mainly dead plants, making use, for instance, of the ready-made sugars and proteins in the dead leaves lying around it. These are processed and fed to it by the special microscopic fungus, the mycorhizal growth, which lives on its roots. Other orchids are fed by mycorhiza only as seedlings, but the bird's nest is permanently dependent.

Most of its life is lived underground. Nine years are needed before the untidy bundle of roots—the 'bird's nest'—stores enough food to produce its first flowerhead. The orchid can even flower and set seeds underground if the spike is stopped, by a fallen trunk say, on its way to the surface. Each separate root in the cluster can live and flower on its own, which enables the plant to 'move' sideways should the nutrients around its original location be exhausted. The bird's nest orchid is rare in Ireland, but several colonies survive on the less acid soils in Killarney and the species was probably widespread in the centuries before Ireland's forests were destroyed.

Botanists call plants like this, that live off dead matter, saprophytes. The ivy broomrape (*Orobanche hederae*), another plant found in Killarney, also dispenses with the need for leaves and chlorophyll, but it is a parasite. It sucks up nourishment directly from the roots of ivy (*Hedera helix*) so it grows, not necessarily where there is shade, but where there are plenty of hosts. (Ivy is not a parasite. It has its own roots and only uses trees and walls for support.)

Many of the great Killarney oakwoods are in steep dark valleys where the canopies mass upwards at an angle and the summer sunlight hardly reaches the ground at all. Here, and in the black evergreen depths of the yew wood, the field layer consists solely of mosses and liverworts (*Hepaticae*). So far scientists have recorded 186 species in Killarney. These are called the 'bryophytes', differing from each other mainly in the shape of their leaves. Mosses form their leaves either in spirals or in two flat rows. The leaves of liverworts look like little flat, closed hands, or sometimes they stick up in

27,28 *Top Left to Right* Frog orchid; fly orchid.
29,30,31 *Bottom Left to Right* Fragrant orchid, early purple orchid, lesser butterfly orchid.

32 The pine marten.

33 *Top Left* Dense-flowered orchid with mountain avens.   34 *Top Right* Spring gentians.
35 *Bottom* Burren limestone pavement near Black Head.

rows of three fingers. They are ancient life-forms that evolved in a world before flowers, when the ground was covered in tree ferns and quagmires. What they require most is moisture, lots of damp air, and the advantage of not being dried out by sunshine.

As nothing much else can grow in the darker woods, the bryophytes run riot in Killarney, providing one of the most amazing moss displays in the whole of Europe. Under the yew trees, for example, where there is hardly even any leaf litter, the moss lies in a solid blanket, extending almost continuously over many hectares.

Though they all share the desire for damp and shade, the Killarney mosses actually occupy different niches in the darkness. They form communities that are just as distinct, though not as obvious to the layman, as those of the various woodland flowers. So, the dominant moss in the yew wood is a large woolly mop character called *Thamnobryum alopecurum*. It flourishes there because it can spread effectively over bare rock and once established it hosts, in its turn, several smaller species, that grow on top of it.

In the oakwoods on the other hand, bare rock is less common because boulders are more likely to be covered with humus formed from the leaf-litter. Consequently they are colonized by mosses like the beautiful, feathery *Thuidium tamariscinum*, which is a specialist on thin wet peat. Other locations —deeper patches of peat, the bases of tree trunks, even upper branches—all have their own typical groups of bryophytes. Furthermore, many of them, like flowers, appear to be restricted to particular soil types. There are nearly fifty species of mosses and liverworts in Killarney that are only found on the limestone areas and more than sixty that are restricted to the old red sandstone.

Whatever the weather outside the woods, the sheltered microclimate in amongst the Killarney trees is always extremely humid. Everything drips with moisture and soils develop not only on the ground but in crevices on the tree trunks, on dead stumps and on the upper sides of high branches. This aerial humus is the habitat of common polypody (*Polypodium vulgare*), a remarkable plant that in Killarney lives almost exclusively in the hanging world above the ground and whose fronds, attached to oak branches ten metres up, look like the plump fingers of little green martians. Some of the mosses also adopt this lifestyle, as does the tiny, transparent filmy fern (*Hymenophyllum wilsonii*), and many of the oldest trees are festooned with matted 'fur'.

Plants that can grow independently on others like this, without parasitising their food supply or ever being rooted in the ground, are called epiphytes. They are a spectacular feature of the vast rainforests of the tropics but rarely develop in such profusion so far north. Killarney, however, is the warmest place in Europe for its latitude, and it is certainly one of the wettest. These unusual conditions permit one other strategy for coping with deep shade.

36 *Top* A Burren turlough.
37 *Bottom* The River Liffey above Blessington.

Sometimes, in the darkest corners, the plants of the woodland floor simply move up off the ground and closer to the light. An old oak may topple sideways but go on growing. On the gentle slope of its trunk ground mosses take root. They create a substantial acid humus that is ideal for flowers like wood sorrel. This sort of hanging garden can be so 'realistic' that large trees like birches will root themselves in it and grow to tall maturity, poised four or five metres above the ground. Similarly, all the epiphytes will move up a notch or two. So polypodies and lichens that grew at a level of say three metres in the more open woods, climb up and up in the darkness until they are clinging fifteen metres high, just below the topmost leaves of the oaks.

When a Forest Fails to Breed

A forest is not like a mountain. It is not a permanent feature of the landscape but a living entity, like a vast animal laid upon the ground. And though the cycle of its birth, fruition and death is usually too slow for us to perceive the changes as they occur, it is certain that the forest will not live unaltered forever.

Like any living organism woodland must reproduce itself if it is to survive, but the rate of reproduction does not need to be frenetic. The individual cell —the oak tree—is a long lived creature. In its 350-odd years it produces about eighteen million acorns and only one of these has to grow to maturity to take its place.

Indeed, the germination of acorns and the growth of saplings is a haphazard affair. Many acorns have already been eaten away inside by weevils like the *Curculio* species before they fall from the tree. Others will feed wood pigeons, jays, badgers, red squirrels, wood mice and bank voles once they are on the ground. Any that survive and manage to germinate beneath the parent will be too short to compete for light and too shallow-rooted to compete for water.

What an acorn needs is a clearing away from the parent tree. But how can it get there? Occasionally the clearing comes to it—the parent or a nearby tree falls and leaves a space. More often, however, it will be transported by a predator. Red squirrels hide acorns and forget where they have put them. Voles will bury stores for the winter and then get waylaid by foxes before they can return to enjoy them. A wood pigeon, slow and laden with food, is killed in a glade by a sparrowhawk and the undigested acorns in its crop spill out and eventually grow.

The life of the forest depends on such accidents. But in Killarney, this, nature's casual system of gardening, is not working. There are almost no oak saplings and the great ecosystem which seems in all its parts to be flourishing, is in fact dying on its feet. And it is not only the oaks that are suffering; there are hardly any young arbutus and even holly and yew are not reproducing successfully.

The problem is overgrazing. Deer, cattle, sheep and goats have all caused trouble, but the main offender is a species of deer imported from Japan called the sika. Sikas are charming animals. The female is speckled and tawny and the male, almost black in the autumn with slender pointed antlers, does not bark or roar at his mate like other deer. He whistles. No wonder owners of nineteenth-century estates wanted them to ornament their grounds. In 1865, two hinds and a buck were brought to Muckross, home of the Herberts, in Killarney. Now there are over 1000 of them, devouring the undergrowth at a faster rate than it can recover.

The impact of the deer can be shown in contrast if you take a boat and visit one of the remoter islands out in the lakes. There, where grazing animals cannot penetrate, the understorey is lush and saplings quite plentiful.

It is in the nature of forests, of course, to support a population of grazing animals. Red deer have probably always lived in the Killarney forests. Three or four hundred animals roam the hills above the woods roaring and fighting on the moors in autumn and moving down for shelter and food in winter and spring. They are believed to be the last remnants of herds native to Ireland. (Red deer elsewhere in the country have been introduced relatively recently.) Young oaks can cope with a certain amount of browsing. They can grow back their leaves several times in a season. They can build up food reserves in their roots, remaining small and biding their time. It is not unusual to find a sapling half a metre tall and twenty-five years old. But the introduction of extra mouths from abroad has upset the balance.

Overgrazing in Killarney has two consequences which may be irreversible. Firstly, when clearings are no longer recolonized by woody growth they become waterlogged. Without the thirsty roots of young trees there is nothing to soak up the incessant Kerry rain. Even if the sika were removed, the oak trees could not return because they will not germinate in drenched soils. Instead the plants of damp moorland like purple moorgrass invade, and woodland turns to bog. This is a natural process, part of the ebb and flow of habitat development. It has happened before in Ireland when climates changed or when 'catastrophes' like Neolithic man interfered with the environment.

Secondly there is rhododendron. It too was introduced as an estate ornament, probably in the 1830s. Originally from the shores of the Black Sea, rhododendron likes warm acid soils, but it did not really spread until the sika deer had got to work. Unfortunately the deer won't eat it, so as the native undergrowth was grazed away there was nothing to inhibit the rhododendron's advance. Over the last fifty years it has rampaged in close-twined thickets four metres high, choking the ground flora and the holly in the shrub layer, and snaking out across two-thirds of the forest. The only way to reduce it is to cut it with chain saws, burn the whole plant and pluck every new seedling out of the ground.

The almost imperceptible decay of the Killarney woods could mean the dissolution of the most complex ecosystem nature has produced in Ireland. There are important political points to be made: more decisive action should be taken against the sika, more financial encouragement given to the people who organize youth helpers from all over the world to help clear rhododendron in the summer. But aside from these, what we are witnessing is a habitat in the process of changing, of being colonized by new species. Man has simply been a 'biotic factor', an agent in this process, just as he has 'helped' nature create most of our landscape. So the problems of sika and rhododendron in Killarney do not only hold lessons for conservationists; they also teach us about how habitats work.

Men, Trees and Ireland's New Forests

During their 8,500 year tenancy of the Irish landscape, men have changed their minds several times about woodland. At first it was a vast and threatening black hole into which the unwary might disappear, harbouring terrors known and unknown. The wolf, for so long the cause of ignorant nightmares, was not extinguished in Ireland until the eighteenth century. The very last one, it has been said, was torn to shreds by the hounds of a Mr Watson in County Carlow in 1786.

Once early man had become a proficient farmer, he began to regard the forest more as a competitor, a rival for land. It was not until the 1600s, when most of the woods had been cleared, that attitudes changed for the third time and trees began to be valued and finally husbanded as a resource. Oak bark was needed for leather tanning, oakwood charcoal for smelting iron ore, oak planks for making storage barrels, house frames, fighting and merchant ships.

By 1700, established landowners began to realize that if every tree cut down meant money in the bank, so might every tree planted. They developed and managed plantations of oak, diversifying later into ash, beech and Scots pine. But this brief flourishing of mainly deciduous woodland was subject not to nature but to politics. In 1881 the British parliament under Gladstone passed the second Land Act, which was soon to facilitate the transfer of some 25,000 farms from landlord to tenant. Before selling, many landowners cashed in on the trees planted by their grandfathers. Travelling sawmillers, over from England, did a roaring trade right across Ireland.

After the First World War had taken a further toll of Irish trees, less than half a per cent of the country's surface remained as woodland. Over the last sixty years the State Forestry Department has worked hard to reclothe the naked landscape. Although Ireland remains the poorest clad country in Europe, outside the windswept, glaciated folds of Iceland, woodland cover has increased from around 50,000 hectares in 1920 to 480,000 in the 1980s. And the planting trend is gathering pace. Between 1975 and 1982 an impressive 63,000 hectares of new woods were established.

But the twentieth-century forester does not have the patience of his forebears. He favours the quick-growing imported conifers of western North America, trees like the sitka or silver spruce (*Picea sitchensis*) and the lodgepole pine (*Pinus contorta latifolia*). Private tree farmers, draining and terracing the blanket bogs of remoter hillsides like Mount Callan in County Clare have found their conifers can achieve faster growth rates than forests in Britain. So the conifer race is on and Irish forests—once pure deciduous stands of oak, ash and elm—are now almost entirely evergreen.

The new predominance of conifers has a mixed effect on the survival of Ireland's woodland communities. On the plus side, pine martens seem to be benefiting from the additional cover—particular evidence for this comes from Northern Ireland. Red squirrels prefer any trees to no trees, so do woodmice. The impact on bird-life is neutral. Many of the specialized oak-forest birds which might be expected to suffer—the pied flycatchers, redstarts (*Phoenicurus phoenicurus*) and woodpeckers,—are missing from Ireland. Common Irish woodland birds, chaffinches, blue tits, great tits, coal tits, goldcrests, wrens, and tree creepers, adapt well to life among the conifers. Chaffinches remain the most numerous species though coal tits and goldcrests are favoured over blue tits and great tits.

Woodland plants and insects are not so lucky. Because conifers are evergreen, the shade is constant throughout the year and throughout the wood. This reduces the variety of habitats available to flowers, so, botanically, conifer forests tend to be less rich than deciduous woods. The main conifer tree species are introduced, not native. They arrived in Ireland without their natural insect attendants and now constitute a new habitat which has to be colonized from scratch. There has not yet been time—supposing it will ever happen—for the full range of native Irish woodland invertebrates to adapt to the new trees. Consequently the conifer plantations support only a very simplified insect community.

On balance, the decline of deciduous woodland in Ireland continues to mean a decline in the vigour and richness of forest ecosystems. Genetic selection is a means of making oak trees grow faster and more attractive to foresters; simply planting a seedling in a plastic tube can give it greenhouse-type protection in the wild and can more than double its early growth rate. But these techniques are largely ignored in Ireland. Even in Britain, where foresters have, in the recent past, been hostile to deciduous trees—the government poisoned large areas of oak trees in the 1960s to make room for conifers—over a third of woodland is still broadleaf. In Ireland the figure is down to 10 per cent.

The conifer revolution is one of the biggest changes in the contemporary Irish landscape, affecting other ecosystems as well. The drainage and afforestation of blanket bogs in the west has meant a decline, particularly, in bogland plants and invertebrates.

The biology of a conifer also seems to increase the acidity of the woodland soil, partly through its life cycle, partly through the decay of its needles, and partly through its year round tendency to trap acid particles contained in rain. Subsequent rain showers carry this acidity into nearby streams damaging river life; the eggs and young of trout (*Salmo trutta*) and salmon, for example, —fish that travel up into the headwaters near upland forest sites to spawn— are killed by even mildly acid water. Conifers, then, are a mixed blessing, and the loss of deciduous woods is definitely a disaster.

It takes many hundreds of years for a large organism like a new tree species to be fully incorporated within the natural ecosystem. It takes far, far longer for that ecosystem to grow and ramify as it has done in the oak forests of Killarney.

6
Limestone Land: The Colonization
Of The Burren

Along the shores of County Clare, midway down the western coast of Ireland, and stretching away inland for many miles, lies the ancient Barony of the Burren. When I first saw it, it looked an empty landscape: a grey world of shattered rocks strewn to the horizon, vast stone slabs ribbed with green veins of thin turf—a land with no trees, few streams and strong winds.

Its shape is a bit like a table made of limestone tipped up at its north-western corner, where the summit of Slieve Elva rises above 300 metres. The table is cracked and jagged in places, but to the east it folds and slopes gently into wide, flat pavements. To the west, it falls away more sharply to a narrower shelf of coastal pavement, reaching out into the sea and softening southwards into sand dunes.

Its beauty is not so much aesthetic as emotional; it is not a place for sublime vistas or pictures of the well-balanced rural scene. Instead it offers an overwhelming sense of space and freedom, and, in a way, of optimism. For, each spring and summer, its bare rocks, its cliffs and cracks and stony pastures, enjoy the bright blossoming of millions of flowers.

In early May there are yellow fields so full of cowslips that it is almost impossible to walk through without stepping on them. There are discrete mauve lines of early purple orchids and by mid-month rings and clusters of spring gentians (*Gentiana verna*) appear. Their blue colour is like no other blue—it gives them a solid, almost man-made look, like brooches pinned to the clipped turf.

By the end of May thousands upon thousands of snow-white mountain avens (*Dryas octopetala*) have flowered. The western slopes and pavements are dotted with tiny golden rock-roses (*Helianthemum canum*) and every nook is filled with the papery-red, dark-eyed flowers of bloody cranesbill (*Geranium sanguineum*).

Summer brings a succession of orchids—twenty different species will flower in a normal year. Purple thyme and pale eyebrights (*Euphrasia*) grow in mossy profusion on smaller islands of soil, richer meadows crowd with yellow bedstraws (*Galium verum*), clovers and vetches, tufts of rare saxifrages (*Saxifraga*) surround the stones and mile upon mile of rock is scattered with the shrubs of the burnet rose. All this, the flowering of the Burren, has become famous as one of the finest botanical phenomena in Europe. For here, in an area of stark topography covering less than 1 per cent of the surface of Ireland, examples of more than three-quarters of the country's entire native flora can be found.

Such an extraordinary concentration of variety makes the Burren an excellent starting-point for a study of Ireland's plant life. But numbers of flowers alone do not account for the reputation that the Burren has attained. Nor is the real impact of those numbers necessarily always obvious.

This was brought home to me one day when I was leaving Mullaghmore, the last lonely hill on the south-eastern rim of the Burren, surrounded by level limestone pavement and, for me, one of the most beautiful places in Ireland. Presumably I was wearing a suitably botanical expression because I was stopped by two American ladies who explained to me that they were 'looking for the flowers'. Having found no man-eating orchids, tree ferns or elephant-sized lilies, they had resorted to searching for the glass-houses that might denote the presence of a helpful botanical garden or other museum. Could I help them?

When I showed them that the flowers mostly grew only a few inches off the ground, and that their beauty was merely minute and fragile, my new friends were politely disappointed. The idea that the botanical interest lay, not in any curiosity of behaviour—the tendency to snap your finger off, say, or to dance to traditional Irish music—but in the close juxtaposition of plants with different and distant geographical affinities, seemed to them to be overly academic.

It is sad that anyone should be disappointed with the Burren. The fault perhaps lies with tourist brochures and careless descriptions. It is movingly lovely; but the real mysteries of the Burren are technical, involving the reasons for the way plants distribute themselves. To understand them requires a little more knowledge than the casual visitor can be expected to have. Put simply, these mysteries include questions like the following: why do we find 'arctic' plants growing on the Burren, so far south? Why are there 'Mediterranean' plants growing here so far north? How can they survive side by side? Why does the Burren contain flowers that we normally associate with northern Spain or the Swiss Alps?

Many of the Burren's plants have peculiar distributions: some are found nowhere else, or almost nowhere else, in Ireland; some do not grow in Great Britain, and there are even plants that 'ought' to be found on the Burren— that grow in similar conditions nearby—but are not. There are other questions too, concerning the circumstances that affect the more common plants.

Why do high mountain flowers grow at sea level on the Burren? How do plants that require acid conditions come to be growing sometimes within a few inches of lime-loving plants, when acid and lime are diametrically opposite soil types? And, most obvious question of all, how does such a seemingly barren landscape manage to sustain so much life?

To be useful, our definition of any habitat has to show its wildlife community developing along predictable lines. The flora of the Burren contains so many apparent anomalies—there are so many examples of flowers that 'shouldn't' be found where they are—that, at least at first glance, the rules of colonization would seem to be being broken.

The Burren has often been described as a giant rock garden and—like most clichés—it is a good way of putting it. When you are walking around the tip of Black Head, with the Atlantic Ocean behind you and 'arctic' mountain avens and warmth-loving, dense-flowered orchids (*Neotinea intacta*) at your feet, it does sometimes feel as if a mad gardener has been let loose. You can imagine him with his fixed grin and glazed eye, sowing botanical confusion as he scatters a mixed bag of flower seeds from all over Europe, regardless of the conditions.

But the whole point about the Burren is that its flowers are native. No one has planted them. They got there all by themselves and most of them have been there for thousands of years. Archaeologists have shown us, for instance, that the pollen of the rock-rose has been present continuously on the Burren since the end of the last Ice Age, 10,000 years ago. This means that rules of some sort must apply.

We do not yet know what all these 'rules' are, nor precisely how they work together. There is still no explanation which gives a coherent account of all aspects of the Burren's flora. Botanists have worked hard, however, to interpret the region and explain its anomalies. A number of very sensible theories have emerged which shed light on many of the mysteries, and this chapter will examine these as we look at each group of plants—the arctic and the southern plants, the acid and alpine and lime-loving plants—in turn.

The Burren's peculiar diversity of flowers is the result of a number of different influences. These divide into the general—those that have affected the whole of Ireland—and the particular—those that are special to the Burren. General influences include Ireland's geological history, its location out in the Atlantic, its long-term affinities with other parts of Europe and the impact of widescale colonization. As we know, Ireland, like any land mass, has always been bombarded by all sorts of species from outside looking for a foothold.

Particular influences include the unusual combination of a warmish climate, limestone soil and barren topography. These uniquely varied conditions have offered niches, or last refuges, to a vast concentration of 'hopeful' colonizers. Furthermore the history of this colonization has, in a sense, been preserved.

Over the last three or four hundred years men—charcoal burners, farmers, peat cutters, industrialists, builders—have had a significant impact on the rest of Ireland, but, at least until very recently, they have made fewer alterations to the Burren. Its appearance has probably not changed too radically since the final disappearance of its pine trees, believed to have occurred about 1,500 years ago. The fact that many of these influences are discernible makes the Burren a fascinating place to study, not only for its own sake, but because it also tells us how the rest of Ireland was colonized.

Without plants there can be no life on the land, they form the basic constituent of every wildlife community. Plants have come to the Burren not by magic, nor entirely by accident. The impulses that have brought so many different types of species together on the Burren teach us about the forces that enable land to be colonized and ecosystems to develop, about one of Ireland's most interesting natural habitats and about a remarkable place on earth.

What Sort of Habitat is the Burren?

The Burren is a wonderful place for rainbows. It rains somewhere here every other day on average. The wide horizon spreads such a vast expanse of land beneath the eye, and the sun, flashing through the clouds, reflects so glintingly from the rocks that rainbows are bound to be frequent. They stand complete, rising in double strands from the stones, spanning several miles, disappearing into the stones again.

The other phenomenon that emerges from the rocks after rain is a veritable army of snails. The most conspicuous is the brown-lipped snail (*Cepaea*

nemoralis) whose large shells, white, yellow, brown, deep gold, plain and striped, seem to crowd the rocks. But there are also the tall, conical spires of *Balea perversa*, the little bumpy brown shells of pigmy vertigo (*Vertigo pygmaea*) and the minute, translucent *Vallonia excentrica*, just two millimetres wide. They all come out on the damp rocks and the wet turf to feed on the plants and the algae and lichens that cover the stones.

The Burren supports around seventy species of land snails, which is probably more than anywhere in Ireland. Why so many? The answer is that they are making use of the stores of lime laid down for them by their own marine ancestors 340 million years ago. Snails form their shells from calcium carbonate, the mixture of calcium and carbon which makes chalk and lime, the chief constituent of limestone.

The Burren is a block of limestone 1000 metres thick. It is built from billions of generations of seashells and fish skeletons, dating from a period when, for 80 million years, (from 350-270 million years ago) Ireland was almost entirely covered by warm ocean.

The shells, deposited as sediment on the ocean floor—this is why limestone is called a sedimentary rock—were compressed into stone by the weight of the waters, the pressure of the earth's upheavals, and the slow passage of time. A few of the exposed slabs of the Burren still hold the fossilized imprints of the last layer of marine animals and plants. Occasionally, with careful scanning of the stone surface you can find the spiral of an ammonite, the clustered marks of coral or the filigree pattern left by a sea fan.

All this expanse of limestone, however, had to undergo many geological adventures before being stripped and revealed to the modern eye as the Burren. The piles of sea skeletons rose so high that the water became shallow enough for sand spits to form. By 270 million years ago these had grown over with swamp-forests, from which Britain derives its valuable 'carboniferous' deposits of coal, and the Burren limestone was covered with sands, siltstone and shale. Then, as we have seen, the whole region—Ireland and Britain included—was raised above the water by the 'Armorican' upheaval, only to disappear under new seas eighty million years later. When Ireland finally reappeared about seventy million years ago, in preparation, as it were, for the sculpting of its present geography, the Burren region had gained a thick covering of clay over layers of shale and sandstone. This was almost all scraped off during the Ice Age, probably less than one million years ago.

This pre-history may not seem relevant now, but it is important in two respects: if the clay and shales were still intact (traces of them still cap the ridge of two hills, Slieve Elva and Poulacapple, while the Burren 'disappears' beneath shales to the south) then the area would be of little interest to botanists; if, on the other hand, the Burren had never had this protective mantle to shield it from the effects of weathering then the Burren itself would, quite simply, no longer exist.

Limestone is a soft rock. It can soon be eroded by the wind and it dissolves comparatively easily in rainwater. The weather we have now is eating down through the Burren at a rate of approximately half a millimetre every year. If it had been exposed as it is now twenty-five million years ago, it would all be gone. The nature of the underlying rock is a definitive influence on any wildlife habitat. The fact that the Burren is limestone, and therefore extremely porous, has, for instance, an extraordinary effect on the way rivers and lakes behave in the region, and they in their turn affect the vegetation. The limestone's way of weathering and its fracture in places into the clints and grykes—the slabs and the cracks between them—that typify limestone pavement, favour the survival of certain plants.

A more significant feature of limestone than either of these, however, is the presence of lime as the chief ingredient in the soil. Lime supports a very large and characteristic group of flowers. You would find many of these, if you looked carefully, on other limestone areas in Ireland. So, although the Burren is famous for its mysteries and its peculiarities, these aside, it can be looked at first as simply a limestone habitat.

The Limestone Habitat

Limestone soils support more species of flowers than any other type of soil in Ireland, or in Britain for that matter. Why is this?

Firstly, there are a large number of plants like cowslips and bloody cranesbills that only really thrive on alkaline—that is lime-rich—soil. Botanists call them calciloles—from the Latin words *Calx*, meaning chalk, and *colo* meaning I inhabit. Most of Ireland's orchids fall into this category. It may be that some calcicoles are rather like the snails and require purer lime than other plants, but this has not been proved. Calcium itself is only used directly by plants for the building of cell walls and in special cellular deposits. All plants require it, but only in minute quantities.

What the lime really does is to help encourage the growth of bacteria. These tiny micro-organisms in the soil help plants to gain access to whatever nutrients exist in the ground. In particular, they turn nitrogen from the air into nitrates, and nitrates can be 'swallowed' by plants when they are dissolved in water. On so-called acid soils—acid, remember, being the chemical opposite of alkaline—these microscopic creatures cannot survive so easily, which is why farmers sometimes spread 'lime' on their fields.

But lime is not, strictly speaking, a fertilizer. It helps plants to feed, but it doesn't feed them. Plants need to 'eat', or rather absorb, small amounts of many types of mineral, but to grow fast they must have phosphates (from phosphorus), potassium and nitrates. Because limestone soils are crowded out with calcium carbonate, these nutrients are actually often in short supply. There is always enough for every plant to get a little bit, and the lime ensures that they get it, but there is not enough for any single plant to be greedy.

The result is that quick-growing plants, especially the taller grasses, are held back. Nothing gets too tall in the early part of the growing season and a whole host of smaller, ground-hugging plants, that would otherwise be deprived of light by grasses and shrubs, have time to flower and so survive.

The limestone is very democratic. All calcicoles are roughly equal and because no single plant can easily become dominant in any one area there is always room for variety. In a way, the richness of the Burren's flora is increased by its infertility—if you measure fertility by the sheer quantities of nutrients in the soil. This lack of competition for light on the Burren is its most important feature. But the limestone has other helpful characteristics: it tends to hold whatever warmth is available. Furthermore, the calcium gives even the thinnest soil a healthy, crumbly texture, which facilitates the passage of air, roots and water.

Because rainwater soaks easily away through the limestone rock, the Burren soils stay fairly dry. In a wet climate like Ireland's, this is very useful. It means that the roots of the plants need never be waterlogged and there is no risk of 'drowning'. Because so much of Ireland is bog—for which plants need to be specially adapted—it's not surprising that all sorts of flowers requiring dry conditions crowd into areas like the Burren. The beautiful blue harebell (*Campanula rotundifolia*) is a good example. It doesn't specifically seek limestone—so it's not a calcicole—but it must have a well-drained soil.

Another important feature of limestone soils is that although they are pleasantly dry, they are unlikely actually to dry out. During any extended period without rain, the porous rock begins to draw up moisture from the water-table, back through itself towards the surface, where plant roots can reach it. Such droughts, of course, are rare in Ireland, but in the hot rainless June of 1984 it was noticeable that the Burren turfs remained surprisingly green, its flowers husbanded by this sort of capillary action.

The Burren's Orchids

The Burren's limestone soils are attractive to flowers because they are warm and dry, but never too dry; because they are alkaline and therefore rich in bacteria; because they are crumbly and easy to live in; and because, the competitiveness of longer grasses and shrubs is constrained by the scarcity of nutrients other than lime.

In many ways the lifestyles of the Burren's orchids reflect these conditions. Britain has fifty species of orchid; twelve of these are at the northern edge of their European range and are restricted to the far south and south-east of England. They never reached Ireland and it is not entirely surprising that Ireland in all has only twenty-seven species, at least twenty-two of which are found fairly frequently on the Burren. They include twayblades and helleborines (*Epipactis*), bee and fly orchids, early purple, pyramidal, fragrant and frog orchids (*Coeloglossum viride*). The numerous *Dactylorhiza* orchids include the unusual, white-flowered subspecies of the spotted orchid (*Dactylorhiza fuchsii okellyi*)—which for some reason crops up in west and northern Ireland, in north-west Scotland and the Isle of Man, and there are also great rarities like the dense-flowered orchid.

Nowhere else in Ireland has such a magnificent concentration of orchids. The simple explanation for this is that the Burren is Ireland's finest expanse of limestone and almost all the orchids of Ireland, and indeed of Britain, are either true calcicoles, growing only on limestone, or flowers that show a distinct preference for it. In fact only four species do not grow at all on calcareous soils: the heath-spotted orchid (*Dactylorhiza maculata*), the bog orchid (*Malaxis paludosa*), the lesser twayblade (*Listera cordata*) and, creeping ladies' tresses (*Goodyera repens*). This last is not found in Ireland.

It seems the Burren's limey soils encourage the activities of those particular minute fungi, the mycorhiza which, as we know, nourish orchid seedlings during the long years that can elapse between germination and the production of leaves. The warmth of the limestone is important too because orchids are such long-lived perennials. Although they have devised methods for surviving in the cold—for instance, by storing food for the coming spring underground and allowing their leaves to die back completely after the autumn—winter is a threat. The Burren's mildness is particularly helpful to species like the fly, bee and pyramidal orchids, and the autumn ladies' tresses, whose ranges all have a southerly inclination.

There are two types of limestone grassland, both found on the Burren, both affecting the distribution of orchids. The first consists of medium-sized grasses, thirty to sixty centimetres high, mainly hairy oat grass (*Avenula pubescens*), false oat grass (*Arrhenatherum elatius*) and smooth meadow grass (*Poa pratensis*). Here you will find bright pink pyramidal orchids, which grow easily to thirty centimetres, and so have the height to push themselves up through the grass and attract the butterflies they require for cross-pollination.

The tiny frog orchid, on the other hand, is altogether inconspicuous. It usually grows only a few inches from the ground and relies for pollination on beetles, feeding them with nectar from its sticky pale green petals. It is only likely to survive in the second type of grassland, which has a much shorter turf created by low grasses like sheep's fescue (*Festuca ovina*), blue sesleria (*Sesleria albicans*) and by the slightly taller quaking grass (*Briza media*). These last two are so attractive that they justify diverting our attention from the flowers. Sesleria has beautiful grey-blue flower heads which it waves even from the caps of the bare rocks. It is the most characteristic grass of the Burren since in Ireland it only grows on limestone. Quaking grass is even more lovely and its fragile dancing heads have always been used in dry flower arrangements. Both are fairly delicate, uninvasive grasses that do not really inhibit flower growth.

Many of the Burren orchids are scattered right across the dry limestone, but a few are restricted to damper localities. Apart from the obvious ones like marsh helleborine (*Epipactis palustris*), and the fenland marsh orchids of the *Dactylorhiza* family, there are some interesting species like the fragrant orchid. In its most common form it is a dry land flower but for some reason those on the Burren belong to a special subspecies (*Gymnadenia conopsea densiflora*) that only grows beside fens. The exquisite pink flowers of the fragrant orchid are firm to the touch, like pink sugar-icing, and are pollinated by moths. Lesser butterfly orchids (*Platanthera bifolia*) grow in similar damp terrain. Their flowers, thin white crosses with very long spurs, are pale enough to be visible at dusk and emit their strongest scent in the dark to attract night-flying moths. Moths of course are most common around marshy areas, particularly in the Burren where there is little woodland cover. One other orchid which seems to have a 'moist' distribution is the fly orchid. This species is elsewhere associated with shade and woodland borders and it may be that the damper Burren hollows give it some semblance of shelter.

The Mysteries of Flower Distribution

Limestone is not exactly a uniform rock. In Britain, it ranges in age from ancient pre-cambrian outcrops 600 million years old, scattered in Wales and Scotland, to the more recent Oligocene rocks of the Isle of Wight which date from around forty million years ago. The chemical content of the soils can vary as well. The Southern English chalk downs are pure calcium carbonate, while in East Anglia the chalk is contained in boulder clay and in the North Midlands—in a stretch from Nottingham to the Tyne—the rock consists of a high proportion of magnesium.

These various British limestones support distinct communities of flowers, all calcicoles, but with different plants predominant in different localities. The Burren holds a good cross-section of all these plants mixed up together: madder (*Rubia peregrina*)—common on the Burren—is particularly associated with south-west Britain, with Devon and the Avon Gorge. Squinnancywort (*Asperula cynanchica*)and yellow wort (*Blackstonia perfoliata*), are plants of the southern English chalk downs: squinnancywort almost exclusively so, yet both are numerous on the Burren. Mossy saxifrage (*Saxifraga hypnoides*) and stone bramble (*Rubus saxatilis*) are associated with the northern Peak District, hoary rock-rose and dark-flowered helleborine (*Epipactis atrorubens*) with Denbighshire in North Wales, and the pyramidal bugle (*Ajuga pyramidalis*) with the old limestones of north-west Scotland. All are found on the Burren, even though it consists solely of single-age carboniferous limestone.

This amalgamation of limestone communities that elsewhere are discrete, or separate, must be proof of the enormous range of limestone terrain that the Burren has on offer—from the tall and short grass meadows through fens, through shaded clefts and hollows, to open rock, narrow terraces, scree and cliffs. But it also reflects the wider mixture on the Burren of plants associated with various 'provenances', from all over Europe. It is another reminder that colonization is not a simple process. It has not been a steady advance of a batallion of flowers, moving gradually from Europe to Britain to Ireland to take over the Burren. The Burren did not wake up one mythical morning to find itself covered with the limestone flora. The effect of colonization has been continuous since the last Ice Age, with plants arriving at different times from different locations.

Colonization is not entirely haphazard, but its progress is not always predictable. Some plants just do have rather curious distributions, and the Burren has more than its share of such oddities. Take Irish saxifrage (*Saxifraga rosacea*) as an example. Saxifrages are quite clever at storing water in their fibrous, spongy leaves so they can grow on dry stone, and Irish saxifrage is one of the most beautiful. It has distinguished white flowers on the ends of very upright pink stems about ten centimetres long, and its leaves look a bit like tufts of moss that have gone rusty. It blows gently in lines on rocks near the sea at Black Head on the north-west corner of the Burren, and it is found at intervals along the west coast from Kerry up to northern Mayo. But it is not found in Britain (it had one location in North Wales but seems now to be extinct there). This would not be so surprising if it had not also been identified in places as far apart as Iceland, the Jura mountains, and Czechoslovakia.

Interestingly enough, another of the 'Burren specialities', Irish eyebright (*Euphrasia salisburgensis*), has a rather similar sort of distribution. Eyebrights

—there are lots of them, (fourteen species in Britain and Ireland)—are upright little plants with small, lipped, white flowers usually showing orange at the centre and thin purple veins. Like all of them, Irish eyebright is parasitic. It plugs into the deep roots of thyme and feeds from there. It differs from the others, however, in having very thin, sparse leaves, like little dark green teeth. Irish eyebright likes shallow soil over limestone and, while its headquarters is on the Burren, it can be found elsewhere in the west from County Limerick, up to Donegal. Outside this range, however, its nearest location is 1200 kilometres away on the Vosges mountains of France. It also grows on other mountains in south and central Europe and on lower ground in the county of Gotland in south-east Sweden. An odd array of localities indeed!

A final example of this peculiar sort of peppered distribution is the spring sandwort (*Minuartia verna*). With its small, white, cup-like flowers it might almost be mistaken for a miniature saxifrage. It likes limestone rocks and in Britain is found on most of the famous areas of carboniferous limestone— in Derbyshire, the North Pennines, North Wales and Cumbria. But in Ireland, the only limestone it is found on is the Burren, and mysteriously, the only other place in the whole country that it grows is on patches of basalt up in the north-east.

Arctic-Alpines

Now we come to the heart of the Burren's mystery. One of the most arresting botanical sights in north-west Europe occurs in late May when millions of mountain avens flower up and down the Burren rocks, across the pavements, on the hill-tops and along the shores. They look a bit like giant white buttercups, with bright golden stamens at the heart of the flower surrounded by eight broad, white petals. And when they fruit they produce a whirl of feathery fingers, as if they've plucked the pale down from passing swans.

Mountain avens is an arctic-alpine. That means that it grows up on the tundras of the Arctic and on mountains further south whose upper slopes, above the treeline, resemble tundra conditions. The plant is specially adapted to a strenuous regime of long, cold winters and brief summers. It is not a 'flower' but a dwarf shrub. Like many northern plants it is evergreen. It stores food in its leaves throughout the winter so that it doesn't have to waste time each year in the short growing season producing new ones, and is ready to flower almost as soon as the arctic sun returns. The leaves are thick and dense to provide storage space, hairy to avoid moisture loss in the exposed, windy landscape, and waxed for insulation. They form a more effective pantry than would an underground tuber because, while the ground will be deep-frozen in winter, the insulated leaves are kept relatively warm under a cozy igloo of snow. The top of the leaf is dark green and will absorb sunlight for photosynthesis, but the underside is silver, which gives the leaf some choice in repelling summer heat when it doesn't wish to lose water. The flowers too, when they appear, normally reflect away the sun's warmth. But when the petals are cupped, the heat radiates towards the stamens. The temperature in the flower cup can then be raised by about eight degrees centigrade and this provides an attractive siesta spot for the tundra mosquitoes and other flies charged with the role of pollination.

But why does such an apparently specialized plant grow on the warm lands of the Burren, often, amazingly, at sea level? One clue lies in the behaviour of another spectacular Burren flower, the spring gentian.

The spring gentian is sometimes carelessly referred to as an arctic–alpine, but this is misleading. Although the tip of its range does just extend over the Arctic Circle in north-east European Russia, it is not an arctic flower, and does not occur at all in Scandinavia. We do, however, associate it most often with the high alpine meadows of Switzerland, and in Britain it grows in one place, high up in the Pennines of Teesdale in northern England. Yet in Ireland, where it is confined to the Burren and northwards to areas around Connemara, it resembles mountain avens in growing at sea level.

What seems to appeal to it is that the Burren is a bit like a mountain lying on its back—a mountain without the altitude. It has the bare rock and barren landscape, and the all-important fact that competitive larger plants are absent —as they would be on a mountainside or indeed in the tundra. These conditions are usually produced by a cold climate but on the Burren, as we know, they are a feature of the limestone relief. The same presumably applies way down in Yugoslavia, on the limestone Karst of the north-west region there, where spring gentians also grow near sea level.

If lack of competition is the main factor in the survival of mountain avens and gentians on the Burren, then the Burren's own remarkable rockscape has accentuated the effect. The way the rocks are dressed or undressed with soil, the scoops and ribbons of turf and the terrace formations, provide an almost infinite variety of discrete locations where different plants can flourish without being carpeted over by other enthusiastic calcicoles. This is what differentiates the Burren from other limestone regions. Gentians and mountain avens, after all, do not grow on the chalk downs of southern England.

The question remains as to how and when these plants arrived in the Burren. It may be that the gentian has colonized the area from Europe in the last 7000 years or so, whereas mountain avens could conceivably have survived through the later years of the Ice Age. The pollen record shows that mountain avens was extremely common in late glacial times, but that it disappeared, even from sites where it is abundant now, a few thousand years into the post-glacial era. The assumption is that it retreated to one or two isolated spots on exposed ridges as trees invaded the region. Then as the trees declined it spread back again.

There is no trace of gentian pollen from the Ice Age, nor for several thousand years afterwards, which implies that it arrived more recently. A little piece of supporting evidence is the fact that gentians are found on the limestone islands of Aran—ten miles off the Clare shore—but mountain avens is not. If the gentians had travelled this far it would not be surprising that they continued and colonized the similar habitat on Aran. If, on the other hand, mountain avens actually died out on Aran but not on the Burren, and if it has been gradually extending from a few existing stands, then the sea might have proved a barrier to it.

However we speculate about the arrival of gentians and mountain avens in the Burren it is certain that their presence is entirely natural. Because they are so spectacular they were probably the very first flowers ever to be officially 'observed' on the Burren. Way back in 1650 a clergyman, a Mr Heaton sent his record of them to the English botanist William How who published it that same year in his book *Phytologia Britannica*.

Southern Species on the Burren

There is one extraordinary experience that a naturalist can have on the Burren and nowhere else on earth. It is to stand near the sea, perhaps somewhere round the promontory of Black Head, and look at a patch of turf that contains mountain avens and another little flower, the dense-flowered orchid, growing within a few inches of each other.

For whereas mountain avens is a genuine arctic plant, the dense-flowered orchid has its centre of distribution far to the south, beside the Mediterranean Sea. It looks a modest flower, rarely more than a few centimetres high with small greeny-white flowers, like miniature bonnets, folded tightly round the top of the stem. It is an easy flower to miss and, unlike the conspicuous avens and gentian, it wasn't recorded until 1880. The Canary Islands, Madeira, Portugal and the South of France: these are the sort of areas where it has been recorded outside the Mediterranean region. In Ireland, a few plants have been found northward to east Mayo, eastwards to Offaly, and even in one spot near Cork. In 1969 a little group was also discovered on sand dunes on the Isle of Man. But it does not grow in Britain, nor in any other north or central European country, so why does it have such a stronghold on the Burren?

I have already mentioned the 'warmth' of the limestone as a factor in the survival of limestone plants. This warmth can be explained with the help of the Burren's farmers. In most hillside regions cattle are brought down to the valleys in winter. In the Burren, however, they are moved up, because the limestone retains heat and the grass goes on growing. The ground is actually warmer in the limestone hills than on the lowland shales to the south. The shores of the Burren are washed by the Gulf Stream. Even though the sea looks very cold in winter, at, say, forty-five degrees Fahrenheit, it is actually much warmer than the ground surface nearby which, away from the limestone, may be close to freezing. This difference in temperature is transmitted through the limestone into the Burren which then acts like a storage heater, accentuating the effect of an already mild winter. The average January temperature in Galway, near the north-eastern edge of the Burren is the same as in Rome. Warm and open, the Burren is almost always free of winter frosts, and in spring and summer the limestone absorbs and stores the heat of the sun as well.

It would be a mistake of course, to think of the Burren as a sort of northern hot house. The mountain avens and its alpine friends run no risk of being frizzled. For although the winters are mild, the temperature in July is the same as it is in sub-arctic Finland in the summer.

Although the dense-flowered orchid is the only genuine Mediterranean plant on the Burren, there are others with a definite southern inclination. The delicate maidenhair fern (*Adiantum capillus-veneris*), which grows between cracks in the rocks, has a distribution extending south to the tropics.

Its shapely fronds, with their purplish stems and geometric leaves, have made it a popular houseplant. It was once more common on the Burren than it is now and it seems to have suffered from the careless greed of plant collectors.

Large-flowered butterwort is also found on the Burren. It is one of those plants (discussed in Chapter Two) with Lusitanian or northern Iberian affinities, and is not found in Britain, nor away from south-western Ireland. It grows on a sodden rock face, dripping with algae, a few hundred yards from the holiday spa of Lisdoonvarna. For many years this was its only known station in the Burren and because it was so close to the resort botanists suspected that it had been deliberately planted there. But in 1949 more butterworts were discovered further north on the Burren hill of Cappanawalla, and now, these, marking its most northerly location in Europe, are accepted as surprising but natural.

If we assume that these 'warm-blooded' plants are not relics from one of the warm periods before the final fling of the last Ice Age (Chapter Two), then they must have arrived, like many plants, on the wind or in the stomachs of birds. They are evidence of two things: firstly plants will travel considerable distances for the chance of a life in Ireland; secondly they may come from diametrically contrasting regions of the northern hemisphere.

Life on the Bare Rock

If you could look down from a satellite you would see that almost a fifth of the Burren's surface consists of exposed rock. But even on the barest stone, plant life is taking root. Slight folds and natural depressions in the pavement surface are drilled by the rain and the force of the water with its mildly acidic content dissolves the soft limestone to form hollows. As soon as any small indentations are made, water flows towards them and they deepen. When they are seven to ten centimetres deep their bottoms fill with algae, particularly blue-green algae of the genus *Nostoc*.

Nostoc species tend to form dark bumps and balls of growth which dry up into powdery dust in warm weather. In the deeper hollows this will not blow away and the algae or its residue can form the basis of a 'soil' for mosses to grow in. The droppings of hares and goats blow in from outside bringing some extra nitrogen, as do bits of dead plant, attracting the beetles that feed on them. Flies come in for the shelter, spiders string their webs across the openings and the organic content of the new soil increases.

Gradually the hollows are occupied by larger plants, and become miniature oases among the rocks. But not all the new tenants will be lime-loving plants. The soil in each separate hollow will have a different history. Algae is acidic and where it has formed an effective barrier between the limestone beneath and the soil above, acidity may predominate. So, many hollows are tenanted by wood sage (*Teucrium scorodonia*), a plant that looks a bit like a white nettle, and which tolerates acid soils. Or the soil may be 'neutral' where acid and lime elements have cancelled each other out. The broad leaves and tall spikes of the twayblade are often found in these types of hollow. Or the oasis may have a good covering of wind-blown Burren earth supporting a smart bunch of bloody cranesbills.

This interesting mixture of acid and limestone plants on the Burren spreads over patches of soil more extensive than just the hollows. In fact whole little communities of acid plants, with ling and heath-spotted orchids, are surprisingly frequent on the limestone. One reason is that the limestone is not always pure. It may contain what geologists call chert, a mixture of other minerals. If this has weathered in the past it leaves a sort of clay which can

seal the limestone under it and facilitate a build-up of potentially acidic peat on top.

The Burren soils are too well replenished from beneath by lime to turn acidic through the normal process of leaching (see Chapters Three and Four). But this may not always apply to the very top millimetre or so. Rain may well continue to wash the lime from this very thin layer, leading to 'surface acidification'. A plant like mountain everlasting (*Antennaria dioica*) finds this condition particularly attractive. It has beautiful silvery leaves and furry white flower heads, sometimes called catspaws. In the rest of Europe it likes upland acid locations; in the Burren and elsewhere in Ireland it confuses botanists by growing frequently over limestone.

There are two types of bare pavement on the Burren, the shattered and the smooth. The shattered pavements, more common in the east, have their joints filled with debris and are often littered by 'erratics', the huge boulders of limestone scattered by long-melted glaciers. The commonest plants here are burnet roses, wood sage and blackthorn and the ubiquitous miniature geranium, herb robert, that even clings to the sides of the boulders.

The long pillars of the smooth pavements are split from each other by deep cracks. This is the formation that geographers call clints (the surface) and grykes (the clefts). The smallest grykes provide channels of moisture and are often filled with snaking ivies, or the stubby red and green fronds of rusty-back fern (*Ceterach officinarum*). But many of the grykes are a good foot wide and up to a metre deep. Their cliff-like walls will only support specialists. Hairy rock-cress (*Arabis hirsuta*) for instance, has leaves that are thick for storing water and hairy to deflect winds that might dry the plant out through transpiration.

The floors of the grykes are often earthed with the remains of moist, fertile drift soil. Here, shelter and deep shade enable several woodland plants to grow, like the sinuous emerald green hart's-tongue fern (*Asplenium scolopen-drium*) and the bright wood anemone. These subterranean woodlands are invisible as you look away across the surface of the pavements. But when you peer down into the grykes you find trees growing as well—particularly blackthorn, hazel and whitebeam (*Sorbus aria*). They are always sawn off—by wind and roaming wild goats (*Capra hircus*)—just before they appear above ground level, but they serve to remind us that the Burren was once a forest.

The Lost Woodlands of the Burren

Looking out in July, when the small flowers have finished their business and the richer meadows are a tangle of taller vetches and nodding ox-eye daisies (*Leucanthemum vulgare*), it is hard to believe that the Burren has not always been grassland. But the pollen record tells us that great stands of pine once

covered the hills and that the pavements were once enveloped in woods of
yew and juniper and dense thickets of hazel.

Now, of course, the tallest relics on the open lands are the lonely stone
graves of the ancient folk who cut down the trees. There are wedge tombs
and chamber tombs, their great, erect slabs stripped, like the Burren pavements, of the turf that used to clothe them by 3,000 years of wind and rain.

Scientists are not quite certain about the precise history of the Burren
forests—how much of the region was wooded and how long the trees lasted.
There is evidence, for instance, that native pines—now extinct in Ireland—
survived here into the dawn of the Christian era.

There are, however, some interesting biological clues to help date the
disappearance of the woods. Firstly, of the Irish flowers that are not found
on the Burren, only three are woodland species. As we have seen, the
pavement grykes do provide a sort of woodland alternative, but it may be
significant that so many forest plants have survived in the Burren when there
are so few trees here.

Secondly, such enormous floral variety, though it is explained by the
Burren's extraordinary qualities, is often an indication of a 'disturbed' environment. By this I mean one that has changed in fairly recent times and
has not yet settled into a regular pattern of dominant, subordinate and failed
species. Put rather simply, if the flowers on the Burren have only been
fighting it out for the last 3–4,000 years, rather than 8,000, then fewer of
them have had time to lose the battle for space and disappear.

A third clue to a recent, more extensive woodland past is a butterfly.
The pearl-bordered fritillary (*Boloria euphrosyne*) is a small, orange-brown
butterfly, dabbed and lined with black and with silver 'pearls' painted along
the rims of its wings. In Ireland it is only found on the Burren, but in Britain
it is quite common, especially in the south, and especially in woodland
clearings.

But all these bits of evidence can be read in different ways. After all, the
whole of Ireland was once wooded, and the pearl-bordered fritillary's larvae
feed on violets, which are common all over Ireland. Nevertheless, violets
have a role all of their own on the Burren (see Turloughs). The brown
hairstreak (*Thecla betulae*) is another little hedge and woodland butterfly that
in Ireland is mostly confined to the region round the Burren, yet its caterpillars
feed on blackthorn, one of the commonest trees in the country. As we have
seen there are many factors at play producing the Burren's uniqueness.

Nevertheless, we know the forests were there and that now they are gone.
What remains, are scrub woods of hazel. Left to their own devices these
patches of hazel, mostly isolated in deeper hollows of soil, can spread quickly
and in time would probably become the dominant climax vegetation on the
Burren. But for many hundreds of years the hazel has been kept at bay by
another legacy of man, the feral goat. Herds of goats, long since turned to

the wild, still rattle across the Burren stones, pruning any tree plucky enough to stick its head up, and browsing away at any gains made by the scrub.

The goats, in fact, do a great service to botanists by maintaining the *status quo* in favour of the smaller flowers. Indeed any attempt to destroy or remove the goats—and people have been doing this—could be a botanical disaster.

The Burren woods, or their absence, also have a significant influence on the rest of the wildlife, particularly the birds. The hazel scrub provides some limited breeding sites for hedgerow birds: chaffinches, song thrushes, wrens, robins, dunnocks, yellow hammers (*Emberiza citrinella*) and blackbirds. But since they are all tree- or at least shrub-nesting species, they don't take full advantage of the larger invertebrate populations that feed on the flowers out on the pavements. With so many snails you might have thought the Burren would be bristling with thrushes and blackbirds, but their lustrous singing is rarely heard far from the bushes.

Instead, it is the ground-nesting birds of open land that benefit from the insect bonanza, species like skylarks, meadow pipits and wheatears. You'll see a lonely pair of wheatears on almost every mountain in Ireland, but in the Burren their numbers get quite congested. On the lower slopes of Mullaghmore I have sometimes found three nests—all in holes under the pavements—within a single square kilometre. As the young are getting ready to fledge, the most convenient food is provided by the fat grubs of chafers. Rose chafers (*Cetonia aurata*) and garden chafers (*Phyllopertha horticola*) are especially common on the Burren, maturing, as they do in their millions, just in time to munch through the full flowers of the burnet roses.

The high density of meadow pipits ensures, as it did on the Murlough sand dunes, that cuckoos are calling frantically all through the main flowering season. Higher up the food chain, there are ravens and hen harriers and, on the one or two suitable rock-faces, peregrine falcons.

The Burren is a mountain landscape with the mildness and productivity —in terms of insects and floral variety—of a lowland grassland. So, this character is reflected in its flowers: the curious mixture of alpine and lowland limestone plants; and in its birds: upland species, not much variety, but unusually large numbers.

The Pine Marten

Apart from the feral goats, the two most obvious mammals on the Burren are Irish hares and stoats. Hares are common because of the rich grazing, and like the goats they play an important ecological role in keeping the turf mown. Stoats have innumerable hiding places among the stones and prey on the young hares, on rabbits, and on the mice that eat the bulbs and fruits of the plants. Their diet is also amply supplemented in summer by all the small ground-nesting birds.

Foxes and badgers are less often seen, but are as common on the Burren as they are elsewhere in Ireland. Otters are always elusive, but they are here, where there's water, and they quite often appear bobbing offshore round the coast.

There is one species of mammal, however, that has its last Irish stronghold on the Burren: the pine marten. It's a beautiful creature with an alert, pointed face, expressive black eyes and furry, wide-set ears dabbed inside with cream. No two are ever quite the same. Their soft, thick brown pelts can vary from pale chocolate to almost black and on their throats each has a patch of creamy fur which can be large or very small, mottled or clear, oblong or squarish.

Like stoats, badgers and otters, the pine marten is a member of the weasel family. It is lithe and quick, and long—a large one can grow to a metre in length, a third of which is bushy tail. It can race up trees, swing from the branches, bound and undulate over the rocks and squeeze into cracks and holes.

Pine martens are still quite common on the Burren because of the hazel scrub. Although the hazel no longer covers vast areas, there are still plenty of small patches. Many of these are completely undisturbed. Each one is a safe island surrounded by plentiful food. The martens live in the denser thickets, producing their litters of three or four young in early April, mostly in the tree-holes or rock cavities. But they do their hunting along the edges of the scrub and the pavements.

Although, if you're lucky, you might stumble on a pine marten sunbathing out on the warm stones, you are unlikely to see it feeding since it hunts at night. But we can find out what pine martens eat by investigating the faeces they leave behind on the rocks and fallen tree limbs. Irish scientists have recently examined many hundreds of faeces gathered in County Clare and they reveal interesting aspects of the animal's diet. They eat a lot of fruit: not only the autumn fruits, like hazelnuts, blackberries and crab apples, but the berries of ivy and hawthorn and rowan (*Sorbus aucuparia*) that last later into the winter. This sort of seasonal preference has also shown up in Russian stoats. A winter study in the arctic Kola Peninsula found berries, mostly juniper in 71 per cent of the faeces there. Ground beetles are another major ingredient, and they too are plentiful on the Burren, while the rest of the diet consists, not surprisingly, of meat—mostly mice and the small birds, particularly wrens and robins, that live in the hazel scrub.

Eating fruit and vegetable matter may well help the pine marten to fatten up before winter and may be an important factor in its survival. Another dietary habit, however, seems to have contributed to its catastrophic decline over most of the rest of Ireland. Pine martens will eat carrion. During the 1950s and '60s there was a rise in sheep-farming in Ireland, especially on poorer land. The lethal poison strychnine was put out in dead carcasses to poison would-be predators. Despite long-term deforestation, and continual pressure from gamekeepers and trappers (martens were valued for their pelts), Ireland's pine marten population did not really collapse until the poisoning began.

County Clare was never an important sheep farming region and common grazing rights, and therefore indiscriminate poisoning campaigns, have not been normal practise there. The Burren has kepts its pine martens, so have Connemara and Mayo. In Ulster, there are a few recent records from all counties, particularly Fermanagh and Armagh. Elsewhere in Ireland, however the picture looks bleak, with only isolated populations in Meath, Offaly, Cork and Kerry.

In 1976, the pine marten was protected in Ireland—a measure that was desperately needed. But poisoning remains a threat and, on the Burren, so does the grubbing up of hazel scrub for agriculture, for the scrub is often located on usable soil. Recent forest plantations across the country may offer a new habitat and in 1983 the Forest and Wildlife Service began a captive-breeding programme with the aim of rehabilitating the species. But pine martens are shy and though they can occasionally become quite tame, they are easily frightened during the breeding cycle. So far young have been produced, but not successfully reared.

Turloughs

We have looked at the significance of limestone on the Burren flora, at the effect of the montane landscape, the mild climate, and the character of woodland and scrub. But what about the behaviour of water? Water in the Burren isn't like water elsewhere. Because the limestone is so porous the underground water-table carves out strange subterranean cave systems, armed, as it were, to the teeth with stalagtites and stalagmites. Consequently, upland streams, which might be expected to trickle visibly down hill, sink into one hillside terrace and emerge on the one below. That is why the hills are never as dry as they look. Rivers, like the River Fergus, which should travel on the surface, have a disconcerting habit of disappearing underground for a mile or so, while waters that belong underground regularly seep to the surface to fill the Burren's beautiful turloughs.

The word turlough, from the Irish words *tuar* and *lough*, means literally 'dry lake'. It is here, in these wide, grassy hollows that the strange fluctuations in the Burren's water-table have their most dramatic influence. For after heavy rains, water from beneath wells up into the turloughs through swallow holes in their floors.

In winter the turloughs may remain filled for weeks, drawing in flights of winter duck, of Shoveler (*Anas clypeata*) and wigeon (*Anas penelope*), and groups of whooper swans (*Cygnus cygnus*) down from the Arctic, or the occasional Greenland white-fronted geese (*Anser albifrons flavirostris*). But the flooding can occur at any season and sometimes the turlough will fill and empty again in the space of a few days or even hours.

The turlough's peculiar status, sometimes lake, sometimes pasture, makes it the most exclusive plant habitat on the Burren. The floor is generally carpeted with a rich sward of 'submersible' plants like silverweed (*Potentilla anserina*) that flourish when the turlough is dry and survive when it is not. The other turlough plants occupy distinct zones according to their distance from the floodline. The upper limit of regular flooding is marked by the bushes of potentilla (*Potentilla fruticosa*). With its large, yellow, rose-like flowers and its narrow silvery-green leaves, potentilla grows almost in rings round the rims of some turloughs, and occasionally forms quite dense shrubberies. Yet it is found in few other locations in west Ireland and in only two places in Britain (the Lake District and Upper Teesdale). Apart from these other isolated stands, you would have to travel to the Alps or to south-east Sweden to find it again and the Burren population, so closely tied to the turloughs, is reckoned to be the largest in the whole of western Europe.

Above potentilla grow plants—and these include all the turlough shrubs and trees—that cannot tolerate frequent inundation. Below it grow the flowers and grasses that can.

Although the 'shrub-limit' is a clear line of demarcation, a more detailed record of flooding is provided by the mosses. A blackish, blotchy moss called *Cinclidotus fontinaloides* grows just at the level where all (or almost all) flooding ceases. This is usually several feet above the shrub limit. Usually around three to four metres below *Cinclidotus* the level of more regular flooding is marked by the water-moss, *Fontinalis antipyretica*, a leafy, lighter green submergible, sometimes called willow moss.

But the best way to appreciate the turlough's plant zones is to look at where its four species of violet grow. Furthest from the flood line, under pockets of denser scrub, you find the wood violet (*Viola reichenbachiana*). Being a woodland plant it flowers early—usually mid April—to catch the sunlight before the leaves on the trees shade it out. It is best identified by its slender, dark purple spur sticking out behind its large petals. Closer to the water, in more open ground, and therefore flowering three weeks or so later, grows the common dog violet (*Viola riviniana*). Another big violet, it has a stouter, much paler spur. Both these 'dryland' violets have large, rounded leaves.

The other two violets, occurring on or below the regular floodline, must wait for the turlough to empty before they can flower. The upper species is the heath dog violet (*Viola canina*). It has smaller flowers and narrower leaves than the upper two violets, and a yellowish spur. It flowers in mid May when the water level has fallen.

Finally in June, when the turlough is likely to be all but dry you may spot the last and rarest of the violets, the tiny fen violet (*Viola persicifolia*). It has very pale, china-blue flowers, white spurs and noticeably long pointed leaves, and it grows almost down to the turlough's floor. The species is nearly extinct in the fens of Britain, and is disappearing from its other main haunt, the Burren. It used to flower in sheets beside some of the larger turloughs, but very recently intensive grazing by cattle seems to have decimated it.

The invertebrate life of these unpredictable 'dry' lakes has only just begun to be investigated by Irish scientists. Although there seems to be no abundance of species it is believed that the unique conditions may produce one or two specimens—creatures like freshwater shrimps—that are new to scientific discovery here. Turloughs are probably responsible for one other Burren phenomenon. That is the presence of a seaside wading bird like the ringed plover, breeding out on the dry stone pavements, twenty-five miles inland.

Conclusion

Wags and wits have said of New York that to get to know the city two days are fine, two weeks are better, two years are not enough. This is even more true of the Burren. In two days in late May you can appreciate the dazzling variety of flowers and you will have time to recognize that they are an odd mixture. In two weeks you can come to grips with some of the explanations and begin to make sense of the paradoxes. But after two years you realize that explanations can only go so far, that you can understand some of the curious distributions of the plants but not all, that the Burren really is a bit of a mystery.

So there are two points to be made with this chapter. Firstly, the colonization of a piece of land will be attempted by organisms from many regions, and is controlled by the combination of many different local conditions. Understanding this involves the careful analysis of all the ingredients of the habitat. Secondly, nature doesn't always obey the superficial rules that scientists make for it and understanding this involves a certain humility. For both these purposes, the Burren is a wonderful and exhilarating example.

Post-Script

Ireland contains the largest continuous area of carboniferous limestone in Europe. Most of the centre and west of the country is limestone (see map on p28) and it is Ireland's most significant geological formation. But the eastern half is covered with drift soil—better for farmers than for small flowers—while much of the rest is bog.

Limestone only emerges on or near the surface in the west. Wherever it does so, interesting plants appear. The eastern rims of the main Killarney lakes in Kerry are limestone and they support the country's last native yew woods and rarities like the strawberry tree. The eastern margin of Connemara contains a cross-section of Burren flora, and limestone outcrops up in County Mayo are the only Irish locations for the rare limestone polypody fern (*Gymnocarpium robertianum*). Sligo's magnificent, flat-topped Ben Bulben, and its surrounding limestone plateau is particularly remarkable. It has many interesting plants including three species of very rare arctic-alpines: arctic saxifrage (*saxifraga nivalis*) and chickweed willow herb (*Epilobium alsinifolium*), which are found nowhere else in Ireland, and fringed sandwort (*Arenaria ciliata*) which is found nowhere else in Ireland or Britain either.

The Burren, however, is more astonishing than all these places. I believe it is Ireland's most important and most unusual natural habitat. So it is very sad that in the last five years E E C grants have been channelled towards the provision of fertilizer to increase the Burren's grazing capacity. Unlike the complexities of the region's flora, the effect of fertilizer is very simple: it makes the grass grow. And when the grass grows it shades out the flowers and they disappear. This is a very serious threat to the Burren—and a completely unnecessary one. The E E C is now producing more milk and butter and meat than it can even afford to store. Farmers, of course, must be encouraged to stay in the Burren and they need to make a living. A new E E C scheme exists, however, which would permit grants to be paid to farmers, in areas of special ecological importance, to farm in traditional ways that would not damage the natural environment. To date, Ireland has not taken advantage of this scheme.

7
Aspects Of Water:
Irish Wetlands And The River Liffey

Ireland is a wonderful place for water. The great forests that might once have drunk up half the rainfall before it ever reached the ground have disappeared. Their standing-room has grown waterlogged and turned into the vast bogs of the west, rich in their legacy of sodden peat. The country's concave saucer shape and its endless rainy days ensure that the moisture lies heavy on the land, filling interminable streams and rivers and swelling the banks of long lines of lakes.

Every stretch of Irish water is important to wildlife, and some of that wildlife is so unusual that it must be thought of as important to the world. There's the Shannon, Ireland's grandest river, which rises far up on the Leitrim plateau, and winds its way through the still waters of three great lakes, Lough Allen, Lough Ree and Lough Derg, before merging with the sea beyond Limerick. Its estuary alone is eighty kilometres long and is bordered by hundreds of square kilometres of inter-tidal mudflats. In winter these are crowded with birds, with ducks and waders whose numbers sometimes include dizzy concentrations of rare black-tailed godwits (*Limosa limosa*). A distinct subspecies of this beautiful, rufous, long-legged wader, called *islandica*, breeds far to the north on the summer water-meadows and marshes of Iceland. In autumn they head south and at the end of the winter half the total population of these special Icelandic birds can be found on their way home, feeding on the Shannon.

The Shannon is famous too for what are known as its 'callows'. In its middle to lower reaches, between Lough Ree and Lough Derg in County Offaly, the river's flow is slow and meandering and its tributaries are often choked with water-lilies (*Nymphaeaceae*). From November to April the seeping river spreads over the flood-pastures, the 'callows', on either bank and the drowned grasses feed gangs, 7,000 strong, of bright-coloured wigeon. The area is so wet and wild in winter that no one really knows how many tens of thousands of plovers, of pert

38 *Top* Sandwich terns squabbling.
39 *Bottom* Roseate tern, the rarest European tern.

golden plovers (*Pluvialis apricaria*) and black and white lapwings it holds.

In Ulster there's Lough Neagh, one of the largest freshwater lakes in western Europe, covering 383 square kilometres. It is the remains of a sort of rift valley created 65 million years ago by the Antrim volcanoes. They spilled out such a weight of lava—which itself hardened into a sheet of basalt sometimes 800 metres thick—that the earth's crust split. The space in between the faults sagged to form the basin of the Lough. This is now kept topped up by no less than six major rivers which draw their water from the Sperrin Mountains to the west, from the Antrim Hills in the north-east and the Mournes away to the south.

In the few places where the marshy banks of Lough Neagh have not been drained or mastered by flood control schemes, they provide a habitat for the rare and peculiar orchid, *Spiranthes romanzoffiana*, known as Irish lady's tresses. This slender orchid has long creamy flowers that grow in a spiral. It differs from the more common autumn lady's tresses (*Spiranthes spiralis*) in having leaves on its stem and three rows of flowers up the flowerhead rather than one. It is particularly interesting, however, because of its distribution: in Europe it is only found beside Lough Neagh, in Cork, in Kerry and in a few localities in Scotland, but across the Atlantic in North America it grows all the way from Alaska and Canada to Pennsylvania and out west to Colorado and California.

On any winter's day the bobbing waters of Lough Neagh will be home to at least 50,000 ducks. But because of its grebes the lake is even more remarkable in summer. For the great crested grebes (*Podiceps cristatus*) of Lough Neagh, instead of nesting singly or in small groups like most grebes, breed in colonies. The reed beds round a single lake island can hold the reed-woven, raft-like nests of eighty or 100 pairs.

Then there is Lough Corrib, the long beautiful lake that stretches away north of Galway. Lough Corrib is something of a phenomenon. Most lakes and rivers can be classified according to two simple criteria: like soils, they are either rich in nutrients or poor in nutrients depending largely on the geology of their beds. If they lie on limestone or, like Lough Neagh on basalt and clay, they will be rich, mildly alkaline, and will support plenty of life. If they lie on granite or, like many of the lakes of the uplands and the west, embedded in peat and fed by peaty streams, they will be poor, acidic and comparatively bare of plants, of insects and therefore of birds. Ecologists describe the rich waters as *eutrophic* (from the Greek word *eu* meaning good) and the poor waters as *oligotrophic* (from *oligos*, the Greek word for few). Lough Corrib, however, belongs to another, much rarer, mixed category. It has both small oligotrophic patches and large eutrophic areas but in its southern half it is a 'marl' lake. Marl lakes occur where the bed is pure chalk or limestone, and where the consequent level of calcium carbonate in the water is so unusually high that it actually appears, out of solution, forming

40 *Top Left Above* Wigeon (male and female).
41 *Top Left Below* Whooper swans with wigeon and mallard.
42 *Top Right* Grey heron.
43 *Bottom* Male and female common newt.

a layer on the lake bottom. This layer, precipitated out of the water, is the 'marl', and for chemical reasons it takes with it most of the water's phosphorus. Without phosphorus the clouding microscopic plants—phytoplankton—cannot grow. The water therefore remains crystal clear, almost blue, and with so much light, larger submerged aquatic plants can grow at much greater depths than is normal. Marl lakes usually contain rich growths of stonewort (*Nitella* and *Chara spp*), a straggling weed which is the favourite food of coots (*Fulica atra*) and pochard (*Aythya ferina*), the commonest ducks on Lough Corrib, and of the wild whooper swans that visit in winter.

Because Ireland has so much limestone, marl lakes are more common here than in most parts of Europe. They include Loughs Owel and Derraveragh in Westmeath, Lough Derg and other parts of the Corrib complex like Loughs Mask and Carra. Limestone, as we saw on the Burren, can also produce turloughs. The most famous, and the largest surviving turlough is Rahasane which lies away from the Burren proper, south-east of Galway. It is a magnificent place to hear the high whistling of thousands of wigeon, and in winter to see all three species of swan, the mute (*Cygnus olor*) and whooper swans and the smaller and much rarer Bewick's swan (*Cygnus bewickii*) which flies here from Siberia.

There are also the marshes of the south-east, the Wexford Slobs, which have formed at the mouth of the river Slaney: 1,900 hectares of wet pastures on the north and south of the estuary reclaimed by draining the rich mud brought down by the river over thousands of years. These, along with the estuarine mudflats and the sandy islands in Wexford harbour provide the most important habitat for water birds in the whole of Ireland. Almost all the ducks are there in large numbers: mallard and wigeon, teal (*Anas crecca*), pintail (*Anas acuta*) and shoveler, pochard and shelduck (*Tadorna tadorna*), tufted duck (*Aythya fuligula*) and the rarer scaup (*Aythya marila*). Winter brings waders like curlews, whimbrel (*Numenius phaeopus*), dunlin (*Calidris alpina*) and knot (*Calidris canutus*), black-tailed and bar-tailed godwits (*Limosa lapponica*), grey plovers (*Pluvialis squatarola*), and, again, vast numbers of lapwings and golden plovers, their flocks swollen in harsh weather by birds from Britain seeking a kinder refuge. There are redshanks (*Tringa totanus*) and spotted redshanks (*Tringa erythropus*), geese and more Bewick's swans. Until the late 1970s, the sand-reef of Tern Island held the largest colony of terns in Ireland and the largest colony of the very rare roseate tern (*Sterna dougallii*) in all Europe. Sadly the island has been heavily eroded and though the commoner terns have moved elsewhere the roseates have disappeared altogether and seem to be plummeting in numbers throughout most of the Northern Hemisphere.

The other great rarity on the Wexford Slobs is the Greenland white-fronted goose (*Anser albifrons flavirostris*) (p146). This is a handsome grey goose, with a white forehead and black stripes on its belly. It looks like the Eurasian white-fronted goose (*Anser albifrons*) except that it has a yellow rather than a pink beak. There are only 20,000 left, breeding on the tundra lands of Greenland, which means it is the rarest goose which visits either Ireland or Britain. In autumn over half the population head south for Ireland, most of them going to the Slobs where they spend six months of the year. The remaining 8,000-odd birds visit Islay off the west coast of Scotland.

One reason for the bird's scarcity is that its reproductive abilities have been declining, probably through disruption and hunting pressures. This is revealed when ornithologists conduct winter counts. They discover that only about one in eight of the birds in any flock are 'first year' juveniles born the previous summer. Most geese are slow to reproduce and they compensate for this, like human beings, by living for a long time—for twenty years or more which is long for a bird. Nevertheless, the Greenland white-front's reproduction rate is dangerously low. The Eurasian form, for example, is much more successful, a third of its population consisting of 'first year' birds.

In 1982 the Irish government placed a temporary moratorium on hunting Greenland white-fronts and in 1985 the Greenlanders were persuaded to stop shooting them as they arrived to breed. Numbers have edged upwards and Irish hunters have pressed for resumed shooting rights. But the increase in the goose population of the Slobs is not entirely due to the ban on shooting. It is part of a long-term change in the bird's behaviour pattern. Until about twenty-five years ago they used to scatter in small groups across Ireland feeding on thousands of separate, undisturbed little bogs. But now that drainage and turf cutting have removed so many peatlands, searching for those that remain becomes an inefficient way of life. Instead the geese concentrate on the Slobs. In a sense, the Greenland white-front is a symbol of what has happened to wetlands—drainage, destruction, development and disturbance—all over Ireland and indeed also over Europe.

Finally we come to Ireland's magnificent salmon rivers: the Foyle, which over the last hundred years has been one of the most productive salmon fisheries in the world; the beautiful Cork Blackwater whose middle reaches between Fermoy and Lismore are considered to be among the finest angling waters anywhere; the Corrib, the Slaney, the Bann, the Bandon, the Burrishoole and many more. What do these Irish rivers have that can nurse a tiny egg, laid high up in the gravelly beds near the headwaters and upper loughs, and power the young salmon as it grows from alevin to parr to smolt, turns silver and heads for the open sea? And what do they have that brings it back —the full grown 5, 10 or even 15 kilogram fish—from the shelves off Greenland where it has fed for two or three years? Why does it risk the Danish oceanic trawlers and the miles of illegal monofilament nets spread round the Irish coast to catch it, all for the mystique of breeding in the river where it was born? The answer is that, like all of us, the salmon wants its offspring to have the same advantages that it enjoyed in its youth. For a young salmon these are increasingly rare commodities: clean water full of oxygen, and a natural community of freshwater invertebrates to feed on— in short, the unspoilt ecosystem of an Irish river.

At the Mouth of the Liffey

I began this survey of Ireland's habitats in the city of Dublin, so that's where I'll end it, with a portrait of Dublin's river, the River Liffey.

One of the pleasures of a winter's afternoon in Dublin is to walk out along the north wall of the Liffey estuary towards Bull Island. If you look back at the city you can watch the incongruous gangs of black and white brent geese (*Branta bernicla*) flocking back and forth in front of the painted facias of the terraced waterfront houses. If the tide is out, the sand and mudflats ripple and glisten like spread silver, with the godwits picking their way daintily through the sparkling water-light. Weaving and turning, clouds of small waders, dunlin and knot, rise and fall like gnats, searching for the ebbing waterline. And as the sun sinks behind the gaudy red and white striped chimneys of Ringsend power station it throws out scarlet beams to catch the heavy-billed curlews in shimmering silhouettes.

This, like any fine estuary, is one of the richest feeding grounds that birds can find. Way up river, the Liffey rises in the Wicklow Mountains, winding down through the limestones and shales of the Kildare and Dublin plains. When it isn't being polluted, like so many Irish rivers, by careless effluent from farm and factory, the river acts like a food conveyor belt, nourishing plants and animals all along its route, and when it reaches the sea it is still carrying a generous load of nutrients. Out into the broad arms of the river mouth the current spills the mineral salts it has lifted from the river bed, the myriad tiny organisms it has torn from their moorings upstream and the nitrogenous sewage effluent it has picked up from human habitations.

This microscopic bounty settles and sifts into the sands and mud of the estuary where it helps to feed the crowded connurbations of brackish and salt-water invertebrates. For although the mudflats may have a still and empty look, beneath the surface the damp silt is busier than any city. It contains the inch-wide shells of edible winkles (*Littorina littorea*) which have grown from eggs laid far out to sea and left to develop and disperse alone on the currents. There are smaller rough winkles (*Littorina saxatilis*) that sometimes travel up river and produce live young that they actually 'brood'. There are edible cockles (*Cerastoderma edule*), typical 'bivalve' molluscs that breathe and feed by siphoning the salt water, drawing it in through one valve and expelling it through the other. Beautiful slim tellins (*Tellinas tenuis*), another species of bivalve mollusc, are responsible for the quarter-inch pink, yellow or cream-coloured shells that litter the strandline. Lugworms (*Arenicola marina*), too leave a familiar signature. They live in U-shaped burrows in the mud and as they swallow the sand in front of them and push out the waste at their tails, they create a pattern of dips and coiled worm castes across the sand. Much less sedentary is the busy ragworm (*Nereis diversicolor*), which like the lugworm can grow to ten centimetres in length and more. The minute estuarine snails *Hydrobia*, however, have one of the most interesting feeding methods. When the tide falls they slide over the mudflats feeding on the detritus that remains before burrowing under the surface in preparation for feeding strategy number two. Then as the tide returns six hours later the snails emerge to secrete a sort of raft of mucus on which they can float while they feed directly from the water.

Despite its wealth of nutrients, the estuary is not an easy place to live in, since the endless influx of freshwater and the variation of the tides create inconsistencies in the water's salinity. The normal salinity of the sea exceeds thirty parts of salt in a thousand parts of water. Near the river mouth, though, the salinity may be as low as three parts per thousand. Because most species are adapted either to salt or fresh water, the variety of organisms that can cope in an estuary is limited. Even those that can manage the conditions may have narrow tolerances. The freshwater louse *Asellus* for example can survive in salt water but cannot breed in levels higher than five parts per thousand while the little marine crustacean *Corophium volutator*, which can live in three parts per thousand, needs five to moult and eight to reproduce. Only the indestructable freshwater *Tubifex* worms, seem almost as indifferent to salt as they are to pollution.

Without variety there is less competition so the well-fed mudflat invertebrates exist in astounding quantities. One study found, in a single square metre of estuarine mud, no fewer than 596 ragworms, 128 lugworms, 10 shore crabs (*Carcinus sp*), 132 cockles, 22,000 *Corophium* crustacea and 47,000 *Hydrobia*!

No wonder such a large group of birds took to the water and became waders. In order to exploit the estuarine invertebrate resources to the full,

different species of wader have developed different methods of feeding and have even evolved different shapes to help them. The red legs and beaks of the redshank, for instance, are relatively long, enabling it to feed in deeper water and pick up organisms buried in the mud. The short-billed, shorter-legged, ringed plover, on the other hand, is a strandline specialist. It moves very fast, chasing the sand hoppers or stands on one leg tapping the mud with the other to stimulate the lugworms beneath into moving and so betraying themselves. The snipe has short legs and an extremely long beak, it feeds round the boggy edges of the brackish pools, probing far into the mud, locating its food by touch. Like many long-billed waders, the end of its beak is packed with a network of nerves known as Herbst's corpuscles which make it extremely sensitive. It can also manipulate the tip of the bill to pick food up, without having to open the rest and risk getting a mouthful of mud underground. The small, black and white turnstone (*Arenaria interpres*), with its lovely summer plumage of chestnut scapulas, has a tough, wedge-shaped bill strong enough to smash the plates of a barnacle. Turnstones feed on the carrion and invertebrates that they find under pebbles and weed. They are adept at rolling up quite heavy carpets of seaweed by thrusting their heads beneath it at an angle and running up and down along its length. Occasionally, when faced with an awkward task like flipping over a large fish, they will team up into groups of three or more and do the job together.

There are even differences within species. Curlews have the longest bills among the Irish waders. Their regal, down-curved mandibles are the perfect instrument for seizing, squashing, washing and swallowing a crab without any risk of getting their toes pinched. But when it comes to feeding in the deepest mud the female curlew has an advantage over the male since her beak can be a good four centimetres longer.

The ultimate specialist, however, is the oystercatcher. There are generally two schools of thought among oystercatchers: hammerers and stabbers. The first use their magnificent, red, reinforced beaks to smash their way into mussel shells, the second use them to prise open the molluscs at their joints. The technique either of hammering or stabbing is learned from the parents and becomes a fixed habit. Occasionally, however, ingenious families break through the frontiers of knowledge. One fortunate ornithologist witnessed two crafty oystercatchers teaching their young to carry their mussels thirty feet up into the air and drop them on a road!

The wealth of the estuary, its conspicuous teeming bird life, is a quintessential aspect of the healthy river. The fundamental unit of 'wealth' is the minute, apparently insignificant invertebrate. Similarly the herons (*Ardea cinerea*) and the trout, the otters, grey wagtails (*Motacilla cinerea*) and dippers, which we associate with the inland stage of the river, are sustained by equally complex, equally 'invisible' communities of invertebrates living in the fresh water back up stream.

Invertebrates: Five Ways of Life in Fresh Water

It might seem eccentric to have started at the end of the river and be working backwards, but I am doing this to emphasise the importance of the current.

The birds and mammals that feed in the river are just exploiting its facilities. They are really land animals at heart. They breed on dry land and they can go up and down stream at will using the river banks. But the invertebrates and fish that live out their lives in the water have to reckon constantly with the flow of the current. To them the river's current must seem like an inexorable downhill escalator which they have continually to ascend just to stay still. If they give up and relax they will be carried far away and may even end up out at sea. This is one reason why salmon and sea trout struggle up to the headwaters to lay their eggs, so their young have the maximum leeway to make a mistake with the current. Indeed the whole life of the river faces upstream.

In the city stretches of the Liffey gangs of black-headed gulls flutter and dip, picking debris and the remains of little invertebrate tragedies from the moving face of the water. Further up, among the fields of Palmerstown, mute swans tip themselves and dabble at the waterweed and hooded crows squabble along the freshwater mussel beds below Lucan. But all these lower lengths of the river are comparatively bare, not because of pollution but because of Lucan's massive hydro-electric dam. The periodical torrents of water released at the flood gates regularly sweep the lower river clean of invertebrates. There is, of course, a second major dam system below the Blessington lakes and the Liffey does not reveal a truly natural flow until you travel above that. A few miles above Lucan, however, in the waters around the little village of Celbridge, you find the first significant rafts of water crowfoot, and wherever that grows it creates breathing space for the development of a reasonable invertebrate community.

The watercrowfoots (*Ranunculus spp*) belong to a large family of aquatic buttercups containing at least ten species, all very similar to each other. They produce beautiful small white flowers with yellow centres which stand, sometimes in their hundreds, just above the surface of the water. Crowfoots have a clever way of dealing with the current: they form two types of leaf. The main 'working' leaves grow under water and are long and threadlike so they can stretch out with the flow of the water without the risk of being torn off or swept away. The second leaf-type is completely different. It is much broader and floats on the surface where it helps to support the flowerheads.

Crowfoot forms a sort of vegetative barrage, modifying the flow of the river. In some cases, like on the River Bandon in County Cork, the crowfoot rafts are so dense and extensive that the water is almost brought to a halt. On the Liffey the strands are much more modest but where they occur, immediately downstream an eddy of calmer water exists in which invertebrates can flourish.

The river provides five different types of invertebrate habitat. First there is the open water inhabited by the floaters, the minute organisms that we call plankton. Some are plants and classed as phytoplankton, some are tiny animals, or zooplankton. Although we still know little about it, the world of plankton seems to be as complicated in its way as the world of birds, mammals, or higher plants, and a short stretch of slow-moving water or lake can hold many dozens of species.

Most of the phytoplanktons are only visible when they come together to form patches of green or blue-green algae. If you look at them under a microscope, however, they can be extremely beautiful. The most important free-floating forms in the river are the diatoms which have an infinitely thin glassy shell. Of these, one called *Asterionella* grows in an attractive eight-legged star shape while *Diatoma* is like a string of delicate cylinders threaded together.

Among the zooplankton, there are numerous single-celled animals, or protozoa, but more conspicuous are the mini crustacea: the *Cladocera* or water fleas and copepods. Water fleas like *Daphnia*, which most children manage to fish out of the local river or pond at some stage in their scientific career, are oval-shaped rather like fleas with fat tummies and bristly antennae.

Copepods—a common one is called *Cyclops*—have longer, segmented bodies like microscopic lobsters, and they often carry two bunches of eggs attached to their rear legs and held either side of their tails. Both copepods and water fleas can regulate their depth in the water by flailing their antennae, but they are not true swimmers. This lack of mobility renders them extremely vulnerable. Their only protection is their minute size and their ability to reproduce in huge numbers in suitable conditions.

Together the planktons provide the basis for all aquatic life, forming the vast, anonymous bottom of the watery food chain. Phytoplanktons, like all plants, derive their energy from the sun, making their food through photosynthesis and using nitrogen and phosphorus in the water. Zooplankton feed on dissolved organic matter which they ingest by endless drinking.

The second invertebrate habitat, particularly important in still water, is the surface film. Small water snails can travel along its underside, feeding on the plankton below it. Midge larvae can hang in the water suspended by it while slender water-measurers (*Hydrometra*) and pond skaters (*Gerris spp*) live out their lives on top. They use the surface film like a spider's web, both as a trap and a telegraph system. They devour other insects that fall into the water and as soon as they sense a disturbance they converge on it, the pond skater whizzing along on four legs while its other two are ready to grab the prey, and the water-measurer using all six legs to walk across the water.

The third habitat consists of the footholds offered by the weeds in the water and the stones at the bottom. These will be coated by fixed rather than floating algae, and so become important grazing grounds for aquatic snails like the large pond snail (*Lymnaea stagnalis*). Anchored to some of the plants will be animals like the *Hydra*, a sort of freshwater 'sea-anemone', whose cotton-thin, half-inch tentacles can catch and paralyse with poison any passing water fleas and copepods. The larvae of all sorts of chironomid midges also live attached to water plants. Some make holes in the stems and then spin a sort of net across the exit. By fidgeting in its tunnel the larva can persuade the water to swill across its net which collects organic particles. When the larder is full the larva gobbles it up and spins a new one. Down amongst the stones, you will also find the larvae of stoneflies (*Plecoptera*) and caddisflies (*Trichoptera*), to be discussed later in the chapter, and crustacea like the freshwater shrimp (*Gammarus*) and the freshwater hog-louse (*Asellus*). The real tigers of this zone, however, are the two-inch nymphs of the dragon flies. Twenty-two out of forty-four of the British dragonflies and damselflies are regularly recorded in Ireland and of these all but three have been found in or near the Liffey system. (This of course reflects the number of competent observers as well as the richness of the fauna.) Some of the commonest species are the large red damselfly (*Pyrrhosoma nymphula*), the so-called common blue damselfly (*Enallagma cyathigerum*) and the sturdy-looking brown hawker (*Aeshna grandis*). Dragonfly nymphs hide in the weeds and they have extraordinary, hinged jaws which they can literally throw out at smaller insects, grabbing them as they pass and munching them up.

The silty river bottom, the fourth habitat, is used by burrowing invertebrates. These include the nymphs of numerous species of mayflies (*Ephemeroptera*), the slender creatures with diaphanous wings that fishermen imitate as lures. Mayflies are unique among insects because they go through a form of 'moult' in the winged state. When the nymphs crawl out of the water to hatch they emerge first as a 'sub imago', the angler's 'dun'. This has wings but it is covered in a fine down of hairs to keep it waterproof as it struggles from the nymphal skin. These are what give it its dull colouring. Unlike most winged insects the emerging 'dun' can fly immediately. This permits it to move to a safer location, further from the water where within hours, or sometimes minutes, it can moult again into the spick-and-span shiny adult that fishermen call a 'spinner'. Mayfly spinners do not feed. They are produced solely to mate. This they do as they hatch out in clouds, the females dropping their eggs into the water like little bombs. Within twelve hours most are dead and they drift away down river as the 'spent gnats' so beloved of trout.

Freshwater worms (*Annelidae*), like small, thin earthworms also burrow into the silt and mud, as do the large swan-mussels (*Anodonta cygnaea*) and tiny pea-mussels (*Pisidium amnicum*). These burrowers are an essential part of the water's self-cleaning system. When the myriads of plankton die they sink to the river bottom. There some are disposed of by fungi and bacteria, just as dead matter is dealt with on land, under the oak trees for instance. The rest are devoured by the water hog-lice and the burrowers. The mussels feed by trapping the food particles in their gills. From there the tasty bits are allowed to slide on a slip-stream of the mussel's own mucus to its mouth.

Water, as we know, is for swimming in. But this, in effect the fifth habitat, is scarcely used by invertebrates. Only diving beetles like the formidable waterboatmen (*Notonecta*) are really effective swimmers. Their scooped, flattened, seed-like bodies, their hard moulded wing-cases, large eyes and oar-like legs make them powerful movers, able to chase their insect prey across open water. They are not, however, true 'aquatics', like the pond snails and some of the other freshwater invertebrates because they cannot get their oxygen from the water. Instead they have to travel intermittently to the surface to fetch a bubble of air which they then use like an aqualung. But this makes them buoyant so if they stop still they have to cling onto something, like a piece of weed. In fact, the true swimmers are not invertebrates at all, they are the fish and the mammals, the vertebrates at the top of the river's food chain.

The River, its Fish, Mammals and Birds

When Ireland's waters began to move again during the centuries following the end of the Ice Age, they contained only a small contingent of fish. They had to be species that liked cold water and could tolerate salt since Ireland was soon isolated by salt water. The earliest colonizers—or in places perhaps survivors—were subarctic fish like the charr (*Salvelinus alpinus*) and the whitefish (*Coregonus autumnalis*) and the three-spined stickleback (*Gasterosteus aculeatus*). Anadromous species—fish that spawn and develop in fresh water but feed as adults at sea—were also present. They included salmon and trout and the two lampreys, *Petromyzon marinus*, the sea lamprey, and the river lamprey (*Lampetra fluviatilis*). These were later joined by the more southerly anadromous species, the allis shad (*Alosa alosa*) and the twaite shad (*Alosa fallax*). Finally there was the eel (*Anguilla anguilla*) which is what we call a catadromous fish—one that lives in rivers but goes to sea to spawn.

These few species formed the basis of Ireland's native freshwater fish fauna and for thousands of years they enjoyed exclusive dining rights over the bulk of the invertebrate communities of Ireland's rivers. In time the trout populations separated, as they always do, into silvery sea-running forms (sea trout) and redder river forms (brown trout). The latter, isolated in their river systems, developed many slightly different genetic strains. Sadly, most of these have been erased by interbreeding with new stocks introduced for angling but numerous forms of charr and whitefish still survive, landlocked in Irish lakes. There is, for example, a unique strain of charr in Lough Coomasahann in County Kerry, and more surprisingly a twaite shad (*Alosa fallax Killarniensis*) known as the goureen, which seems to have got stuck in Lough Leane and adapted to full-time freshwater living.

The 'coarse fish', like perch (*Perca fluviatilis*), pike (*Esox lucius*), minnow (*Phoxinus phoxinus*) and loach (*Noemacheilus barbatulus*), all prefer warmer water to breed in. Having failed to reach Ireland in the cold early post-glacial period they stayed away. As late as the twelfth century Giraldus Cambrensis, in his list of Irish fauna, still specifically mentions their absence and most of Ireland's coarse fish did not arrive until the last 300 years. Deliberate introductions have now resulted in the country having a fairly full complement, including pike, perch, carp (*Cyprinus carpio*), gudgeon (*Gobio gobio*), tench (*Tinca tinca*), minnow, loach, brook lamprey (*Lampetra planeri*), dace (*Leuciscus leuciscus*), rudd (*Scardinius erythrophthalmus*), bream (*Abramis brama*) and ten-spined stickleback (*Pungitius pungitius*). They are not all welcome. One of the most recent arrivals, the small, red-finned roach (*Rutilus rutilus*), has an alarming capacity for breeding. They like the pools below weirs and a typical colony can lay hundreds of millions of eggs along a fifty metre stretch of river. From original introductions in Cork they have spread to many waters in the last twenty years, including the Liffey, and in some areas they are beginning to displace the native trout.

Because all the coarse fish like warmish water, they tend to congregate in the slow, muddy, lowland reaches of rivers. Ecologists actually call this the 'coarse zone'. Above it comes the 'minnow reach', then the cooler, faster-moving and highly oxygenated 'trout reach', and finally the precipitous upland threads of the headwaters to which fish rarely penetrate.

Sustained by their rich diet of aquatic insects, Ireland's river fish in turn feed several species of mammal and bird. Since the early 1960s American mink have been escaping from mink farms and they are now well-established predators on the Liffey, in the Mournes, on the Shannon, the Boyne and the Slaney and in many parts of the north and north-west. Stoats, too, have been seen taking fish on the lower Shannon, but the sleekest, finest Irish fisherman is, of course, the otter.

Ireland probably has more otters than any comparable area of Europe. A twelve month survey from 1980-1 found them present at 92 per cent of 2,373 sites examined. Their signs are regularly found in Galway and Cork and on the Liffey on the outskirts of Dublin, but they are very clever at keeping out of sight. Just occasionally, though, they do something eccentric and people see them. One July morning in 1986 an otter walked into the Post Office in the village of Kanturk, County Cork, and holed up for a few hours in the post mistress's bedroom before being chased out. Unfortunately, this particularly disorientated animal did not survive. A local youth was seen thrashing it with a stick and we found its body a few days later beside the River Allow. Normally, however, otters feed and travel by night, only betraying their presence to us by the smears of their shiny black faeces. These, known as 'spraints', have a sweetish musty scent and are deposited as deliberate 'trademarks' on anything prominent—on stones and bricks, on the low ramparts under bridges, or in drainage pipes. On the open river bank the otter will also construct a special platform by scrabbling the grass into a pile with his forepaws. An experienced naturalist can follow the spraints and the distinctive prints left in the mud by the animal's webbed, five-toed paws, and so estimate the number of otters in a district and the extent of their wide nocturnal wanderings from river system to river system.

Otters are beautifully designed for aquatic activity. Their eyes are set rather high on their heads so they can swim under their prey and watch them against the paleness of the sky above. They are also protected by see-through flaps which come down over the eyes when the animals submerge. Their nostrils too are positioned high up so they can lie in the water and breathe with only their noses showing. They are long and streamlined, with warm, waterproof coats and strong rudder-like tails and are powerful enough to overtake most species of fish. An average male otter measures about 1.2 metres from nose to tail and a female a few centimetres less. Yet observations show they prefer to catch quite small fish—mainly young eels under thirty centimetres long and a wide variety of fish of about twelve centimetres in length. Examination of the faeces has revealed them to have a surprisingly varied diet, exploiting all the facilities of the river. They are very fond of crayfish (*Astacus pallipes*) and will eat all sorts of smaller invertebrates including earthworms, beetles, slugs, and freshwater shrimps. Some make a speciality of feeding on marine molluscs, spending most of their time around the coast, occasionally even getting caught in lobster pots, while in late winter others frequently head up into the hills to feast on frogs gathering in upland ponds to spawn.

Any naturalist who has been lucky enough to watch otters has been struck by their playfulness. I once saw six swimming together in a river, weaving in and under and round each other as if they were all one animal. Whether it's a mother teaching her two or three cubs to swim—which she cannot do until their underfur is fully developed and 'waterproofed' at about three months—or a solitary male tossing a twig in his dextrous forepaws, an otter conveys an infectious sense of exuberance and enjoyment of life.

So, in a different way, do kingfishers (*Alcedo atthis*) with their sparkling azure wings and red bellies, glimpsed as they streak along the river bank and shrill out their piercing whistle. Kingfishers are perfect diving machines, able to plunge like arrows deep into the water and seize fish 5 centimetres long in their beaks. It is not always a safe method of fishing, however, and I remember finding a bird that had smashed its beak so badly on a stone that the lower mandible was only hanging on by the skin. Nevertheless, it survived like this for at least three weeks and seemed otherwise perfectly healthy!

Altogether more sombre, but equally well adapted to the life of the fisherman is the grey heron. It can stand for long minutes motionless, in water a foot deep waiting with its sinuous neck coiled for a strike. The inside of a heron's beak is rough and striated to help it hold onto slippery fish and eels. It also has an interesting shape to its middle toe. The nail is decorated with little teeth, like a comb, and these are used to clean fish and eel slime from its feathers. Several other fish-eating birds have the same equipment including gannets, shags and bitterns (*Botaurus stellaris*).

There are two other typical river birds in Ireland, both of them common on the Liffey, though neither of them feeds on fish. The first is the stumpy brown and white dipper. It is a bird of the upper reaches, with a liking for fast-moving, shallow waters. It takes up a conspicuous station in the middle of the river usually on a large stone where it bows quickly up and down. Then it slips into the water and creeps submerged against the current picking up beakfuls of mayfly and stonefly larvae which it can see because its eyes, like the otter's, are sheathed in a transparent film.

Dippers tend to nest in crevices under bridges, often side by side with the other little river bird, the elegant grey wagtail. The male grey wagtail is a beautiful bird. In the breeding season his back is blue-grey, his throat is pitch black and the area under his tail is a brilliant yellow. Both he and his more dull-coloured female flick their tails constantly uttering bright little peeps whenever they fly. They also feed on invertebrates but they don't compete with the dipper, for though they share precisely the same habitat they don't share the same habits. Grey wagtails feed above the surface of the water, hurrying among the stones of the shallows or on the rafts of crowfoot and sometimes fluttering up to snap at alderflies (*Sialis spp*) and mayflies in the air.

On the Liffey, it is the dippers and grey wagtails that probably suffer most from the disruption caused by the hydroelectric dams. We watched one afternoon by the old stone bridge at Ballymore-Eustace where the river valley, having made its wide loop through the lowlands from Celbridge to

Newbridge, starts to climb up towards its source in the Wicklow Mountains.
A mile upstream the gates of the Blessington dam had just been opened and
the grey wagtails that a moment before had been feeding among the stones
at our feet flew up into the willows for refuge. Then a three-foot wall of
water rushed through, drowning the feeding grounds and the tall monkey
flowers on the bank, plucking at the lower branches of the trees just below
where the birds sat and swilling past within inches of the startled wagtail
chicks huddled in their nest beneath the bridge. We wondered how many
nests had been lost before the parents learned to build so high above the
natural floodline and how they coped for food each time their insect dinners
were so rudely swept away.

To the Reservoir and the Lakeside Vegetation

Many Irish rivers have to pass through lakes at some stage of their journeys.
Of course the broad straggling basin above Blessington is a reservoir created
by the hydro-electric dam at its south-west corner. In many ways however,
it resembles a natural lake, filled as it is by the Liffey's headwaters. Nor is
this the first time that the ecosystem of the Liffey has had to adapt to a change
in course. Geologists believe that, before the Ice Age, the river headed due

west to join the River Barrow. Glaciation blocked its path with the dense
gravel deposits of the Curragh—now the home of the Irish Derby—so the
Liffey developed its curious loop to turn back east for Dublin Bay.

The still waters of lakes tend to be richer in plankton than rivers and lake fish
like charr sometimes feed almost exclusively on zooplankton. Blessington
Lake has most of the typical aquatic invertebrates and its shallow western
fringes are excellent for dragonflies. Birds like little grebes (*Tachybaptus rufi-
collis*), mallards, tufted ducks and moorhens are common breeders, joined in
winter by a wider assortment of ducks that arrive to feed.

But it is the plant life of Blessington and of lakes in general that I
want briefly to talk about. Water plants occupy specific niches, just as the
invertebrates do. Duckweeds (*Lemna*) for instance, are like little boats; trailing
their roots in the water they produce their minuscule flowers as they bob
along on the surface. The pondweeds (*Potamogeton*) are submerged plants,
rooted in the lake or river bottom and conducting all their business under
water. The crowfoots, as we have seen, are something of a mixture, as are
the water-lilies. The white water-lily (*Nymphaea alba*) actually germinates
beneath the water. Each seed is wrapped in a sort of air-filled sponge. This
floats away from the parent and then decays, leaving the seed to sink and
develop at a suitable distance. The fruits of the rarer yellow water-lily (*Nuphar
lutea*) have to form above water and don't begin their voyages until they
have become embryos.

All these plants are capable of growing in mid-current or in open water.
The so-called 'emergent' plants, on the other hand tend to grow in the
shallows by the banks. These are the bulrushes and the bur-reeds (*Spargan-
ium*), the highly poisonous hemlock waterdropwort (*Oenanthe crocata*) a white
umbellifer beloved of hoverflies, the primitive, fern-like marestail (*Hippuris
vulgaris*), the blue-flowered brooklime (*Veronica beccabunga*)—a type of speed-
well—and the beautiful yellow iris—all plants that indicate the margin
between water and dry land.

In most rivers this margin is constantly maintained by the endless flow of
the water. On the Liffey the turbulent flooding from the dams weeds out
much of the midstream vegetation; there are few patches of reeds and
emergent plants only grow in profusion on the backwaters. Along the disused
millraces below Palmerstown for instance, there are fine stands of irises and
a careful look will also reveal one of the most beautiful of all the river plants,
the tall delicate pink flowering rush (*Butomus umbellatus*), which is something
of a rarity in Ireland.

But the warm, lush upper banks of the Liffey, more or less untouched by
regular flooding, are wonderfully rich in riverside—as opposed to emergent
—plants. There are the fleshy spikes and purplish flowers of butterbur
(*Petasites hybridus*) whose enormous leaves were once used for wrapping
butter. There is clustered, white-flowered meadowsweet, marsh valerian

(*Valeriana dioica*) and ragged robin whose flowers look like shreds of pink ribbon. The lilac petals of cuckoo flower, or lady's smock—the favourite food of the maytime butterfly, the orange tip (*Anthocharis cardamines*)—are also a common sight as are the handsome yellow bells of the naturalized American plant, the monkey flower (*Mimulus guttatus*), each individually coloured with a stain of 'rust'.

On the borders of lakes the zones that plants inhabit become more easily blurred. Round the roots and stems of the emergent vegetation silt and mud collects. The lake edges grow shallower, marshland plants invade the fringes, emergent plants spread further into the middle, and eventually most shallower waters are colonized and covered over. Already you can see this happening on the north-western edge of Blessington Lake where the red fingers of amphibious bistort (*Polygonum amphibium*), humming in summer with bumble bees, are extending in dense profusion across the shallows.

This slow evolution from water to dry land often involves an eventual shift from alkaline to acid conditions—a mineral-rich water becomes a base-rich fen and then its new hummocky edges, cut off from spring water, become peaty and acidic. This is often the first stage in the formation of a raised bog (see chapter four).

These subtle ecological nuances are well reflected by the habits of *Dactylorhiza* orchids, the spotted and marsh orchids, which grow close to the Liffey. This is a notoriously 'difficult' group of plants much given to brain-teasing hybridisation. But the occurrence of the different species usually tells us something about the state of evolution of any particular lake or fen.

The rarest is the narrow-leafed marsh orchid *traunsteineri* which is found near Prosperous, about five miles from the Liffey. It is tall, with purplish, well-separated flowers and only grows in the most base-rich, 'young' fens. The early marsh orchid *incarnata*, recognizable by pale pink flowers whose top petals have a pinned-back look, is more widespread, requiring 'average' older fens. The common broad-leafed marsh orchid *majalis*, a scarlet flower, likes most wet ground that is not actually acidic so it will be found in fens that are turning into bogs. Finally, the common spotted orchid *fuchsii* prefers dry ground and will tolerate neutral soils while the last, the heath spotted orchid, *maculata*, is a true dry acid specialist, appearing on the new-formed peat.

This, of course, is something of a simplification but it helps to emphasise the dynamic nature of lakeside vegetation. When we look at most lakes, as opposed to rivers, we are witnessing a stage in an ongoing process of colonization.

The Headwaters, the Source and the End of the Journey

Above Blessington, the course of the Liffey makes its final ascent into the hills. Here, as its bed steepens, the river travels over granite and the nutrients that have fed such masses of life downstream become scarcer. Fish life falls away and even hardy little brown trout rarely make it up the last stony miles.

The current, which has always been a force to reckon with, now grows more torrential as the river grows narrower and narrower. The water rushes and spills, tumbling loose stones in front of it and creatures that live in these scurrying headwaters require particular tenacity. Most typical are the stoneflies. These are long-winged, rather thick-bodied insects, usually about twelve mm long and brown or blackish in colour. The adults live for two or three weeks—long enough to mate, anyway—crawling on the stones and streamside vegetation, feeding, if at all, on exposed algae. The nymphs, however, have a much longer life-span, developing in the water. They are distinguishable from similar mayfly nymphs because they have two rather than three 'cerci', the tail-like appendages owned by most primitive insects and familiar to us as the pincers on the rear-ends of earwigs (*Dermaptera*). The bodies of these nymphs are specially flattened so the current flows safely over them, allowing them to feed on the river bed even in fast water.

Stonefly nymphs, like mayfly nymphs, cannot grow gradually as we do. Instead they have to grow in stages. Each time they want to expand they have to split and shed their external skeleton, swell a little and then grow a new one. One of the larger carnivorous stoneflies (most of the others eat algae), is called *Dinocras cephalotes*. Its adult has a fifty mm wing-span and has been observed undergoing thirty-three of these 'moults' over a three-year period. In nutrient-poor upland waters, growth is necessarily slow. Nevertheless, most stoneflies reach adulthood in one or two years.

There is at least one family of mayflies, the *Ecdyonuridae*, that are also quite common in headwaters and they too have the flattened shape of the stonefly nymphs. The other characteristic insects of this region are the caddisflies of the family *Agapetus*. Their larvae weigh themselves down against the current by rolling themselves up in a fine case of sand and granite fragments.

The source of the Liffey, a flat, boggy scrape where the diminished trickle of river seems almost to be sucked back into the peat, lies some 500 metres up, a little way north of the Sally Gap, the main pass in the northern Wicklow hills. This is a mountain land, an acid land, one of bog-cotton, of sundew and butterwort. Up here the more traditional Dublin and Wicklow men still vie for turf allotments, cutting the peat with the old long-handled, L-bladed spade or *slean* of the region and leaving the blocks in piles to dry beside the road.

And if you climb to the round bare summit of Kippure nearby, 750 metres high, you can look north to the threaded streets of Dublin and the Liffey estuary. You can look eastwards to the long coastal dunes while away to the west you can see the wide landscape of the lowlands—the lakes and grasslands and hedgerows—the habitats of Ireland.

Bibliography

General

Angel, H. 1981. *The Natural History of Britain and Ireland*. London, Michael Joseph.

Arnold, E. N. and Burton, J. A. 1978. *A Field Guide to the Reptiles and Amphibians of Britain and Europe*. London, Collins.

Chinery, M. 1976 (2nd. ed.). *A Field Guide to the Insects of Britain and Northern Europe*. London, Collins.

Cramp, S. and Simmons, K. E. L. 1977. *Handbook of the Birds of Europe, the Middle East and North Africa. Vols I–IV*. Oxford, Oxford University Press.

Doogue, D. and Harding, P. T. 1982. *Distribution Atlas of Woodlice in Ireland*. Dublin, An Foras Forbartha.

Fairley, J. 1975 (Rev. ed. 1984). *An Irish Beast Book*. Belfast, Blackstaff.

Garrard, I. and Streeter, D. 1983. *The Wild Flowers of the British Isles*. London, Macmillan.

Howarth, T. G. 1973 (Rev. ed. 1984). *Colour Identification Guide to Butterflies of the British Isles*. Harmondsworth, Penguin.

Hubbard, C. E. 1954 (Rev. ed. 1984). *Grasses*. Harmondsworth, Penguin.

Huxley, A. 1978 (Rev. ed.). *Plant and Planet*. Harmondsworth, Penguin.

Imms, A. D. 1947. *Insect Natural History*. London, Collins.

Jermy, A. C., Arnold, H. R., Farrell, L. and Perring, F. H. 1978. *Atlas of Ferns of the British Isles*. London, Botanical Society of the British Isles and British Pteridological Society.

Kerney, M. P. and Cameron, R. A. D. 1979. *A Field Guide to the Land Snails of Britain and North-west Europe*. London, Collins.

Lack, P. 1986. *The Atlas of Wintering Birds in Britain and Ireland*. Calton, Poyser.

Mitchell, F. 1976. *The Irish Landscape*. London, Collins.

Ní Lamhna, E. 1979 (2nd. ed.). *Provisional Distribution Atlas of Amphibians, Reptiles and Mammals in Ireland*. Dublin, An Foras Forbartha.

Ní Lamhna, E. 1980 (3rd. ed.). *Distribution Atlas of Butterflies in Ireland*. Dublin, An Foras Forbartha.

Perring, F. H. and Walters, S. M. 1962. *Atlas of the British Flora*. London, Botanical Society of the British Isles.

Phillips, R. 1980. *Grasses, Ferns, Mosses and Lichens of Great Britain and Ireland*. London, Pan.

Praeger, R. Ll. 1909. *A Tourist's Flora of South-west Ireland*. Dublin, Hodges, Figgis.

Praeger, R. Ll. 1937. *The Way That I Went*. Dublin, Hodges, Figgis.

Praeger, R. Ll. 1941. *A Populous Solitude*. London, Methuen.

Praeger, R. Ll. 1950. *Natural History of Ireland*. London, Collins.

Royal Irish Academy. 1979. *Atlas of Ireland*. Dublin, Royal Irish Academy.

Sharrock, J. T. R. 1976. *The Atlas of Breeding Birds in Britain and Ireland*. Berkhamsted, Poyser.

Skinner, B. 1984. *Colour Identification Guide to Moths of the British Isles*. Harmondsworth, Penguin.

Smith, A. J. E. 1978. *The Moss Flora of Britain and Ireland*. Cambridge, Cambridge University Press.

Southern, H. N. 1964. *The Handbook of British Mammals*. Oxford, Blackwell.

Tansley, A. G. 1968 (2nd. ed.). *Britain's Green Mantle*. London, George Allen and Unwin.

Turrill, W. B. 1948. *British Plant Life*. London, Collins.

Tutin, T. G., Heywood, V. H., Burges, N. A., Moore, D. M., Valentine, D. H., Walters, S. M. and Webb, D. A. 1964–1980. *Flora Europaea. Vols 1–5*. Cambridge, Cambridge University Press.

Warren, A. and Goldsmith, F. B. 1983. *Conservation in Perspective*. Chichester, Wiley.

Webb, D. A. 1977 (6th. ed.). *An Irish Flora*. Dundalk, Dundalgen.

Whittow, J. B. 1974. *Geology and Scenery in Ireland*. Harmondsworth, Penguin.

Chapter One

Chinery, M. 1977. *The Natural History of The Garden*. London, Collins.

Jackson, P. W. and Skeffington, M. S. 1984. *The Flora of Inner Dublin*. Dublin, Royal Dublin Society.

Mabey, R. 1973. *The Unofficial Countryside*. London, Collins.

Teagle, W. G. 1978. *The Endless Village*. Shrewsbury, Nature Conservancy Council.

Threlkeld, G. 1726. *Synopsis Stirpium Hibernicarum*. Dublin.

Chapter Two

Cambrensis, Giraldus. Transl. O'Mara, J. J. 1982 (Rev. ed.). *The History and Topography of Ireland*. Portlaoise, Dolmen.

Harris, M. P. 1984. *The Puffin*. Calton, Poyser.

Hutchinson, C. D. 1981. Cape Clear Bird Observatory 1970–1980. *Irish Birds*. 2,1: 60–72.

Lack, D. 1969. The Number of Bird Species on Islands. *Bird Study*. 16: 193–209.

MacArthur, R. H. and Wilson, E. O. 1967. *The Theory of Island Biogeography*. Princeton, Princeton University Press.

Sharrock, J. T. R. 1973. *The Natural History of Cape Clear Island*. Berkhamsted, Poyser.

Sleeman, D. P., Devoy, R. J. and Woodman, P. C. 1986. Proceedings of the Postglacial Colonization Conference. *Occ. Pub. Ir. Biogeog. Soc*. I.

Yalden, D. W. 1981. The Occurrence of the Pigmy shrew (*Sorex minutus*) on moorland, and the implications for its presence in Ireland. *J. Zool. Lond*. 195: 147–56.

Yalden, D. W. 1981. When did the mammal fauna of the British Isles arrive? *Mammal Rev*. 12: 1–57.

Chapter Three

Buchanan, K. 1975. *Some effects of trampling on the flora and invertebrate fauna of sand dunes*. M.Sc. thesis. University of London.

Mills, S. P. 1986. 'Rabbits breed a growing controversy'. *New Scientist* 109, 1498: 50–54.

The National Trust. 1978. *Murlough National Nature Reserve Management Plan*. Ballynahinch, National Trust.

Quinn, A. C. M. 1977. *Sand Dunes: Formation, Erosion and Management*. Dublin, An Foras Forbartha.

Chapter Four

Bellamy, D. 1986. *Bellamy's Ireland: the Wild Boglands*. Bromley, Helm.

Evans, E. E. 1967 (2nd. ed.). *Mourne Country*. Dundalk, Dundalgen.

Jeffrey, D. W. 1984. *Nature Conservation in Ireland: Progress and Problems*. Dublin, Royal Irish Academy.

McKelvie, C. L. 1985. *A Future for Game?* Hemel Hempstead, George Allen and Unwin.

Mills, S. P. 1984. Unique Irish bog may be dug up. *New Scientist*. 101, 1401: 7.

Newton, I. 1979. *Population Ecology of Raptors*. Berkhamsted, Poyser.

O'Connor, R. J. and Shrubb, M. 1986. *Farming and Birds*. Cambridge, Cambridge University Press.

O'Meara, M. 1979. Distribution and numbers of Corncrakes in Ireland in 1978. *Irish Birds*. 1, 3: 381–405.

O'Meara, M. 1986. Corncrake declines in seven areas, 1978–85. *Irish Birds*. 3: 237–244.

Pearsall, W. H. 1950. *Mountains and Moorlands*. London, Collins.

Ratcliffe, D. A. 1980. *The Peregrine Falcon*. Calton, Poyser.

Raven, J. and Walters, M. 1956. *Mountain Flowers*. London, Collins.

Chapter Five

Bellamy, D. 1982. *Woodland Walks*. London, Hamlyn.

Elton, C. S. 1966. *The Pattern of Animal Communities*. London, Chapman and Hall.

Kelly, D. L. 1975. *Native Woodland in Western Ireland with Especial Reference to the Region of Killarney*. Ph.D. thesis, University of Dublin (Trinity College).

Kelly, D. L. 1981. The Native Forest Vegetation of Killarney, South-west Ireland: An Ecological Account. *Journal of Ecology*. 69: 437–472.

McCracken, E. 1971. *The Irish Woods Since Tudor Times*. Newton Abbot, David and Charles.

Mills, S. P. 1983. 'Forestry in Britain: planting for alternative futures'. *New Scientist*. 99,1369: 336–341.

Neal, E. 1948. *The Badger*. London, Collins.

Peterken, G. F. 1981. *Woodland Conservation and Management*. London, Chapman and Hall.

Rackham, O. 1980. *Ancient Woodland*. London, Arnold.

Simms, E. 1971. *Woodland Birds*. London, Collins.

Turner, J. S. and Watt, A. S. 1939. The Oakwoods (*Quercetum Sessiflorae*) of Killarney, Ireland. *Journal of Ecology*. 27: 202–233.

Wilson, J. 1977. Some Breeding Bird Communities of Sessile Oak Woodlands in Ireland. *Polish Ecological Studies*. 3,4: 245–256.

Chapter Six

Bellamy, D. 1983. *Grassland Walks*. Feltham, Country Life.

Duffey, E., Morris, M. G., Sheail, J., Ward, L. K., Wells, D. A. and Wells, T. C. E. 1974. *Grassland Ecology and Wildlife Management*. London, Chapman and Hall.

Lousley, J. E. 1950. *Wild Flowers of Chalk and Limestone*. London, Collins.

O'Sullivan, P. J. 1983. The distribution of the pine marten (*Martes martes*) in the Republic of Ireland. *Mammal Rev*. 13: 39–44.

Summerhays, V. S. 1951. *Wild Orchids of Britain*. London, Collins.

Warner, P. and O'Sullivan, P. 1982. The food of the pine marten *Martes martes* in Co. Clare. *Trans. intern. Congr. game Biol*. 14: 323–330.

Webb, D. A. and Scannell, M. J. P. 1983. *Flora of Connemara and the Burren*. Cambridge, Cambridge University Press.

Chapter Seven

de Buitlear, E. 1985. *Irish Rivers*. Dublin, Country House.

Freethy, R. 1986. *The Natural History of Rivers*. Lavenham, Dalton.

Hammond, C. O. 1983 (2nd. ed.). *The Dragonflies of Great Britain and Ireland*. Colchester, Harley.

Haslam, S. M. and Wolseley, P. A. 1981. *River Vegetation: its identification, assessment and management*. Cambridge, Cambridge University Press.

Hutchinson, C. 1979. *Ireland's Wetlands and Their Birds*. Dublin, Irish Wildbird Conservancy.

Macan, T. T. and Worthington, E. B. 1951 (Rev. ed. 1972). *Life in Lakes and Rivers*. London, Collins.

Mills, S. P. 1982. 'Salmon: demise of the landlord's fish'. *New Scientist*. 93, 1292: 364–67.

Mills, S. P. 1982. 'Hunters threaten the goose from Greenland'. *New Scientist*. 94, 1308: 634.

Mills, S. P. 1982. 'Britain's Native Trout is Floundering'. *New Scientist*. 96, 1333: 498–501.

Ruttledge, R. F. and Ogilvie, M. A. 1979. 'The Past and Current Status of the Greenland White-fronted Goose in Ireland and Britain'. *Irish Birds*. 1, 3: 293–363.

Townsend, C. R. 1980. *The Ecology of Streams and Rivers*. (*Studies in Biology, 122*). London, Arnold.

Yonge, C. M. 1949. *The Sea Shore*. London, Collins.

Index

Plants and animals are indexed fully, by English and by scientific names (where both are found in the book).
Technical terms are indexed primarily for the pages that show their meaning.
Principal people and places, and broad topics, are given key references only.
Main references are in **bold** type.
spp. means 'various species'.
ff after a page-number means that the subject is treated in passing over the following pages as well.